Sundays and Festivals
with the
Fathers of the Church

Sundays & Festivals
with the
FATHERS OF THE CHURCH
—— *or* ——
HOMILIES OF THE
HOLY FATHERS
on the GOSPELS *of all the* SUNDAYS and CHIEF FESTIVALS *of the* ECCLESIASTICAL YEAR

BY THE REV. D.G. HUBERT
Foreword by Hugh Barbour, O.Praem.

Nihil Obstat:
Daniel Canonicus Iles, S.T.L.

Imprimatur:
✠ Herbertus Cardinalis Vaughan,
Archiepiscopus Westmonast.

Die 4 Junii, 1901

First Published in 1901 by Benziger Bros.
Foreword © Hugh Barbour 2019
2019 © by Arouca Press

All rights reserved:
No part of this book may be reproduced or transmitted,
in any form or by any means, without permission

ISBN 978-1-9991827-7-9 (pbk)
ISBN 978-1-9991827-8-6 (hardcover)

Arouca Press
PO Box 55003
Bridgeport PO
Waterloo, ON N2J3G0
Canada
www.aroucapress.com
Send inquiries to info@aroucapress.com

Book and cover design
by Michael Schrauzer

CONTENTS

FOREWORD BY FR. HUGH BARBOUR, O.PRAEM xi
INTRODUCTION xv

1 *First Sunday of Advent* 1
   Homily by Pope St. Gregory 1

2 *Second Sunday of Advent* 9
   Homily by St. Jerome 9

3 *Third Sunday of Advent* 13
   Homily by Pope St. Gregory, ... 13

4 *Fourth Sunday of Advent* 21
   Homily by Pope St. Gregory 21

5 *Christmas Day* 27
   Homily by Pope St. Gregory 27

6 *The Feast of St. Stephen, the First Martyr* 31
   Homily by St. Jerome 31

7 *Sunday Within the Octave of Christmas* 35
   Homily by the Venerable Bede 35

8 *The Feast of the Circumcision* 41
   Homily by St. Ambrose 41

9 *The Epiphany of Our Lord* 43
   Homily by Pope St. Gregory 44

10 *First Sunday After Epiphany* 51
   Homily by St. Ambrose 51

11 *Octave Day of the Epiphany* 55
   Homily by St. Augustine 55

12 *Second Sunday After Epiphany* 61
   Homily by St. Augustine 61

13 *Third Sunday After Epiphany* 67
   Homily by St. Jerome 67

14 *Fourth Sunday After Epiphany* 71
    I. Homily by St. Jerome 71
    II. Homily by St. Augustine 72

15 *Fifth Sunday After Epiphany* 75
    Homily by St. Augustine 75

16 *Sixth Sunday After Epiphany* 79
    Homily by St. Jerome 79

17 *Septuagesima Sunday* 83
    Homily by Pope St. Gregory 84

18 *Sexagesima Sunday* 91
    Homily by Pope St. Gregory 91

19 *Quinquagesima Sunday* 97
    Homily by Pope St. Gregory 97

20 *Ash-Wednesday* 105
    Homily by St. Augustine 105

21 *First Sunday in Lent* 109
    Homily by Pope St. Gregory 109

22 *Second Sunday in Lent* 115
    Homily by Pope St. Leo the Great 115

23 *Third Sunday in Lent* 121
    Homily by the Venerable Bede 122

24 *Fourth Sunday in Lent* 129
    Homily by St. Augustine 130

25 *Fifth Sunday in Lent, or Passion Sunday* 137
    Homily by Pope St. Gregory 138

26 *Sixth Sunday in Lent, or Palm Sunday* 145
    Homily by St. Ambrose 146

27 *Good Friday* 151
    Homily by St. Augustine 155

28	*Easter Sunday* 159	
	Homily by Pope St. Gregory 159	
29	*Easter Monday* 165	
	Homily by Pope St. Gregory 166	
30	*First Sunday After Easter, or Low Sunday* 169	
	Homily by Pope St. Gregory 170	
31	*Second Sunday After Easter* 175	
	Homily by Pope St. Gregory 175	
32	*Third Sunday After Easter* 181	
	Homily by St. Augustine 181	
33	*Fourth Sunday After Easter* 187	
	Homily by St. Augustine 187	
34	*Fifth Sunday After Easter* 193	
	Homily by St. Augustine 193	
35	*Ascension Day* 199	
	Homily by Pope St. Gregory 199	
36	*Sixth Sunday After Easter* 209	
	Homily by St. Augustine 209	
37	*Whit-Sunday, the Feast of Pentecost* 215	
	Homily by Pope St. Gregory 215	
38	*Whit-Monday* 223	
	Homily by St. Augustine 223	
39	*Trinity Sunday* 227	
	Homily by St. Gregory of Nazianzus 227	
40	*First Sunday After Pentecost* 229	
	Homily by St. Augustine 229	
41	*Feast of Corpus Christi* 235	
	Homily by St. Augustine 235	
42	*Second Sunday After Pentecost* 239	
	Homily by Pope St. Gregory 239	

43	*Third Sunday After Pentecost*	247
	Homily by Pope St. Gregory	247
44	*Fourth Sunday After Pentecost*	255
	Homily by St. Ambrose	255
45	*Fifth Sunday After Pentecost*	261
	Homily by St. Augustine	261
46	*Sixth Sunday After Pentecost*	265
	Homily by St. Ambrose	265
47	*Seventh Sunday After Pentecost*	271
	Homily by St. Hilary	271
48	*Eighth Sunday After Pentecost*	275
	Homily by St. Jerome	275
49	*Ninth Sunday After Pentecost*	279
	Homily by Pope St. Gregory	279
50	*Tenth Sunday After Pentecost*	285
	Homily by St. Augustine	285
51	*Eleventh Sunday After Pentecost*	289
	Homily by Pope St. Gregory	289
52	*Twelfth Sunday After Pentecost*	293
	Homily by the Venerable Bede	294
53	*Thirteenth Sunday After Pentecost*	297
	Homily by St. Augustine	297
54	*Fourteenth Sunday After Pentecost*	301
	Homily by St. Augustine	301
55	*Fifteenth Sunday After Pentecost*	305
	Homily by St. Augustine	305
56	*Sixteenth Sunday After Pentecost*	311
	Homily by St. Ambrose	311
57	*Seventeenth Sunday After Pentecost*	315
	Homily by St. John Chrysostom	315

58 *Eighteenth Sunday After Pentecost* 319
     Homily by St. Peter Chrysologus 319

59 *Nineteenth Sunday After Pentecost* 323
     Homily by Pope St. Gregory 323

60 *Twentieth Sunday After Pentecost* 329
     Homily by Pope St. Gregory 329

61 *Twenty-First Sunday After Pentecost* 333
     Homily by St. Jerome. 333

62 *Twenty-Second Sunday After Pentecost* 335
     Homily by St. Hilary 335

63 *Twenty-Third Sunday After Pentecost* 337
     Homily by St. Jerome. 337

64 *Twenty-Fourth Sunday After Pentecost* 341
     Homily by St. Jerome. 342

65 *Feast of Ss. Peter And Paul, Apostles* 347
     Homily by St. Jerome. 347

66 *The Assumption of the Blessed Virgin Mary* 351
     Homily by St. Augustine 351

67 *The Feast of All Saints* 357
     Homily by St. Augustine 357

FOREWORD

STUDY OF THE AUTHORITATIVE COMMENTATORS on Sacred Scripture, and most particularly of the pericopes to be read out at the Sacred Liturgy has long been the custom of any of the places and communities where the celebration of the Divine Office or the "Liturgy of the Hours" is celebrated. This is true of the several liturgies of both East and West. Just as in the Old Testament Church, so too in the Church of the New Testament, it was unthinkable to approach the inspired word without some example or gloss or commentary. Thus did St Augustine learn to interpret the Sacred Scriptures, which at first seemed to his fine rhetor's ear to be so lacking in both dignity and content, by listening assiduously to the preaching of St. Ambrose in the cathedral of Milan. Ambrose's homilies struck deep into the heart of the North African seeker, and brought him finally to the instant crisis of his conversion to a life of chastity.

Yet this moment of conversion has much to teach us about the real power of Sacred Scripture to heal and encourage the sinner, and much we might not expect if we were to keep our sights at the simply homiletic level of a sermon or exposition. A broader and more flexible model might be at hand.

What I mean is that in fact the efficacious movement of the heart that comes from reading or hearing about the scriptures does not always show itself best in reading and instruction, but in holy *conversation*.

What, after all, was the event of the conversion of St Augustine? He had heard of the manner of life of St Anthony of Egypt by some new monastic recruits who had come down from Trier. He longed to undertake the same, but had not the strength to do so. He had discussed this at length and even—for Alypius his good friend who was present—with disconcerting passion. He was truly at a breaking point when he remembered the *example* of St Anthony, how he was converted to the monastic life simply on hearing the deacon sing at Sunday Mass the invitation of the Lord to follow Him. So Augustine approaches the codex of the epistles of St Paul which was sitting on a gaming table, and read the first passage which his finger indicated. And all was changed after all those years of struggle. Here was no homily or liturgy, or even much reading, only two friends in an intense discussion.

The power of the word of God, operating as a sacramental instrument to heal, and enlighten, and liberate a heart. This is the core of all the rest of our uses of scripture: the hearing of the lessons at Holy Mass and Divine Office, the devout assistance at homilies, sermons, and instructions given by our hierarchically established clergy. All of this will only bear its best fruit if we make use of the means which we have in our private lives to receive the effects, the saving influence of the sacred text.

Holy conversation first, then sacred reading on our own (called *lectio divina*), will fit our hearts to receive the riches of the Fathers and the Holy Gospels.

So my advice to you, good reader, is to take up this lovely and useful volume which God in his Providence has placed in your hands and make it a locus of holy conversation with family and friends, fellow seekers of the truth. Holiness and enlightenment come largely to us through our friends of like mind. To be sure, solitude is also needful, but even there we are not alone, but are surrounded, as the Apostle says, "by a cloud of witnesses."

In our own very difficult times it is sometimes hard to find edification in the preaching we hear in church on Sunday. There are not too many Ambroses about! But we still have the means, and among them is this little book and others like it.

Pray to Our Lady and the Apostles to find you such friends as those who went sorrowing on the road to Emmaus, discussing the events of the triduum of Easter as truly breaking news. Their holy and mournful conversation drew the Lord Himself into their midst and they were enlightened indeed. Had He not said "Where two or three are gathered together in my Name, there I am in the midst of them?" He broke the Holy Bread with them, and brought the discussion back full circle! He will do that for us as well.

Our Lord Jesus wants you to enter into a holy conversation with Him and your brethren, and then you will most happily be enlightened and fed with the Bread of Life at Holy Mass. Perhaps your family could discuss the gospel lesson on the way to Mass or the evening before. There is always a way and the Lord will come with his presence fulfilling His promise which cannot fail.

Hugh Barbour, Ph.D.
Norbertine Canon of St. Michael's Abbey
Orange, California

INTRODUCTION

THE CHRISTIAN'S RULE OF LIFE IS CONTAINED IN the Gospels. They are *the* Book on which he should meditate, and the teaching of which he should endeavour to put into practice all the days of his life. Yet, it is to be feared that, in reading this Book, he might not have the necessary light from above, and perhaps might attach to the sacred words a meaning that was not intended by the Divine Teacher, nor by His disciples. To prevent such possibility, many learned men, well versed in Holy Writ, have carefully explained the meaning of the Gospels, and have thus imparted to Christians a greater taste and love for the reading of the Word of God. Hence we have their commentaries, meditations, lives of Jesus Christ, and divers essays on the Holy Scriptures, the titles of which alone would form a large volume. Many of these works are thoroughly well written, and the reader can be but greatly edified and instructed by them. However, it is strange, that from the beginning it never occurred to any one to go up to the very source. Among spiritual books the oldest are the best and the surest. It seems, therefore, that the works of the holy Fathers should have obtained the preference, for they are nearly as old as the Church, and in them the tradition is preserved in all its strength and purity.

Indeed, when we follow these wise teachers in their writings from century to century, we are astonished that Christian Faith, enlightening us now, should be always one and the same, and that the doctrine of faith, taught by the Church, and the doctrine of morals, preached in the world, have never undergone any change in the succession of centuries. We see that the true Church, our glory and the foundation of our hope, has always remained calm in the midst of storms, victorious in the fiercest struggles, unhurt amidst the most powerful attacks, and always preserved from the arrows of her enemies. We see that the Bride of Jesus has always been holy and infallible in her precepts and commands, always wise and enlightened in her teaching, always prudent and reasonable in her discipline, and always pure in her religious practices. We recognise that the Church, built upon the Rock, has been, and will be to the end of the world, holy and immaculate, because she is protected by the infinitely powerful and eternal God, and guided by the Holy Ghost.

It is, therefore, a subject of astonishment that, what the holy Fathers have written and preached about the Gospels, has not more often been translated and published in modern times. Was it not quite natural to think of this pious duty, especially as they are often quoted in sermons and instructions, and consulted, when difficult passages of Holy Scripture have to be explained? Are not they our teachers, under whose guidance we cannot fall into error? There are no better sources from which to draw with greater safety. What eloquence and diversity in their works! Who would not admire the grace and strength of a St. John Chrysostom, the fecundity and sublimity of a St. Augustine, the clear penetration and depth of a St. Ambrose, the vast learning of a St. Jerome, or the penetrating knowledge of a St. Gregory? What dignity and authority in St. Leo, and what beauty in the writings of the Venerable Bede!

The works of the Fathers of the Church form a rich library. Yet this field, so fertile in an abundance of delicious fruits, remains sterile for the greater number of the Catholic people, who perhaps know not what to choose, or are ignorant of the language of these holy writers. It seems to me that a collection of Homilies from different Fathers, arranged according to the Sundays and principal festivals of the ecclesiastical year, would be a great spiritual help to all Christians. This is the reason why I undertook this collection, and I have carefully endeavoured that it should be useful to all.

Before every Homily is placed the respective part of the Gospels, thus showing the intimate relation existing between the one and the other. The literal, spiritual, allegorical, and figurative meaning of the Holy Scriptures is explained in these discourses. Their style is clear and simple, yet elegant; the comparisons are most

INTRODUCTION   xvii

beautiful and instructive, for they are natural. Simplicity is their ornament, and this simplicity pervades the whole discourse. The present book is, therefore, a selection of different essays which, by their number and diversity, form a collection presenting the doctrine of faith and morals, and containing the principal truths of our Holy Catholic Religion.

This is the notion or idea which may be formed of these Homilies. I have endeavoured to render, in a natural and simple style, the sublime and forcible eloquence of the holy Fathers, without weakening their thoughts. For I am of opinion that a literal translation, often dry and tiring, could not give a clear idea of the beautiful expressions found in these Homilies. A dogmatical work is not to be translated like a history or an ordinary speech.

It is to be hoped that this book will be of great and general utility, specially as priests and others, whose duty it is to instruct the faithful, have not always the time to consult the Fathers, even should they possess their works. The duties of priests in parishes, the time they spend in the confessional, their visiting the sick and the poor, the administration of the Sacraments, will not allow them to do so. Besides, would it not require a long time to find out the special subject? For, in order to discover in the writings of the Fathers a few pages, or even one passage, directly explaining the Gospel, a whole essay or a whole book must sometimes be read, the greater part of which has no direct reference to that Gospel. Again, there are many priests, whose duty it is to preach and instruct, who do not possess the works of the Fathers, who have a few books only: their small means not allowing them to buy any more.

We also offer this book to all Christians who spend some time, specially on Sundays and Feast-days, in spiritual reading. The Homilies are also offered to all those who, through sickness or the nursing of the sick, are prevented from assisting at the instructions of their Pastor. The clergy and the laity will find in them a source of instruction and edification. As to the writer, he will be rewarded by the thought that he has placed in the hands of a great many a selection of solid instructions, a great portion of which has never been translated. Two words will explain why this book ought to be dear to all good Christians: it contains the essential parts of the Gospels, and the most important parts of the works of the Fathers.

D.G. Hubert.
Bath,
October, 1901.

1. FIRST SUNDAY OF ADVENT

GOSPEL: Luke 21: 25-33. *At that time:* Jesus said to His disciples: There shall be signs in the sun and in the moon and in the stars, and upon the earth distress of nations, by reason of the confusion of the roaring of the sea and of the waves, men withering away for fear and expectation of what shall come upon the whole world. For the powers of the heavens shall be moved, and then they shall see the Son of Man coming in a cloud with great power and majesty. But when these things begin to come to pass, look up, and lift up your heads, because your redemption is at hand. And He spoke to them a similitude: See the fig-tree and all the trees, when they now shoot forth their fruit, you know that summer is nigh; so you also, when you shall see these things come to pass, know that the kingdom of God is at hand. Amen, I say to you, this generation shall not pass away till all things be fulfilled. Heaven and earth shall pass away, but My words shall not pass away.

HOMILY BY POPE ST. GREGORY, PREACHED IN THE CHURCH OF ST. PETER
First Homily on the Gospels

I. AS OUR ADORABLE SAVIOUR WILL EXPECT AT His coming to find us ready, He warns us of the terrors that will accompany the latter days in order to wean us from the love of this world; and He foretells the misery which will be the prelude to this inevitable time, so that, if we neglect in the quietness of this life to fear a God of compassion, the fearful spectacle of the approaching last judgment may impress us with a wholesome dread. A short time before He had said: *Nation shall rise against* nation, and kingdom against kingdom. And there shall be great earthquakes in divers places, and pestilences and famines (Luke 21: 10, 11). Now He added: *And there shall be signs in the sun and in the moon and in the stars, and upon the earth distress of nations.* Of all these events we have seen many already fulfilled, and with fear and trembling we look for the near fulfilment of the rest. As for the nations which are to rise up one against the other, and the persecutions which are to be endured on earth, what we learn from the history of our own times, and what we have seen with our own eyes, makes a far deeper impression than what we read even in Holy Scripture. With regard to the earthquakes converting numberless cities into lamentable heaps of ruins, the accounts of them are not unknown to you, and reports of the like events reach us still from various parts of the world. Epidemics also continue to cause us the greatest sorrow and anxiety; and though we have not seen the *signs in the sun and in the moon and in the stars*, mentioned in Holy Scripture, we know, at least, that fiery weapons have appeared shining in the sky, and even blood, the foreboding of that blood which was to be shed in Italy by the invading barbarian hordes. As to the terrible *roaring of the sea and of the waves*, we have not yet heard it. However, we do not doubt that this also will happen; for, the greater part of the prophecies of our Lord being fulfilled, this one will also see its fulfilment, the past being a guarantee for the future.

II. Moreover, we say this, beloved brethren, to encourage you to unceasing watchfulness over yourselves, so that no false confidence may take possession of your souls, leaving you to languish in ignorance; but that, on the contrary, a true and wholesome fear may drive you on to do good, and strengthen you in the carrying out of good works. Take special notice of the following, added by our Saviour: *Men shall wither away for fear and expectation of what shall come upon the whole world. For the powers of heaven shall be moved.* What is meant by our heavenly Teacher when speaking of *the powers of heaven*, but the angels and archangels, the thrones, principalities and powers, that will appear on the day of vengeance of that severe Judge, Who will then demand from us with severity the homage and submission, which He now, as our Creator, although unseen, asks for in love as His due. *Then they shall see the Son of Man coming in a cloud, with great power and majesty.* Which means that the people will then see Him, whom in His meekness and humiliations they would neither listen to nor recognise, coming in power and majesty. In that day they will feel the more compelled to acknowledge His power, since in the present time they deny Him, and refuse to submit themselves to His yoke, to which He so patiently invites them.

III. As, however, these words of our Saviour are spoken to the lost, so are the following uttered for the comfort of the elect: *When these things begin to come to pass, look up and lift up your heads, because your redemption is at hand.* Truth Itself teaches the chosen ones in these words, and seems to say to them: When you see the calamities which portend the end of the world increasing; when fear of that awful judgment day takes possession of even the bravest hearts at the sight of the shaken powers of heaven, then lift up your heads, that is, rejoice with your whole heart, because the end of this world, so little loved by you, announces to you the wished-for freedom to be enjoyed by you hereafter. The head is often used in Holy Scripture for the soul, and in this way, by warning us to lift up our heads, it reminds us to rouse up our souls to the thought of the heavenly home which is awaiting us. Those, therefore, who love God, are commanded to rejoice when they see the end of the world approaching, because, when this world, which they have not loved, is destroyed, they will find themselves in possession of Him, Who is the one true object of their love. We are assured that among these true believers, who have a real longing to see God, there is not one who will not be deeply moved by the fearful events accompanying the end of the world. For we know from Holy Scripture that *Whosoever will be a friend of this world, becometh an enemy of God.* (James 4: 4) Therefore, to show no pleasure at the approach of the end of the world is as much as to declare that we love this world, and that we are the enemies of God. This wicked clinging to the world must be far removed from the hearts of good Christians, and of those who by faith are convinced that there is another life, and by their good works deserve that life. Let those weep over the destruction of the world, whose hearts are given to it, and whose hopes are fixed upon it, and who, far from seeking this new life, refuse to believe that there will be another life. As for us who believe in this heavenly home and in its eternal bliss prepared for us, let us hasten to reach them. We should wish to attain this home as soon as possible, and endeavour to find the shortest way thither. For, are we not surrounded in this world by a great many misfortunes? Do we not experience many troubles and calamities? What, indeed, is this mortal life but a painful way? Consider, beloved brethren, what folly it would be in a man walking along a toilsome and difficult road until overcome with fatigue, and yet not wishing to see the end of it! Moreover, our Saviour teaches us by His wise similitude that this world does not deserve our affection, but that, on the contrary, we should despise it. He says: *See the fig-tree and all the trees. When they now shoot forth their fruit, you know that summer is nigh. So you also, when you shall see these things come to pass, know that the kingdom of God is at hand.* Is it not as though He said: In the same way that you conclude by the trees bearing fruit that summer is near, so by the downfall of the world you will know that the kingdom of God is not far off? These words show us plainly enough that the fall and destruction of this world are its real fruits, since its rise and increase are closely connected with its fall, and since it brings forth those things only which are destined to perish. If, on the contrary, we consider the kingdom of God, we are aware that we may in all truth compare it with the summer, when all the clouds of our afflictions will be dispersed and be followed by happy days, lighted up by a never disappearing sun of bliss.

IV. And that we should never doubt these truths, our Lord confirms them with an oath, saying: *Amen, I say to you, this generation shall not pass away, till all things be fulfilled. Heaven and earth shall pass away, but My words shall not pass away.* Among all corporeal things and beings nothing is more durable than heaven and earth; in the same way nothing disappears more quickly than the word. Before the word is expressed it exists, and hardly is it said than it

1. FIRST SUNDAY OF ADVENT

has disappeared; for the word cannot attain its perfection without at the same instant losing its existence. Now *heaven and earth shall pass away,* says the oracle of eternal truth, *but My words shall not pass away.* It is as if our Saviour said: Learn ye, that everything among you, that seems to be durable, has not been made to last for ever or to continue without any change; whereas what seems to pass away quickly, is firmly and forever established. For even the words I speak, and which fly away, contain in themselves irrevocable utterances.

V. Now, beloved brethren, to return to what you have heard about this world being filled with continual daily increasing evils, consider what remains of the immense nation that has sustained the calamities of which I am speaking. Meanwhile, the troubles have not yet left us; we are still oppressed by lamentable and unforeseen calamities, and we are grieved and afflicted by new losses. Strip, therefore, your hearts from the love of this world which you enjoy so little; and for this purpose take to heart the precept of the Apostle: *Love not the world, nor the things which are in the world. If any man love the world, the charity of the Father is not in him* (1 John 2: 15). What we have experienced these last three days is not unknown to you; how suddenly raging storms have rooted out the largest and strongest trees, have pulled down houses and destroyed churches! Many of the inhabitants, who at the end of the day quietly and in good health projected new plans for the morrow, were taken away by a sudden death during the night, and buried under the ruins of their dwellings.

VI. I beseech you, beloved brethren, be careful! If the invisible Judge is letting loose the stormy winds in order to produce these terrible effects; if He only needs to move the clouds of heaven and thus to shake the whole earth, and to overthrow and ruin the strongest buildings; what can we expect from this Judge when in His wrath He comes to take revenge and to punish sinners? If a mere cloud raised by Him against us is sufficient to strike us down, how shall we be able to resist His almighty power? St. Paul, thinking of the infinite power of the Judge appearing on this awful day, exclaims: *It is a fearful thing to fall into the hands of the living God* (Heb. 10: 31). The Royal Prophet expresses himself with the same force, when in his psalm he says: *The God of gods, the Lord hath spoken; and He hath called the earth. From the rising of the sun, to the going down thereof, God shall come manifestly: our God shall come, and shall not keep silence. A fire shall burn before Him; and a mighty tempest shall be round about Him. He shall call heaven from above, and the earth, to judge His people. Gather ye together His saints to Him; and the heavens shall declare His justice, for God is Judge. Hear, O My people, and I will speak; O Israel, and I will testify to thee; I am God thy God. Understand these things you that forget God; lest He snatch you away, and there be none to deliver you* (Ps. 49). It is not without a special reason that this severe judgment will be accompanied by fire and storms; for it will weigh, as in scales, men who were devoured by the natural fire. Therefore, beloved brethren, keep this great day before your mind's eye, and whatever seems difficult and troublesome, will soon become light and easy, when you compare the one with the other. The prophet Sophonias says to us: *The great day of the Lord is near, it is near and exceeding swift; the voice of the day of the Lord is bitter; the mighty man shall there meet with tribulation. That day is a day of wrath, a day of tribulation and distress, a day of calamity and misery, a day of darkness and obscurity, a day of clouds and whirlwinds; a day of the trumpet and alarm against the fenced cities, and against the high bulwarks* (Soph. 1: 14-16). And the Lord God has spoken of this day through His prophet: *Yet one little while, and I will move the heaven, and the earth, and the sea, and the dry land* (Agg. 2: 7). But, as we have already remarked, if the earth could not resist the force of the wind set in motion, how will man be able to resist the motions of the heavens? For what are all these terrible events causing us so much uneasiness and fear, but heralds announcing to us the wrath of God following them? From all this we conclude that between the evils oppressing us now, and those which will come in the latter days, there is as great a difference as between the power of the highest Judge and the power announcing Him. Therefore, beloved brethren, think of the last day with renewed attention; amend your lives; steadfastly resist all temptations leading you to sin, and wipe out with your tears the sins you have committed. Then the more you have endeavoured, through salutary fear, to anticipate the severity of His judgments, the greater will be the confidence with which you will witness the coming of this Immortal King.

2. SECOND SUNDAY OF ADVENT

GOSPEL: Matt. 11: 2-10. *At that time*: When John had heard in prison the works of Christ, sending two of his disciples, he said to Him: Art Thou He that art to come, or look we for another? And Jesus making answer, said to them: Go and relate to John what you have heard and seen. The blind see, the lame walk, the lepers are cleansed, the deaf hear, the dead rise again, the poor have the Gospel preached to them; and blessed is he that shall not be scandalized in Me. And when they went their way, Jesus began to say to the multitudes, concerning John: What went ye out into the desert to see? A reed shaken with the wind? But what went ye out to see? A man clothed in soft garments? Behold, they that are clothed in soft garments are in the houses of kings. But what went ye out to see? A prophet? Yea, I tell you, and more than a prophet. For this is he of whom it is written: Behold, I send my angel before thy face, who shall prepare thy way before thee.

HOMILY BY ST. JEROME
On St. Matthew 11

I. WHEN JOHN THE BAPTIST SENT HIS DISCIPLES to Jesus, in order to question Him about His mission, he was not ignorant either of His advent or of His dignity as the Messiah. He knew that Jesus was *the Lamb of God Who taketh away the sin of the world,* for he had shown Him to others who had no knowledge of His divine nature. Indeed, the precursor had heard the almighty voice of the Father giving testimony: *This is My beloved Son, in Whom I am well pleased* (Matt. 3: 17). Now we know that our Saviour asked the Jews to show Him the place where Lazarus had been buried, though He knew it well, so that those who would accompany Him thither, should begin to believe in His divine mission, when witnessing the miracle of the raising of Lazarus, that was to follow. In the same way John, who was to be condemned to death by Herod, sent his disciples to Jesus, that by witnessing His miracles and the operation of His divine and almighty power, they might believe in Him, as well as receive instruction from the Divine Teacher Himself, Whom they could then question as their personal teacher. It seems that St. John's disciples were angry with our Lord; for the question shortly before addressed to Him by them, sufficiently disclosed their pride and envy. The Evangelist tells us how the disciples of John came to Him saying: *Why do we and the Pharisees fast often, but Thy disciples do not fast?* (Matt. 9: 14). At another time the same disciples complained to John and said to him: *Rabbi, He that was with thee beyond the Jordan, to Whom thou gavest testimony, behold He baptizeth, and all men come to Him.* (John 3: 26). It was as if they said: We are a small number and almost forsaken, for the multitude are with Jesus Christ, and they follow Him.

II. St. John does not say to our Lord: Art Thou He that is come? But he asks: *Art Thou He that art to come?* As if to say: Let me know whether, after announcing Thy coming into this world, I shall not also announce Thy coming into Limbo, whither I shall soon be going? For is it right and just that the Son of God should die? And is it not Thy own wish to send someone to the just in Limbo and announce to them the mystery of Thy advent?

III. And Jesus answered the inquiring disciples and said to them: *Go and relate to John what you have heard and seen. The blind see, the lame walk, the lepers are cleansed, the deaf hear, the dead rise again.* John had through his disciples asked this question of Jesus: *Art Thou He that art to come, or look we for another?* Yet, instead of answering this question, instead of removing with one word whatsoever had scandalized them, Jesus mentioned His miracles and said to them: Go and relate to John the miracles you have seen; speak of the blind who now see, of the lame who now walk, and of all other miraculous cures you have witnessed. And tell him another fact, no less astonishing, that *the poor have the*

Gospel preached to them. Under the name of *poor* our Saviour meant both the poor in spirit and the poor deprived of the goods of this world; for there will not be any difference between rich and poor, nobleman and serf, when the Gospel is preached to them. This also shows how just and wise and true the Divine Teacher is, Who, when working for the salvation of their souls, considers them all equal. And the words which He added, *Blessed is he that shall not be scandalized in Me,* contain a reproof addressed to the disciples of John, as we shall see later on.

IV. And when these messengers went their way, *Jesus began to say to the multitudes, concerning John: What went ye out into the desert to see? A reed shaken with, the wind? But what went ye out to see? A man clothed in soft garments? Behold they that are clothed in soft garments are in the houses of kings.* Had our Lord condemned St. John by these words, *Blessed is he that is not scandalized in Me,* as many pretend, why does He overwhelm him with praises? Indeed, Jesus praised John the Baptist, because the multitude did not understand the meaning of the disciples' question, and thought that even John was still in doubt as to whether Jesus really were the Messiah, though he had already pointed Him out as the true Lamb of God. In order, therefore, to give the multitude to understand that John did not send his disciples for the purpose of clearing up his doubt, but to have them instructed, our Lord said: *What went ye out into the desert to see?* Was it to see a man who like a reed is shaken with every wind; an inconstant man who is still in doubt about the mission of Him Whom he had already announced? Do you think he envies Me, and that by his preaching he seeks only his own honour and glory and even personal interest? And how could riches and dainty dishes delight one who makes his food of locusts and wild honey? Would soft garments be more useful to him, since he is clothed with camel's hair and a leathern girdle about his loins? Such food and such garments are the appanage of those who look for no other dwelling than a prison; for this will be the abode of them that preach the truth. Flatterers and self-interested people, that is, those who are eager in the pursuit of money and of luxurious living, you find them and their desires in the houses of kings. All this clearly shows that those who lead a severe and penitential life, and who announce the truth in all its purity, without deceit and flattery, must remain away from royal courts and from the palaces of sensual people.

V. The testimony which Truth Itself gave to John the Baptist, saying that he was more than a prophet, exalted him above all other prophets, because, whilst other prophets had, many hundreds of years before, announced again and again the coming of Jesus, John had pointed Him out as already come. Moreover, he was distinguished above all other prophets by the privilege accorded to him of baptizing Jesus in the waters of the Jordan. And in order to point out to all the special dignity of John, our Lord added: *This is he of whom it is written: Behold, I send My angel before thy face, who shall prepare the way before thee* (Mark 3: 2). Not that John possessed the angelic nature, but that, announcing to us the coming of the Saviour, he performed one of the duties of the celestial messengers.

3. THIRD SUNDAY OF ADVENT

GOSPEL: John 1: 19-29. *At that time*: The Jews sent from Jerusalem Priests and Levites to John to ask him: Who art thou? And he confessed and did not deny; and he confessed: I am not the Christ. And they asked him: What then? Art thou Elias? And he said: I am not. Art thou a Prophet? And he answered: No. They said, therefore, unto him: Who art thou, that we may give an answer to them that sent us? What sayest thou of thyself? He said: I am the voice of one crying in the wilderness, *Make straight the way of the Lord*, as said the Prophet Isaias. And they that were sent were of the Pharisees. And they asked him and said to him: Why then dost thou baptize if thou be not Christ, nor Elias, nor the Prophet? John answered them, saying: I baptize with water, but there hath stood One in the midst of you Whom you know not. The same is He that shall come after me, Who is preferred before me; the latchet of Whose shoe I am not worthy to loose. These things were done in Bethania, beyond the Jordan, where John was baptizing.

HOMILY BY POPE ST. GREGORY, PREACHED IN THE CHURCH OF ST. PETER
Seventh Homily on the Gospels

I. THE WORDS OF THIS GOSPEL, BELOVED BRETHren, teach us highly to esteem the humility of St. John. His heroic virtues were so well known, that he was believed by the multitude to be Jesus Christ Himself; yet, far from being led astray by the high estimation in which he was held, or holding a good opinion of himself, he preferred to know himself and to remain in his humble position. *He confessed and did not deny; and he confessed: I am not the Christ*. However, by saying that he was not the Christ, Whom they believed him to be, he did not deny that which he in reality was, and so in truth he became a member of Him Whose name he would not assume. He renounced the name and the high dignity of Jesus Christ, and thus deserved to be a member of Christ; for the confession of his humble condition raised him up to a greatness published and confirmed by our Lord Himself. If now we meditate on some words of Jesus which we find in another part of Holy Scripture, we shall have to clear up a most important question. When the disciples of our Lord asked Him about the second coming of Elias, *He, answering, said to them: Elias indeed shall come. But I say to you, that Elias is already come, and they knew him not, but have done unto him whatsoever they had a mind. Then the disciples understood that He had spoken to them of John the Baptist* (Matt. 17: 11-13). Now, ask John the Baptist if he be Elias, and he will answer: *I am not*. Who can explain this mystery, beloved brethren? Why does the Prophet of truth contradict Him who is the Eternal Truth? For there is a great contradiction between these two testimonies. And if John does not agree with the Truth, who shall be recognised as the Prophet of truth? Yet, when we examine the meaning of these words, which seem to be contradictory, we at once recognise that, although apparently announcing opposite things, they really are in perfect agreement. When the angel, appearing to Zacharias, said that John shall *go before the Lord in the spirit of Elias* (Luke 1: 17), he wished to convey the meaning that John would come into this world with the spirit and power of the prophet Elias, in order to precede the *first* coming of the Redeemer, as Elias would precede His *second* coming. Elias will be the precursor of the great Divine Judge, as John was the precursor of the Divine Redeemer. John was Elias in spirit but not in person; therefore, he could deny to be the person of one whose spirit was in him, according to the testimony of the Lord. Besides, it was proper that Jesus, answering His disciples, should speak of the spirit of St. John; whereas the Baptist, answering a multitude of rough and sensual people, spoke of his body and person, and not of his spirit. In this manner his words do not

3. THIRD SUNDAY OF ADVENT

depart from the way of truth, though at first sight they seem to contain a contradiction.

II. When he promptly added that he was not a prophet, he wished to declare that he had not only the power to announce the Redeemer of the world, but was also able to point Him out; and he declared his mission, saying: *I am the voice of one crying in the wilderness.* You know, beloved brethren, that the only-begotten Son is called the Word of the Father, as St. John the Evangelist tells us, saying: *In the beginning was the Word, and the Word was with God, and the Word was God* (John 1: 1). Now you certainly notice that, when you speak, the sound of the voice strikes the ear before the word is distinctly heard. In the same sense John declares himself to be the voice, because he precedes the Word, for his coming preceded that of the Redeemer; therefore he was the voice through which the Word of the Father was heard. He is also the voice of one crying in the wilderness and announcing to the hopelessly forsaken Judea, the approaching consolation of the Saviour. Lastly, he teaches the meaning of his cry by adding: *Make straight the way of the Lord, as said the prophet Isaias* (Isa. 40: 3). Now, the way of the Lord is made straight and prepared in our hearts, when we hear the word of truth in humility and resignation. His way is also made straight, when through the purity of our life we prepare ourselves to accept the teaching of His truth. Thus Jesus Christ said: *If anyone love Me, he will keep My word, and My Father will love him, and We will come to him, and will make Our abode with him* (John 14: 23). Consequently, he that extols himself in pride and is governed by avarice; he that gives himself up to luxury and lust, closes his heart against truth, opens the door to passions, and shuts every entrance of his soul against the Lord, Who then cannot take up His abode with him,

III. These same men sent by the Jews to St. John, inquired of him why he baptized, since *he was not Christ, nor Elias, nor the Prophet?* But it was envy, not the desire of knowing the truth, that led them to speak. This is sufficiently clear from the words of the Evangelist, who says: *And they that were sent were of the Pharisees*, just as if he had said: They inquired into the doings of John with such eagerness as to show that they wished to find in them something blamable, and that they did not care for his teaching, which only aroused their envy and jealousy. However, since the spirit of meekness and holy zeal does not forsake the saints, even when the envious and wicked question them, we see that John the Baptist answered with words of life and salvation the questions inspired by envy and hatred, and said: *I baptize with water; but there hath stood One in the midst of you Whom you know not.* The baptism of John was only a baptism with water, as he himself confessed, therefore it did not give the Holy Ghost. It had not the power of forgiving sin; only of purifying the bodies, but not the souls, of those who received it. He gave this unfruitful baptism only to fulfil his office of precursor, preceding by this baptism the one of the Redeemer, just as in his birth he had preceded the coming of Jesus into this world. Even in his preaching he had come before the Saviour. Thus by the representation of this sacrament he signified the real Sacrament instituted by our Lord. While announcing the mystery of the Redeemer to the multitude, John taught them that this Redeemer, Whom they knew not, stood in the midst of them. For He Who was God had taken human nature, was like us in everything, and was visibly among men; yet the splendour of His Divinity was hidden from their eyes. And when he added: *The same is He that shall come after me, Who is preferred before me,* he wished to teach us, that if Jesus Christ, as to His birth, has come after him, according to His dignity He was infinitely preferred before him. And he gives the reason of this preference in the preceding words, *He was before me,* and declares that He Who was born after him far surpasses him, because time cannot enclose Him in its bounds. Though He was born of His Virgin Mother in time, yet He was begotten of His Father from all eternity. However, to show even more clearly the esteem and reverence which were due to the Redeemer, he confessed in deep humility that he was not worthy to loose the latchet of His shoe. Among the ancients there was a custom that, when a man would not accept the bride allotted to him by law, this bride was to take off his shoes. This clearly indicates that, when Jesus came to abide among men, He also showed Himself as the Bridegroom of the Holy Church, according to the words of John himself, saying: *He that hath the bride is the bridegroom* (John 3: 29). Now, in order to combat the opinion, according to which some thought that the person of Jesus was John the Baptist, he positively declares that he was not even worthy to loose the latchet of the Redeemer's shoe, acknowledging by this that, as he could neither assume the name nor the nature of the Bridegroom, so neither had he the power to uncover the feet of the Redeemer. There is yet another meaning in these words. Everyone knows that what serves to cover the feet is taken from the skin of dead animals. Now, our Saviour, taking a body like ours, appeared in this world with the covering of our mortal and corruptible nature. Who is able to understand the mystery of the Incarnation of the Word of God? Who can comprehend how the highest Spirit, giving life to everything, received life in the womb of a mother? How was He, who had no beginning, but is eternal, and showed Himself in time, conceived? And as the obscurity of this mystery is signified by the latchet of the Saviour of the world, we understand why John the Baptist declared that he had not the power to loose it. Though he had recognised by his prophetic spirit the Incarnation of the Word, his human mind was not able to conceive this great mystery. When he tells us that he is not worthy to loose the latchet of the Saviour's shoe, he wishes to teach us that he acknowledges his ignorance, and that we are not to be astonished at seeing that He, Who was born after him, was preferred before him; because the mystery of our Saviour's nativity was far beyond his conception and understanding. Lastly, this confession of St. John tells us that, though he might have possessed the required knowledge imparted to him in the gift of prophecy, he still remained in ignorance concerning this incomprehensible mystery.

IV. Beloved brethren, our special attention is called to the way in which the saints endeavour to preserve the virtue of humility. As soon as they are aware of the extraordinary wisdom and knowledge imparted to them, they consider all the things which they do not know, so that the consideration of their weakness may keep them humble, since the knowledge of their perfection might engender pride in them; they are convinced that, knowledge being a virtue, humility is its best preservative. For, be the mind ever so enlightened by extraordinary attainments, it must be humbled deeply, that the blessings received and acquired by knowledge may not be blown away by the wind of pride. Therefore, beloved brethren, when you do good works, remember the evil you have done in past years; for if you keep your faults before your eyes, you will never feel vain delight nor take thoughtless pleasure in any merit you may possess. Consider yourselves less than others, especially less than those not entrusted to your care. Should you notice faults in your neighbour, consider that he possesses virtues which you do not see. Everyone is intended to acquire a certain degree of eminence through his merits; yet in a certain sense he must not recognise this, lest he lose through pride the virtue he has attained. *Woe to you,* says the prophet Isaias, *that are wise in your own eyes, and prudent in your own conceits* (Isa. 5: 21). St. Paul confirms these words when he says: *Be not wise in your own conceits* (Rom. 12: 16). When Saul was puffed up with pride God said to him: *When thou wast a little one in thy own eyes, was thou not made the head of the tribes of Israel?* (I Kings 15: 17). That is, when thou didst esteem thyself but little among others, I exalted thee above all of them; but now, as thou thinkest thyself great, thou hast become little in My eyes. On the contrary, we see David who, in spite of his power and glory, thought but little of himself, dancing before the ark and saying: *Before the Lord . . . I will both play and make myself meaner than I have done, and I will be little in my own eyes* (2 Kings 6: 22). But who is he that would preserve himself from pride? had he done such heroic deeds as this King, and counted in his life so many wonders as we read in the history of this King? He had, by the strength of his arms, struck down lions and bears and cut them to pieces; he was preferred to his brothers, though the last of them, and was chosen to wear the royal crown; he was anointed by the prophet, in order to take the place of a reprobate King, and to govern the kingdom of Israel. With one single stone he had overthrown a powerful giant, the terror of Saul's army. Yet,

3. THIRD SUNDAY OF ADVENT

in spite of these brilliant deeds, and in the midst of his triumph and exaltation, this powerful King, as seen by his humble words and feelings, thought but little of himself. If the greatest saints, amidst their wonderful deeds, thought themselves worthy of contempt, how will those who do not practise the least virtue excuse their vanity and pride? For should we deserve praise for our good works, yet they must be considered as nothing, unless humility give them their value. Virtue will lower, not exalt us, when humility is wanting. The Christian who heaps up virtues without the accompanying humility is like a man exposing dust to the wind; it will be carried away by the wind and thrown into his own eyes. Therefore, beloved brethren, cling to humility in all your actions, as to the root of all good works. Do not consider those whom you surpass in merits, but fix your eyes on those who excel you in virtues; then you will place before you as models those who are most perfect, and by your own humility you will attain the highest degree of perfection.

4. FOURTH SUNDAY OF ADVENT

GOSPEL: Luke 3: 1-6. Now, in the fifteenth year of the reign of Tiberius Caesar, Pontius Pilate being Governor of Judea, and Herod Tetrarch of Galilee, and Philip his brother Tetrarch of Iturea and the country of Trachonitis, and Lysanias Tetrarch of Abilina, under the high priests Annas and Caiphas, the word of the Lord was made unto John, the son of Zachary, in the desert. And he came into all the country about the Jordan, preaching the baptism of penance for the remission of sins, as it was written in the book of the sayings of Isaias the prophet: 'A voice of one crying in the wilderness: Prepare ye the way of the Lord; make straight His paths. Every valley shall be filled, and every mountain and hill shall be brought low; and the crooked shall be made straight, and the rough ways plain. And all flesh shall see the salvation of God.'

HOMILY BY POPE ST. GREGORY, PREACHED IN THE CHURCH OF ST. JOHN THE BAPTIST
Twentieth Homily on the Gospels

I. THE GOSPEL, SPEAKING OF THE ROMAN Emperor Tiberius and of the different Princes governing Judea and Galilee and other provinces, has no other motive but to tell us the year in which *the word of the Lord was made unto John*, the Precursor of the true Messiah. He was to announce to the world Him Who would save some among the Jews and a great number of Gentiles; therefore the time of his ministry is given by the name of the Emperor who reigned over the Gentiles and by the Princes governing in Judea. The enrolment which had taken place in the world, indicates that the Gentiles were to be united, whilst the faithless nation of the Jews would be dispersed. For the Romans recognised but one supreme chief, whilst Judea was divided into four provinces under as many Princes. Thus was verified among the Jews the word of the Redeemer: *Every kingdom divided against itself shall be brought to desolation* (Luke 11: 17). And the names of the high priests are given after those of the Kings, because John the Baptist announced the Messiah, who was both Priest and King. St. Luke, mentioning in his Gospel the ministry of the Precursor, speaks at the same time of the office of priests and rulers.

II. *John came into all the country about the Jordan, preaching the baptism of penance for the remission of sins.* From the words of Holy Scripture it appears that St. John not only preached the baptism of penance, but also administered it to some of the Jews. His baptism could not forgive sins, for only the baptism instituted by Jesus can do that. However, he preached the baptism of penance; for, though he had not the power to give the baptism which sanctifies, at least he announced it to the world. This great prophet had preached, in the ministry of the Word, the Saviour Who, being the uncreated Word of the Father, was made man for us; and now he represented by his sterile baptism the Sacrament of the real Baptism, which alone can sanctify, truth and reality being preceded by shadows and symbols.

III. And the Gospel adds: *As it was written in the book of the sayings of Isaias the prophet: A voice of one crying in the wilderness: Prepare ye the way of the Lord; make straight His paths.* When John was asked by the priests and Levites: *Who art thou?* he answered: *I am the voice of one crying in the wilderness* (John 1: 23). He was called by the prophet a voice, as we have shown elsewhere, because by his voice he had preceded the Divine Word. We also know the words uttered by this voice, for the prophet himself tells them, saying: *Prepare ye the way of the Lord; make straight His paths.* We learn from all this that he, who preached the true faith and the necessity of good works, wished also to prepare the hearts of those who listened to him, that is, to prepare the way by which the Lord was coming. For he removed from men's hearts whatever could prevent the grace of God from entering into and illuminating

4. FOURTH SUNDAY OF ADVENT

them by the Divine light. The minister of the word makes the ways straight for the steps of the Redeemer, when he awakens pious thoughts in the mind of his hearers. Therefore, when it is said: *Every valley shall be filled, and every mountain and hill shall be brought low,* we understand that the humble are meant by the valleys and the proud by the mountains. We know now why at the coming of the Saviour of the world the valleys were to be filled and the mountains to be brought low, for He Himself said: *Everyone that exalteth himself, shall be humbled; and he that humbleth himself, shall be exalted* (Luke 14: 11). A valley, which is filled up, rises and increases; whilst a mountain or hill brought down will decrease. Thus we see that the Gentiles, who in all humility received the faith in Jesus Christ, the Mediator between God and man, received the fulness of grace; whilst the Jews, puffed up and filled with pride and vanity, lost the grace of God through their faithlessness. The valleys are filled, because the humble, receiving into their hearts the word of salvation, obtain at the same time grace to help them to practise virtue, according to the words of the psalmist: *Thou sendest forth springs in the vales* (Ps. 103: 10); and again: *The vales shall abound with corn* (Ps. 64: 14). The water running down the mountains represents those proud men who have forsaken the doctrine of truth; but humble souls receive the truth preached to them, like the valleys receive the waters which render them fertile. Indeed, we recognise this fact when we consider those whose meekness and simplicity are despised by the world, but who are nourished and filled with the bread of Divine truth.

IV. When the multitude saw the extraordinary holiness of John the Baptist, they believed him to be the firm and high mountain announced in Holy Scripture: *It shall come to pass that the mountain of the house of the Lord shall be prepared in the top of mountains, and high above the hills; and the people shall flow to it* (Mich. 4: 1). These words were applied to St. John the more confidently since, according to the Gospel, he was taken for Christ Himself: *The people were of opinion, and all were thinking in their hearts of John, that perhaps he might be the Christ* (Luke 3: 15). The multitude, thinking this in their hearts, insisted on an answer, and said to him: *Art thou not Christ?* But John the Baptist, through his own humility, was in his own eyes like a deep valley. He was, therefore, filled with the grace of the Holy Ghost, and, making known the opinion he had of himself, he answered: *He that shall come after me is preferred before me, the latchet of whose shoe I am not worthy to loose.* Again he said: *He that hath the bride is the bridegroom; but the friend of the bridegroom, who standeth and heareth him, rejoiceth with joy because of the bridegroom's voice. This my joy therefore is fulfilled. He must increase, but I must decrease* (John 3: 29, 30). We see, therefore, that John the Baptist, on account of his great virtues, was taken for Jesus Christ by those who saw and heard him. In order to bring them out of this error, he answered that he was not only not Christ, but that he was not even worthy to loose the latchet of His shoe, that is, to investigate and understand the great mystery of the Incarnation. They also imagined, when taking John for Jesus Christ, that the Church was His Bride. However, he formally declared that the true Bridegroom was He who possessed the bride, as if to say: I am not the bridegroom, only the friend of the Bridegroom, giving us to understand that his only joy consisted in hearing the Bridegroom's voice, and that he did not glory in his own voice. For the joy which St. John felt in his heart did not come from the fact that the multitude listened to him in sincere humility, but from the hope that the voice of truth had gained their hearts, and that by his teaching he would then unfold the truth more fully to them. He could, therefore, say that his joy was full; for he that rejoices only because his voice was listened to, cannot possess real and entire happiness.

V. St. John, speaking of our Redeemer, added: *He must increase, but I must decrease.* Now, let us consider in what our Lord could increase and in what His prophet could decrease. This difficulty is easily overcome when we remember that the people, seeing the wonderful mortification of John the Baptist, and his retirement in the desert far from all intercourse with men, thought he was Christ the Messiah. Whereas, seeing Jesus among publicans, conversing and eating with them, and not avoiding the company of sinners, they took Him for a prophet only, and not for the Christ.

But what John said was literally fulfilled, when the time came that the Redeemer, Whom they had looked upon as a mere prophet, was recognised as the Christ, and that John the Baptist, taken for Christ, was then known only as His prophet. Then, indeed, was fulfilled what John said of Jesus: *He must increase, but I must decrease.* And our Lord increased in the esteem of men as soon as they recognised Who He in reality was; whilst the honour given to John decreased, when it became known that he was only the prophet of the Messiah. Thus the holiness of John the Baptist was preserved, because he remained humble. The greater number of those who wish to attain to greatness, very often by their proud thoughts and sentiments, fall deeply, and verify in their lives these words: *Every valley shall be filled, and every mountain and hill shall be brought low.* For God is with the humble, and gives them His richest blessings; whereas He forsakes the heart of the proud man.

VI. Again it is said: *And the crooked shall be made straight, and the rough ways plain.* These words will be fulfilled when the wicked, whose hearts are corrupted by injustice, endeavour to return to God by practising Christian justice. And the rough ways are made plain, when hard and passionate hearts are softened and become peaceful through the grace of God. When the word of truth is not received, but finds an insensible heart, it is withdrawn, on account of the obstacles placed in its way. Whereas, when through the unction of the grace of God, we are softened and willingly receive the instructions and exhortations of God's ministry, the truth they announce, instead of finding rough ways, finds them smooth and plain, and thus easily penetrates the heart.

VII. *And all flesh,* continues the Evangelist, *shall see the salvation of God;* that is, all men shall see Jesus Christ. But in this life all men cannot see the Redeemer. It seems, therefore, that the prophet spoke of the future, that he saw heaven open before him, and Jesus in His glory, surrounded by angels, apostles and saints, as He will come to judge the world. Then all men, both the just and the unjust, will see the Judge. The just, that they may receive the due reward of everlasting happiness; and the wicked, that they may be punished in everlasting torments for their sins and vices. Amen.

5. CHRISTMAS DAY

GOSPEL: Luke 2: 1-14. And it came to pass that in those days there went out a decree from Caesar Augustus that the whole world should be enrolled. This enrolling was first made by Cyrinus, the Governor of Syria. And all went to be enrolled, every one into his own city. And Joseph also went up from Galilee out of the city of Nazareth into Judea, to the city of David, which is called Bethlehem, because he was of the house and family of David, to be enrolled with Mary, his espoused wife, who was with child. And it came to pass, that when they were there, her days were accomplished that she should be delivered. And she brought forth her first-born Son, and wrapped Him up in swaddling-clothes, and laid Him in a manger, because there was no room for them in the inn. And there were in the same country shepherds watching and keeping the night-watches over their flock. And behold an angel of the Lord stood by them, and the brightness of God shone round about them; and they feared with a great fear. And the angel said to them: Fear not; for behold I bring you good tidings of great joy, that shall be to all the people; for this day is born to you a SAVIOUR, Who is Christ the Lord, in the city of David. And this shall be a sign unto you: You shall find the Infant wrapped in swaddling-clothes, and laid in a manger. And suddenly there was with the angel a multitude of the heavenly army, praising God, and saying: Glory to God in the highest, and on earth peace to men of good will.

HOMILY BY POPE ST. GREGORY, PREACHED IN THE CHURCH OF OUR LADY ON CHRISTMAS DAY
Eight Homily on the Gospels

I. SINCE BY THE MERCY OF GOD WE ARE TO SAY three Masses today, there is not much time left for preaching on this Gospel; at the same time the festival of the Lord's Nativity obliges us to speak a few words. Let us first ask why, when our Lord was to be born, the world was enrolled? Was it not clearly to show that He Who was to come into this world and be made man would one day enroll His elect and inscribe their names in the book of eternity? For the prophet, speaking of the reprobate, says: *Let them be blotted out of the book of the living; and with the just let them not be written* (Ps. 68: 29). Then it is not without a special reason that the Lord is born in Bethlehem. For the name *Bethlehem* signifies the *House of Bread*, and this is the birthplace of Him Who said: *I am the living Bread, which came down from heaven* (John 6: 51). We see then that the name of Bethlehem was prophetically given to the place where Christ was born, because it was there that He was to appear in the flesh, by the eating of which the souls of the elect are fed unto life everlasting. He was born, not in His mother's house, but away from home. And this is a mystery, showing that by assuming our mortality He was born in a strange country. We say strange, considering the Divine nature of our Redeemer, and not His Divine power. For, referring to this power, Holy Scripture says that, when the Lord came into this world, He came unto His own. But, when thinking of His Divine nature, and knowing that He was begotten of the Father before all worlds, we may say that by taking our nature in time, He came into a strange country. Again, considering, as the prophet says, that *all flesh is grass* (Isa. 40: 6), we easily understand how Jesus, taking this flesh, changed it into wheat, since He said of Himself: *Unless the grain of wheat falling into the ground die, itself remaineth alone* (John 12: 24). This is the reason why the Divine Child is seen in a manger after His birth, that His flesh, like pure wheat, may draw to Him the faithful, as mysterious animals, to be fed and filled with eternal wisdom. And when it is said that the angel showed himself to the shepherds keeping the night-watches, and that a wonderful light surrounded them, we learn from this that those, who carefully attend to the flocks entrusted to them must be favoured with deeper knowledge, since their ministry is highly meritorious. For, whilst they carefully watch over their flocks, they are enlightened by God with graces more abundant than those given to others.

5. CHRISTMAS DAY

11. The angel announced that a King was born, and suddenly there was with the angel a multitude of the heavenly host praising God and saying: *Glory to God in the highest, and on earth peace to men of good will.* Before the Incarnation of the Son of God there was disagreement between the angels and men. Original sin and the crimes daily committed in the world were the cause of this division. It was only just that the angels, being the friends and faithful servants of God, should look upon men as strangers and have no communication with them on account of their transgressing the commandments. But since man submitted to God and recognised Him as his lawful Master, the heavenly spirits consider mankind as their fellow-citizens. Though highly superior to us, they do not despise our weakness, since the King of heaven and earth came down and took upon Him this human weakness. These blessed spirits, forgetting their former aversion, wish to live in friendship with us. Instead of despising us as frail humanity, they look upon us as their fellow-creatures. We read in Holy Scripture that Lot and Josua prostrate on the ground worshipped the angels sent by God; but when St. John fell down to adore before the feet of the angel he was prevented from doing so, for the angel said: *See thou do it not, for I am thy fellow-servant and of thy brethren* (Apoc. 22: 9). Why did the angels, before the coming of the Redeemer, see men prostrate before them and prevent them not? And why were they unwilling, after the birth of our Saviour, to receive such honour? Was it not because they saw the human nature, which they had before despised, now exalted high above their own in the person of Jesus, true God and true man? Also because they dread to see the human nature humbled, since they adore that humanity in the person of the King of Majesty, their own King. Lastly, the angels consider man as their equal because they adore God made man, sitting at the right hand of the Father. Let us, therefore, beloved brethren, beware of every sin, by which we might be made unworthy of that heavenly city, which God has prepared for us as well as for His angels. Let us lead such good lives that they may correspond with our dignity. Avoid, therefore, impurity and lust, even every sinful thought. Let not wickedness soil the purity of

your souls; let not the poison of envy and hatred penetrate your hearts. Keep your souls free from pride, covetousness and anger, and especially from the desire of tasting the sinful pleasures of this world. Remember that you have been called *the sons of the most High* (Ps. 81: 6). Defend in yourselves the glory of God by avoiding sin, for God was made man in order to honour us and make us partakers of His eternal glory. Amen.

6. THE FEAST OF ST. STEPHEN, THE FIRST MARTYR

GOSPEL: Matt, 23: 34-39. *At that time:* Jesus said unto the Scribes and Pharisees: Behold, I send to you prophets, and wise men and scribes; and some of them you will put to death and crucify, and some you will scourge in your synagogues and persecute from city to city; that upon you may come all the just blood that hath been shed upon the earth, from the blood of Abel the just even unto the blood of Zacharias, the son of Barachias, whom you killed between the temple and the altar. Amen, I say to you all these things shall come upon this generation. Jerusalem, Jerusalem, thou that killest the prophets and stonest them that are sent unto thee, how often would I have gathered together thy children as the hen doth gather her chickens under her wings, and thou wouldest not. Behold, your house shall be left to you desolate. For I say to you, you shall not see Me henceforth till you say: Blessed is He that cometh in the name of the Lord.

HOMILY BY ST. JEROME
Commentary on St. Matthew 23, Bk. IV

I. THE WORDS ADDRESSED TO THE JEWS BY OUR Redeemer, when He said: *Fill ye up the measure of your fathers* (Matt, 23: 32), especially refer, as we have already remarked, to Himself, whom the Jews afterwards put to death. In a secondary sense they may also be applied to His disciples, of whom He says: *Behold, I send to you prophets, and wise men, and scribes; and some of them you will put to death and crucify, and some you will scourge in your synagogues, and persecute from city to city.* Observe that, according to the Apostle writing to the Corinthians (1 Cor. 12: 4), there are diversities of gifts granted to Christ's followers. Some are prophets of that which is to come; some are wise men, who know the suitable season for rebuke or exhortation; some are scribes learned in the law. And of these they stoned Stephen, slew Paul with the sword, crucified Peter, and scourged the disciples, as we read in the Acts of the Apostles (5: 40; 16: 23). When these men, sent by God, saw that they were universally despised, persecuted from one city to another, and lastly driven out of the land of the Jews, they went to the Gentiles. After reproaching the Jews with the blood of so many of their own people which they had shed, our Lord added these words: *Amen, I say to you, all these things shall come upon this generation.* But the multitude listening to Jesus, when He said these words, had not shed the blood of Abel and other saints of the Old Testament unto *the blood of Zacharias.* Why, then, should they be guilty of all that blood? Because, in the language of the Scriptures, all the just are included in one and the same generation, and all the wicked in another generation, of which they are considered to be the offspring. As to the generation of the just we hear the prophet say: *Who shall ascend into the mountain of the Lord, or who shall stand in His holy place?* (Ps. 23: 3). And, after speaking of those who shall ascend into this mountain, he concludes with these words: *This is the generation of them that seek Him, of them that seek the face of the God of Jacob.* The same prophet, speaking in another psalm of all the saints, says that heaven will ever bless the generation of the just. Considering the wicked mentioned in that passage, we see that they are called a brood, or generation, of vipers (Matt. 3: 7), and all these things shall come upon that accursed generation. The prophet Ezechiel, after enumerating all the sins committed in this world, adds these terrible words: *If these three men, Noe, Daniel, and Job, shall be in the land, they shall deliver their own souls by their justice, but the land shall be desolate* (Ezec. 14: 14, 16). The prophet includes under the names of Noe, Daniel, and Job, all the just who by their virtues were like these men. Then, all those who persecuted the Apostles, and imitated Cain and Joas in their sins, are included in the generation of the wicked.

6. THE FEAST OF ST. STEPHEN, THE FIRST MARTYR

II. It is a matter of dispute among commentators, who is meant by Zacharias, the son of Barachias. We read of several persons of the name of Zacharias; but here, in order to prevent any mistake, it is particularly said: *Whom you killed between the temple and the altar.* I have read various opinions in various places upon this question, and I will give each of them. Some hold that Zacharias, the son of Barachias, is the eleventh of the twelve minor prophets, and this opinion is supported by the father's name. But Holy Scripture nowhere tells us that this prophet was slain between the temple and the altar, and it is hardly possible that he can have been so, for in his time it could scarcely be said that even the ruins of the temple still existed. Others maintain that this Zacharias was Zacharias, the father of John the Baptist. This interpretation is derived from the dreams of the Apocryphal Gospels, wherein it is asserted that he was martyred for preaching Christ's coming. Again, others will have it that this Zacharias, the son of Barachias, was that Zacharias of whom we read, that he was killed by Joas, King of Juda, between the temple and the altar. Against this it is to be remarked that that Zacharias was not the son of Barachias, but of Joiada the priest; whence it is written in Holy Scripture: *Joas did not remember the kindness which Joiada, his father, had done to him* (2 Par. 24: 22). The question, therefore, arises, if this opinion be true, why, the name and manner of death both agreeing with the explanation, Zacharias is called, not the son of Joiada, but of Barachias. In Hebrew *Barachias* signifies *the blessed of the Lord*, and Joiada *justice*. In the Gospel used by the Nazarenes the name of Joiada is used instead of Barachias.

III. *Jerusalem, Jerusalem, thou that killest the prophets, and stonest them that are sent to thee.* Let us not imagine that by the word *Jerusalem* our Lord meant the stones and buildings of the city. No, He spoke of the inhabitants, and complained, like a kind father complains of his children's wickedness. In another Gospel (Luke 19: 41) we are told that when Jesus saw the city He wept over it; and by the words added by our Saviour: *How often would I have gathered together thy children*, He teaches us that all the prophets who had arisen among the Jews, in order to convert them, were sent in His name. When, lastly, He tells the Jews that their house would be left desolate, He only confirms what He had already announced to the prevaricating people by the prophet Jeremiah, saying: *I have forsaken my house; I have left my inheritance* (12: 7). Indeed, we see in our time that the house of the Jews, that is, the magnificent temple, considered as one of the wonders of the world, is a forsaken and desolate place, since Jesus Christ abandoned it, and since the Heir was killed by the perfidious nation, which endeavoured to seize upon the inheritance.

IV. In the same manner our Lord addressed Jerusalem and the whole Jewish nation, when He said: *I say to you, you shall not see Me henceforth until you say: Blessed is He that cometh in the name of the Lord*. These last words, which the children used when expressing their joy at the triumphant entry of Jesus into Jerusalem, are taken from the 117th Psalm, in which the royal prophet speaks of Jesus. By these words our Lord wished to tell the Jews, that they would never see Him unless they did penance, and openly confessed that He was the Son of God the Almighty, announced by the prophets. Time was given to the Jews to be converted. Their only duty was to acknowledge and adore Him, Who was sent by the Father to be their King; then they would see Jesus Christ and reign with Him.

7. SUNDAY WITHIN THE OCTAVE OF CHRISTMAS

GOSPEL: Luke 2: 33-40. *At that time*: Joseph and Mary, the mother of Jesus, were wondering at these things which were spoken concerning Him. And Simeon blessed them, and said to Mary His mother: Behold, the Child is set for the fall, and for the resurrection of many in Israel, and for a sign that shall be contradicted. And thy own soul a sword shall pierce, that out of many hearts thoughts may be revealed. And there was one Anna, a prophetess, the daughter of Phanuel, of the tribe of Aser. She was far advanced in years, and had lived with her husband seven years from her virginity; and she was a widow until fourscore and four years; who departed not from the temple, by fastings and prayers serving night and day. Now, she at the same hour coming in, confessed to the Lord, and spoke of Him to all that looked for the redemption of Israel. And after they had performed all things according to the law of the Lord, they returned into Galilee, into their city Nazareth. And the Child grew, and waxed strong, full of wisdom; and the grace of God was in Him.

HOMILY BY THE VENERABLE BEDE
Bk. I, On St. Luke 2

I. IN THE GOSPEL WE SEE THAT JOSEPH WAS called the father of our Saviour; but we know that he was not, according to the erroneous interpretation of the Photinians, the real father of Jesus, but only His reputed father, in order to save the honour of Mary his spouse. The Evangelist knew that the Virgin, though a mother, had conceived by the operation of the Holy Ghost. However, to follow the common expressions used by historians, he made no scruple at calling St. Joseph the father of Jesus. Moreover, we may apply to him the qualifications of a father in the same sense and for the same reasons as we call him the spouse of Mary, though she remained a Virgin in spite of the conjugal bond. Indeed, on account of this bond, uniting Joseph with his spouse, he deserved the title of father of Jesus more justly than if he had adopted Him; and he would have possessed the rights of a father over Jesus, even though not born of his spouse, had he adopted Him according to the law.

II. It was in very truth that Simeon, when speaking of the Redeemer, could say to Mary: *Behold, the Child is set for the fall, and for the resurrection of many in Israel.* Indeed, many will rise through Jesus Christ, the light and the glory of Israel. He Himself teaches us this truth, when He says: *I am the resurrection and the life. And everyone that liveth, and believeth in Me, shall not die for ever* (John 11: 25, 26). And He will be an occasion of fall for many, because He is the stone which, rejected by the builders, has become the head of the corner, and will grind to dust those on whom it falls, those who do not believe in Him. It was of them that He spoke, saying: *If I had not come and spoken to them, they would not have sin; but now they have no excuse for their sin* (John 15: 22). But Jesus is also an occasion of fall for many, not only in His own person, but also in the person of His ministers. Thus we hear St. Paul say: *We are the good odour of Christ unto God, in them that are saved, and in them that perish* (2 Cor. 2: 15). If, therefore, we willingly accept the doctrine of salvation, preached by God through His ministers sent to us, then it will be a good odour sanctifying our soul; whereas the same doctrine will be an odour of death and an occasion of fall for those who neglect or despise it. When the prophecy again tells us that this Child *shall be contradicted*, we know that by these words is meant the faith in the death of our Lord on the cross preached to the world. St. Paul tells us that the Jews, speaking of the Christians, said: *We know that this sect* — those believing and teaching this doctrine — is everywhere spoken against (Acts 28: 22). And the same Apostle says: *We preach Christ crucified, unto the Jews indeed a stumbling-block, and unto the Gentiles, foolishness* (1 Cor. 1: 23).

III. Holy Simeon again said to our Blessed Lady that a sword would pierce her own soul. We easily understand that a sword of sorrow, grief and suffering, resulting from the great sufferings of her Son, was meant by these words; for no tradition relates that Mary died by the sword, which after all has power over the body only and not over the soul. Holy Scripture speaks of this spiritual sword: *Their tongue is a sharp sword* (Ps. 56: 5). Though the Blessed Virgin Mary was fully convinced that her Son Jesus, the eternally Begotten of the Father, could avoid death, though about to accept it willingly, yet, being His Mother, she could not but suffer the most acute pain on seeing His crucifixion. The sword which, according to the prophet, pierced the soul of Mary, clearly indicates the terrible anguish suffered by this sorrowful mother in her own soul. Before the Redeemer appeared in this world, no one could recognise with certitude those Jews who, either received the grace of Jesus Christ, or refused to accept the grace that was offered them. But when the tidings of His birth were spread abroad, then the hidden thoughts of many hearts were revealed. King Herod, hearing this news, *was troubled, and all Jerusalem with him*; whereas the shepherds rejoiced when the angel said: *I bring you good tidings of great joy; for this day is born to you a Saviour* (Luke 2: 10, 11); and they returned, glorifying and praising God for all the things they had heard and seen (verse 20). The splendour of the miracles and Divine doctrine of the Saviour attracted many to Him, and they listened to His words; whereas others called Him a deceiver, and despised Him. And when they saw Him hanging on the Cross, they even blasphemed Him, and esteemed Him worthy of that cruel punishment; whilst the former showed deep sympathy and grief on seeing the Author of life condemned to death. The Church of Jesus has until now felt this sword of suffering, and will be pierced by it till the end of the world; for, as a mark of faith and salvation, she will be continually contradicted. It is with grief and sorrow that the Church sees great multitudes persevering in infidelity and rushing on to perdition, though very many, hearing and obeying the word of God, will rise with Jesus Christ. Her sorrow increases when the thoughts of many hearts are revealed, and when she perceives in the field, in which she has been continually sowing the seed of the Gospel, cockle growing up. Indeed, the knowledge that the cockle of sin and vice is eminently more fertile, that it takes deep root and shoots forth luxuriantly, choking much of the wheat of virtue and innocence, causes her tears to flow in abundance.

IV. Anna, the prophetess, who by her long and holy life was accounted worthy to see the Redeemer of Israel, and to give testimony to the truth that she perceived in her prophetic mind, is the type of the Church, who sees herself deprived of the visible presence of her Bridegroom and Lord, since He left this mortal life. The number of years mentioned by the Gospel as being the age of this widow, represents the time of the exile of the Church in a foreign land. She cannot, on account of this present life in the world, be united with her Lord and Master, Whose coming, like Anna the prophetess, she impatiently awaits at the entrance of the temple, for she trusts in His promise: *We will come to him, and make our abode with him* (John 14: 23). After the testimony given by Simeon to the Redeemer of the world, and given also about herself by a Virgin in the conjugal state, it seems quite natural, in order not to exclude any kind of conditions, that a widow, venerable both by her position and holy life, should appear in the person of Anna and testify to the coming of the Redeemer of Israel, and confirm this by her praises.

V. St. Luke speaks here of the return of Jesus and His parents to Galilee, *after they had performed all things according to the law of the Lord.* He does not mention the flight into Egypt, already recorded by St. Matthew, and which he did not think it necessary to repeat, to the interruption of his narrative. At all events, we know that St. Luke, like the other Evangelists, was enlightened by the Holy Ghost; and we know that, had the things he omitted not been committed to writing, the omission would have been supplied later on by the inspiration of God, so that the reader could place them in their proper position in the Gospel story. As to the words added by St. Luke that *the Child grew and waxed strong, full of wisdom, and the grace of God was in Him,* we remark that Jesus Christ, having taken a human nature, was subjected to all its weaknesses and infirmities, and could as man grow and wax strong. But, considering Him only as the Word of God and God Himself, we know that He could not increase in wisdom. However, in all truth it may be said that He was full of wisdom and grace, since He was filled with grace as the Mediator between God and man, and from His birth was overflowing with grace, on account of the perfect union between God and man in one Divine Person. St. John confirms all this when, speaking of the Son of God made man, he calls Him *full of grace and truth* (John 1: 14), meaning by this expression the fulness of His Divinity, expressed by St. Luke under the name of wisdom.

8. THE FEAST OF THE CIRCUMCISION

GOSPEL: Luke 2: 21. *At that time*: After eight days were accomplished that the Child should be circumcised, His name was called Jesus, which was called by the angel before He was conceived in the womb.

HOMILY BY ST. AMBROSE
Bk. II, On St. Luke 2

I. THE CHILD IS CIRCUMCISED. WHO IS THAT Child? It is the Child of Whom it is said: *A Child is born to us; a Son is given to us* (Isa. 9: 6). *Made under the law, that He might redeem them who were under the law* (Gal. 4: 4). And His parents *carried Him to Jerusalem to present Him to the Lord* (Luke 2: 22). I have explained, in my commentary on Isaias, what is meant by being presented to the Lord; I will not, therefore, enter into the subject again. He that is circumcised in heart has God for his Protector, for *the eyes of the Lord are upon the just* (Ps. 33: 16). You will easily see that, as all the ceremonies of the old law were types of the realities in the new, so the circumcision of the body—a necessary duty—signified the cleansing of the heart from the guilt of sin. But, since the body and the mind of men remain yet infected with a proneness to sin, the circumcision of the eighth day is also a type of that complete cleansing of sin with which we shall be endowed at the Resurrection. This ceremony was also performed in obedience to the commandment of God: *Every male opening the womb shall be called holy to the Lord* (Luke 2: 23). These words were written with special reference to the delivery of the Blessed Virgin. Truly, He that opened her womb was holy, for He was altogether without spot; and we understand that the law was specially written for

Him from the words of the angel: *The Holy which shall be born of Thee shall be called the Son of God* (Luke 1: 35). Indeed, the Redeemer of the world was not born after a human and corporal manner, but by the operation of the Holy Ghost, by Whom He was conceived in the womb of the most pure Virgin Mary.

II. Among all the children born of women the Lord Jesus Christ stood alone, and could in all truth be called holy. From the first moment of His immaculate birth He felt no contagion from human corruption, for His heavenly majesty drove it away. If we are to follow the letter, and say that every male opening the womb is holy, how shall we explain that so many have been sinful? Was Achab holy? Were the false prophets holy? Were they holy on whom Elias justly called down fire from heaven? But He, to Whom the sacred commandment of the law of God is mystically directed, is the Holy One of Israel. He also alone opened the secret womb of His holy virgin-bride, the Church, filling her with sinless fruitfulness to give birth to Christian souls. Therefore, Jesus Christ, on account of the wonderful and supernatural manner in which He was conceived and born, is the only first-born among men. Nor is this surprising, since we remember that He said to His prophet: *I knew thee, and before thou earnest forth out of the womb, I sanctified thee* (Jer.1: 5). Now, the same Who blessed and sanctified the mother, and granted birth to this prophet is He Who by His Divine power came forth holy and without a spot out of the womb of His own mother.

9. THE EPIPHANY OF OUR LORD

GOSPEL: Matt. 2: 1-12. When Jesus therefore was born in Bethlehem of Juda, in the days of King Herod, behold, there came wise men from the East to Jerusalem, saying: Where is He that is born King of the Jews? For we have seen His star in the East, and are come to adore Him. And King Herod, hearing this, was troubled, and all Jerusalem with him. And, assembling together all the chief priests and the scribes of the people, he inquired of them where Christ should be born. But they said to him: In Bethlehem of Juda. For so it is written by the prophet: And thou, Bethlehem, the land of Juda, art not the least among the Princes of Juda; for out of thee shall come forth the Captain that shall rule my people Israel. Then Herod, privately calling the wise men, learned diligently of them the time of the star which appeared to them, and sending them into Bethlehem, said: Go and diligently inquire after the Child, and when you have found Him, bring me word again, that I also may come and adore Him. Who, having heard the King, went their way; and behold, the star which they had seen in the East went before them until it came and stood over where the Child was. And seeing the star, they rejoiced with exceeding great joy; and entering into the house, they found the Child with Mary, His mother, and falling down, they adored Him; and opening their treasures, offered Him gifts, gold and frankincense and myrrh, And having received an answer in sleep that they should not return to Herod, they went back another way into their country.

HOMILY BY POPE ST. GREGORY, PREACHED IN THE CHURCH OF ST. PETER ON THE EPIPHANY
Tenth Homily on the Gospels

I. YOU HAVE HEARD FROM THE GOSPEL LESSON, beloved brethren, how, when the King of heaven was born, the king of earth was troubled. The depths of earth are stirred, whilst the heights of heaven are opened. Now, let us consider the question why, when the Redeemer was born, an angel brought the news to the shepherds of Judea, but a star led the wise men of the East to adore Him. It seems as if the Jews, as reasonable creatures, received a revelation from a reasonable being, that is, an angel; whilst the Gentiles without, not listening to their reason, are attracted, not by a voice, but by a sign, that is, a star. Hence, St. Paul says: *A sign, not to believers, but to unbelievers; but prophecies, not to unbelievers, but to believers* (1 Cor. 14: 22). So the prophesying—that is, of an angel—was given to those who believed, and the sign to them that believed not. We also remark that later on the Redeemer was preached among the Gentiles, not by Himself, but by the Apostles, even as when a little child He is shown to them, not by the voice of angels, but merely by the vision of a star. When He Himself began to speak, He was made known to us by teachers; but when He laid silent in the manger, by the silent testimony in heaven.

II. However, whether we consider the signs accompanying His birth, or His death, this special thing is wonderful, namely, the hardness of heart of the Jews, who would not believe in Him, in spite of both prophecies and miracles. All things in creation bore witness that its Creator was come. Let us reckon them up after the manner of men. The heavens knew that He was God, and sent a star to shine over where He lay. The sea knew it, and bore Him up when He walked upon it. The earth knew it, and quaked when He died. The sun knew it, and was darkened. The rocks and walls knew it, and broke in pieces at the hour of His death. Hell knew it, and gave up the dead that were therein. And yet, up to this very hour, the hearts of the unbelieving Jews do not acknowledge that He, to Whom all nature did testify, is their God, and, being more hardened than rocks, refuse to be rent by repentance. But that which increases their guilt and punishment lies in the fact that they despise that God Whose birth had been announced to them by the prophets, hundreds of years before, and Whom they had seen after His birth in the stable. They even knew the place of His birth, for they spoke of it to the inquiring Herod, and told him that, according to the testimony of Holy Scripture, Bethlehem was to be renowned as the birthplace of the Messiah. They strengthen, therefore, our faith, whilst their own knowledge condemns them. The Jews are like Isaac, whose eyes were overtaken with the darkness of death, when he blessed, but could not see his son Jacob standing before him. Thus the unhappy nation was struck with blindness, and, knowing what the prophets had said about the Redeemer, would not recognise Him, though He stood in the midst of them.

III. When Herod heard of the birth of our King, he betook himself to his cunning wiles, and, lest he should be deprived of an earthly kingdom, he desired the wise men to search diligently for the Child, and when they had found Him, to bring him word again. He said, *that he also may come and adore Him*; but, in reality, if he had found Him, that he might put Him to death. Now, behold, of how little weight is the wickedness of man, when it is tried against the counsel of the Almighty. It is written: *There is no wisdom, there is no prudence, there is no counsel against the Lord* (Prov. 21: 30). And the star which the wise men saw in the East still led them on; they found the new-born King, and offered Him gifts; then they were warned in a dream that they should not return to Herod. And so it came to pass, that when Herod sought Jesus, he could not find Him. Even so it is with hypocrites who, whilst they make pretence to seek the Lord, to adore Him, find Him not.

IV. It is well to know that one of the errors of the Priscillianist heretics consists in believing that every man is born under the influence of a star. In order to confirm this notion, they bring forward the instance of the star of Bethlehem that appeared when the Lord was born, and which they call His star, that is, the star ruling His fate and destiny. But, consider the words of the Gospel concerning this star; they say: *It went before them until it came and stood over where the Child was.* Whence we see that it was not the Child who followed the star, but the star that followed the Child, as if to show that the Child ruled over the star, instead of the star ruling over Him. Let, therefore, the hearts of the faithful be free from the thought that anything rules over their destiny. In this world there is only One Who directs the destiny of man, that is, He Who made him. Neither was man made for the stars, but the stars for man; and if we say that they rule over his destiny, we set them above him, for whose service they were created. When Jacob came out of his mother's womb, and his hand took hold of his brother Esau's heel, the first could not have been perfectly born without the second immediately following. Yet such was not in afterlife the position of these two brothers, whom their mother brought forth at one birth.

V. Should a ridiculous astrologer, according to his principles, pretend that the power of the stars depends on the very moment of the birth to which their whole operation is referred, we answer that the birth of man requires a certain space of time during which the stars continually change their position. These changes would consequently form as many destinies as there are limbs in those who are born during that space of time. There is another fixed rule accepted by the adepts of this pseudo-science, namely, that he who is born under the sign of Aquarius (waterman) will never have any other profession than that of a fisherman. Yet we know from history that the Gatulians never carry on that business. But who will pretend that not one of them was ever born under that special sign of the Zodiac? By the same principle they will say that all those, born under the sign of the Balance, will be bankers or money-lenders. But we know that there are many nations among which these kinds of business are unknown. These so-called learned astrologers must, therefore, confess, either that these nations have not this sign of the Zodiac, or that none of their children are born under this sign. Many nations, as we know, have a law that their rulers must be of royal blood. But are not many poor children in these countries born at the very moment when the one, who is destined to be king, sees the light? Why, then, should there be a difference between those who are born under the same sign, so that some are clothed in purple whilst others are slaves? We wish, in speaking of the star that appeared to the wise men, to say these few words against the deceptions of astrology.

VI. The wise men brought gold, frankincense and myrrh. Gold is a gift suitable for a king, frankincense is offered in sacrifice to God, and with myrrh are embalmed the bodies of the dead. By the gifts, therefore, they presented to Him, the wise men set forth three things concerning Him, to Whom they offered them. The gold signifies that He was King; the frankincense that He was God, and the myrrh that He was mortal. There are some heretics who believe Him to be God, but confess not His Kingly dominion over all things. These offer Him the frankincense, but refuse the gold. There are some others who admit that He is King, but deny that He is God. These present the gold, but withhold the frankincense. Again, there are other heretics who profess that Christ is both God and King, but deny that He took to Himself a mortal nature. These offer Him gold and frankincense, but not myrrh for the burial incident to His mortality. Let us, however, present gold to the new-born Lord, acknowledging His universal Kingship; let us offer Him frankincense, confessing that He Who had been made manifest in time, was still God before time; let us give Him myrrh, believing that He, Who cannot suffer as God, became capable of death by assuming our human, mortal nature. There is also another meaning in this gold, frankincense and myrrh. Gold is the type of wisdom, for, as Solomon says, wisdom is a treasure to be desired, and that it is found in the mouth of the wise (Prov. 21: 20, Septuagint.). Frankincense, which is burnt in honour of God, is a figure of prayer; witness the words of the Psalmist: *Let my prayer be directed as incense in Thy sight* (Ps. 140: 2). By myrrh is represented the mortification of the body, as where Holy Church says of her children labouring in their strife after God even unto death: *My hands dropped with myrrh* (Cant. 5: 5). We offer, therefore, gold to this new King when in His sight we reflect the brilliancy of true wisdom. We offer Him frankincense when our pious prayers, like a sweet odour before God, banish all wicked thoughts and inflame good desires. We offer him myrrh, when by fasting and penance we mortify our passions; for through the effects produced by the myrrh, as we have already remarked, the bodies are preserved from corruption. Our flesh is corrupted when we give up this mortal body to luxury, as the prophet says: *The beasts have rotted in their dung* (Joel 1: 17). The image of these beasts indicates those carnal beings who give themselves up to their shameful desires, and hasten towards their own destruction. We bring, therefore, a present of myrrh to God, when by temperance and mortification we preserve our bodies from all impurity.

VII. The wise men teach us also a great lesson in that *they went back another way into their country*; and what they did, *having received an answer in sleep*, we ought to do. Our country is heaven, and when we have once known Jesus, we can never reach it by returning to the way, wherein we walked before knowing Him. We have gone far from our country by the way of pride, disobedience, worldliness, and forbidden indulgence; we must seek that heavenly fatherland by subjection, by contempt of the things which are seen, and by curbing the fleshly appetites. Let us, then, depart into our own country by another way. They that have by enjoyment put themselves away from it, must seek it again by sorrow. It behoves us, therefore, beloved brethren, to be ever fearful and watchful, having continually before the eyes of our mind, on the one hand, the guilt of our doings, and, on the other, the judgment at the last day. It behoves us to think how that, awful Judge, Whose judgment is hanging over us, but has not yet fallen, will surely come. The wrath to come is before sinners, but has not yet smitten them; the Judge yet tarries, that when He comes there may perhaps be less to condemn. Let us afflict ourselves for our faults with weeping, and with the psalmist, *let us come before His presence with thanksgiving* (Ps. 94: 2). Let us take heed that we be not be fooled by the appearance of earthly happiness, or seduced

9. THE EPIPHANY OF OUR LORD

by the vanity of any worldly pleasure; for the Judge is at hand, Who says: *Woe to you that now laugh, for you shall mourn and weep* (Luke 6: 25). Hence, also, Solomon says: *Laughter shall lie mingled with sorrow, and mourning taketh hold of the end of joy* (Prov. 14: 13). And again: *Laughter I counted error, and to mirth I said: Why art thou vainly deceived?* (Eccles. 2: 2). And yet again: *The heart of the wise is where there is mourning, but the heart of fools where there is mirth* (7: 5). Let us fear lest we do not fulfil the commandments given to us. If we wish to celebrate this feast to His glory, let us offer Him the acceptable sacrifice of our sorrow, for the royal prophet says: *A sacrifice to God is an afflicted spirit; a contrite and humbled heart, God, Thou wilt not despise* (Ps. 1: 19). Our former faults were remitted by the Sacrament of Baptism, yet we have again offended God; and these sins which the water of baptism cannot cleanse, will be forgiven only when in real and deep sorrow we shed tears of contrition. We have gone away from our real fatherland; we have followed the false gods which allured us; let us, therefore, return by another way, the way of suffering, the bitterness of which we shall endure with the grace of God.

10. FIRST SUNDAY AFTER EPIPHANY

GOSPEL: Luke 2: 42-52. When Jesus was twelve years old, they went up to Jerusalem, according to the custom of the feast. And having fulfilled the days, when they returned, the child Jesus remained in Jerusalem, and His parents knew it not. And thinking that He was in the company, they came a day's journey, and sought Him among their kinsfolk and acquaintance. And not finding Him, they returned to Jerusalem, seeking Him. And it came to pass, that after three days they found Him in the temple, sitting in the midst of the doctors, hearing them and asking them questions. And all that heard Him were astonished at His wisdom and His answers. And seeing Him they wondered. And His mother said to Him: Son, why hast Thou done so to us? Behold, Thy father and I have sought Thee sorrowing. And He said to them: How is it that you sought Me? Did you not know that I must be about My Father's business? And they understood not the word that He spoke unto them. And He went down with them, and came to Nazareth, and was subject to them. And His mother kept all these words in her heart. And Jesus advanced in wisdom and age, and grace with God and men.

HOMILY BY ST. AMBROSE
Bk. II, On St. Luke 2

I. WHEN OUR LORD WAS TWELVE YEARS OLD, HE began to dispute, as we read in the Gospel. And the number of His years was the same as the number of His Apostles, whom He afterwards sent forth to preach the faith. He Who, as to His humanity, was filled with wisdom and grace from God, was not careless of the parents of this same humanity, and, after three days, was pleased to be found in the Temple; thereby foreshadowing that, after the three days of His Passion, He, that had been reckoned with the dead, would present Himself living to our faith, on His heavenly throne and in His Divine Majesty.

II. *How is it that you sought Me? Did you not know that I must be about My Father's business?* Thus spoke Jesus to His parents, to teach us that in Him there are two generations one from His Father, another from His mother. That from His Father is His eternal generation as God the Son; that from His mother is that whereby He came into this world to work for us and minister to us. These acts of His, therefore, which are above nature, beyond His age, and different from His custom, proceeded not from the strength of His humanity, but from the power of His Divinity. On another occasion His mother moved Him to work a miracle; on the contrary, here He objects to His mother's words, because she treats as belonging to His humanity what was of His Divinity. On the first occasion it is said that He was twelve years old; but on the other He had already disciples. His mother had witnessed the wonder He worked on an earlier occasion, and had learnt from her Son to call on the mightier nature for a work of power.

III. The Gospel adds: *And He went down with them, and came to Nazareth, and was subject to them.* Who will be surprised to see that the Teacher of all virtues should practise those which were inspired by His devotion to His parents? Let us not wonder, then, how He, Who was subject to His mother, was about His Father's business. His subjection to His mother proceeded, not from weakness, but from dutiful affection. Let the false serpent of heresy lift its head from its cruel lair and spit poison from its venomous breast. For the heretics say that, as the Son was sent by the Father, the Father is, therefore, greater; and if the Father be greater than the Son, it follows that the Son is less; yea, that He Who is sent has of necessity need of some strengthening from outside. He was subject to His mother; had He need of human help? God forbid! He was obedient to His servant who had said: *Behold the handmaid of the Lord* (Luke 1: 38). He also recognised the authority of him who on earth was thought to be His father. Let us not be surprised, therefore, to see that He was obedient to His Heavenly Father; for, if it is a virtue to be subject to human beings, the obedience to God must not be called weakness. The honour paid by Jesus to His parents explains the honour which, as He said, was due to God. The Father honoured the Son, why should not this Son honour His Father? At the baptism of Jesus the voice of the Father was heard, and affirmed this was His beloved Son, in Whom He was well pleased. And this very Son, after assuming our human nature, should not be allowed, according to some heretics, to raise His voice and, expressing the feelings of His heart, publish that the Father is greater than He? We are right when we say that the Lord is infinitely great and worthy of all honour and praise; that His greatness has no limits, and we confess that He can neither increase nor decrease. Why should we not also believe that this Son, after uniting our humanity with His divinity, was obedient, to His Father, specially after the testimony of the honour paid by the Father to His Son?

IV. Let us take this lesson to heart, in order to be convinced of our duty to obey our parents. For we see how the adorable Son of God, being one with the Father in time, in will and in action, nevertheless seems to be obedient to His Father. The person of the Son is not the same as the person of the Father; yet their divine power is the same. Let us also consider that the Son was begotten without labour of the Father from all eternity; whereas our birth was to our parents a cause of many troubles and anxieties. Is not a mother giving birth to a son exposed to many dangers? Is she not for a long time troubled with anxiety and fear? And when her wishes are fulfilled and her pains are over, her anxiety is not at an end, on account of the dangers to which the new-born child will be exposed. What shall I say about the solicitude of the father in providing for his children, about his expenses for their education, and specially about his cares and labours, of which a future generation will reap the benefit? All this shows the duty of children to be obedient and grateful to their parents. And could there be a son so unnatural as to find the life of his father too long and his income too small to share it with him? Let such a one be ashamed of himself, and remember the great love of Jesus, Who deigns to make us His coheirs of the kingdom of heaven.

11. OCTAVE DAY OF THE EPIPHANY

GOSPEL: John 1: 29-34. *At that time:* John saw Jesus coming to Him, and he saith: Behold the Lamb of God, behold Him Who taketh away the sin of the world. This is He of Whom I said: After me there cometh a man, Who is preferred before me; because He was before me. And I knew Him not, but that He may be made manifest in Israel, therefore am I come baptizing with water. And John gave testimony saying: I saw the Spirit coming down as a dove from heaven, and He remained upon Him. And I knew Him not; but He Who sent me to baptize with water, said to me: He upon Whom thou shalt see the Spirit descending and remaining upon Him, He it is that baptizeth with the Holy Ghost. And I saw, and I gave testimony that this is the Son of God.

HOMILY BY ST. AUGUSTINE
Sixth Tract on St. John

I. WHEN JESUS WAS BAPTIZED BY ST. JOHN A DOVE came down from Heaven and rested upon Him. At the same time the three Persons of the Holy Trinity, in Whom we believe, were manifested; for, as the Gospel says: *Jesus, being baptized, forthwith came out of the water; and lo, the heavens were opened to Him, and He saw the Spirit of God descending as a dove, and coming upon Him. And behold, a voice from heaven saying: This is My beloved Son, in Whom I am well pleased* (Matt. 3: 16, 17). We see here, then, the adorable Trinity: the Father, Whose voice was heard; the Son, Who was present in His sacred Humanity; and the Holy Ghost, Who showed Himself in the form of a dove. It was in the name of this Blessed Trinity that the Apostles were sent, and we know well that such was the case. Nevertheless, we are confronted with the fact that there are some heretics who disbelieve this plain truth, or, rather, who close their eyes to the light shining before them; for, indeed, it is clear as the noonday sun that the Apostles were sent forth in the name of the Father, and of the Son, and of the Holy Ghost, to teach and baptize, and also that they were so sent by our Saviour Himself, of Whom it is written: *He it is that baptizeth* (John 1: 33). And Jesus spoke thus by His Evangelist, since He had reserved to Himself that power, the ministry only of which He has delegated to others.

II. Now, St. John was not at first aware of this truth; he only learned it on the occasion of the baptism of our Lord. He already knew that Jesus was the Son of God and the supreme Ruler of the universe, and that He was the Christ, and would baptize with the Holy Ghost. But what he did not know before, but only understood from the dove descending and remaining upon our Lord, was this: that our Redeemer would retain an absolute power over baptism, which He was about to establish as a sacrament; that He would not communicate His power over the Sacrament to His ministers, but would employ them only to minister therein the power which He retains for Himself. And it is in this power Jesus Christ reserves to Himself alone, and is yet daily administered by His priests, that the unity of the Church resides. Indeed, the true Church is likened to a dove in Holy Scripture, for we read: One is My dove, My perfect one is but one; she is the only one of her mother, the chosen of her that bore her (Cant. vi. 8). But were the power of our Saviour in the sacrament of salvation to belong to His ministers, there would be as many baptisms as ministers, and there would no longer be the baptism of Christ.

III. Notice, beloved brethren, that before St. John was allowed by our Lord to baptize Him, he, the Baptist, knew that the Saviour would baptize with the Holy Ghost. But when Jesus had received Baptism, St. John, having seen the dove come down from heaven, learnt something hitherto unknown to him, that is, that though there would be ministers of that power, yet this power to impart the Holy Ghost in Baptism would be reserved to Jesus Christ Himself alone, and would not be communicated to others. This is what St. John learnt on that occasion. But how can we prove that he knew the Redeemer would baptize with the Holy Ghost, and that he understood that this power was not to be transmitted to anyone? The Gospel tells us that John knew Jesus even before He came to him at the Jordan to be baptized, for he then said to Jesus: *I ought to be baptized by Thee, and comest Thou to me?* (Matt. 3: 14). Behold, he knew Him to be the Lord, the Son of God! But how can we prove that he knew Him to be He Who would baptize with the Holy Ghost? Before the Lord came to the river, whither many had betaken themselves to be baptized by John, the Baptist said: *I indeed baptize you with water; but there shall come One mightier than I, the latchet of Whose shoe I am not worthy to loose: He shall baptize you with the Holy Ghost and with fire* (Luke 3: 16). But how could John say, before the coming of the dove, that he knew not Jesus? Are we to call him a liar? God forbid! But when the dove came down and rested on Christ, then it was he first knew that the Lord reserved the power of Baptism as peculiar to Himself, so that, let whomsoever you will, whether just or unjust, baptize with His Baptism, yet the virtue of the Sacrament will proceed, not from the minister, whether just or unjust, but from Him on Whom the dove rested. Thus Christ is the real Baptizer in every Christian Baptism, and will be so to the end of all time. In this sense it is written of Him: *He it is that baptizeth with the Holy Ghost.* Should Peter baptize, the real Baptizer is Christ; should Paul, should Judas, the real Baptizer is still Christ*

IV. For if the sanctity of Baptism depended on the personal holiness of the minister, no two baptisms would be exactly alike; then each recipient of the Sacrament would think himself more or less regenerated, according to the greater or less holiness of the minister of the Sacrament. But, beloved brethren, note this well. The saints, those holy servants of God, who appertain to the dove,

---

* In order to understand this homily, we must bear in mind that St. Augustine's intention was to refute the Donatists. These heretics pretended that in the Holy Trinity the Father was greater than the Son, and the Son greater than the Holy Ghost. They also thought that Catholics should be re-baptized. For this reason St. Augustine repeats over and over again that the three Persons of the Blessed Trinity are equal, that they have one and the same Divinity, and that Baptism is the same Sacrament by whatsoever officiant it be administered.

whose portion is in Jerusalem, those good men in the Church, of whom the Apostle says: *The Lord knoweth who are His* (2 Tim. 2: 19), differ among themselves by diversity of graces and holiness, some-one having attained to one degree of sanctity, another to another. It results, therefore, that though one person be baptized by a saint, and another by a less worthy minister, whose chastity is not so intense, and who has made less progress in the way of perfection, yet, nevertheless, each recipient receives the same grace through the same Sacrament. How could this be, were it not that Christ Himself is the effectual Baptizer? Thus the degree of sanctity and merit of the minister does not result in a more or less perfect Sacrament, which is always one and the same. And for the same reason it is evident that even though the minister be unworthy, yet, either because his unworthiness is unknown to the Church, or because she tolerates him as chaff, which at the harvest will be separated from the corn, the Baptism he administers is identical with that administered by a minister never so worthy, since in every case Jesus Himself is the effectual Baptizer.

V. Let us, then, beloved brethren, recognise this truth, and not act as those blind heretics who do not see it, or pretend not to do so, and thus hasten towards their condemnation. If they would but open their eyes, it would be evident to them that the Apostles and disciples of the Lord were sent by their Master to all the nations of the earth, and commanded to baptize all men in the name of the Father, and of the Son, and of the Holy Ghost. In fact, since our Lord sent them to all nations, He sent them to His inheritance. For we know the prophet referred to Him when he said: *Ask of Me, and I will give thee the Gentiles for thine inheritance, and the utmost parts of the earth for thy possession* (Ps. 2: 8). And it is not unknown to you that *the law came forth from Sion, and the word of the Lord from Jerusalem* (Isa. 2: 3), and also that our Lord preached first at Jerusalem, and that it was thence He sent His disciples, saying: *Going, therefore, teach ye all nations, baptizing them in the name of the Father, and of the Son, and of the Holy Ghost* (Matt, 28: 19). You will notice that our Lord, when sending forth His disciples and commanding them to baptize all nations, did not say in the names of the Father, and of the Son, and of the Holy Ghost, but *in the name of the Father, and of the Son, and of the Holy Ghost*, to give us to understand that there is only one God. The Apostle emphasizes this when explaining God's promise to Abraham: *To Abraham were the promises made and to his seed. He saith not, AND TO HIS SEEDS, as of many; but as of one, AND TO THY SEED, which is Christ* (Gal. 3: 16). These words, as St. Paul remarks, do not refer to the multitude of his descendants, but to one, Who is Jesus Christ, to give us to understand that, as Jesus is one, so also there is but one God the Father, the Son, and the Holy Ghost.

VI. However, do not boast of your baptism, nor be proud on account of that privilege; for, though your baptism was perfectly effectual, as I am bound to acknowledge, and though the dove recognised it, yet she is continually lamenting that, in spite of this sacrament, uniting you with her, you are nevertheless outside her communion, and consequently out of the road to salvation. She sees in you the sign of a Christian and approves of it, but at the same time she sees and deplores your disobedience to the Church; therefore she calls and invites you to return to her. You are wrong in glorying in her Baptism, since you refuse to hear and obey her. The wicked, whom the Church does not recognise as her children, may as well boast of the privilege of her Baptism. Are there not, however, many avaricious and intemperate people, and others who are secretly idolaters, or those, again, who surreptitiously consult fortune-tellers and astrologers, who yet possess the self-same privilege of baptism in which you glory? And all this time the dove, seeing herself among ravens, is lamenting such a state. Cease, then, to boast of a blessing which you have in common with the wicked, and endeavour to practise humility, charity, peace, virtues of which you stand in great need, so that through them the Baptism you have received may be profitable to you.

12. SECOND SUNDAY AFTER EPIPHANY

GOSPEL: John 2: 1-11 *At that time*: There was a marriage in Cana of Galilee; and the mother of Jesus was there. And Jesus also was invited, and His disciples, to the marriage. And the wine failing, the mother of Jesus saith to Him: They have no wine. And Jesus saith to her: Woman, what is it to Me and to thee? My hour is not yet come. His mother said to the waiters: Whatsoever He shall say to you, do ye. Now there were set there six water-pots of stone, according to the manner of purifying of the Jews, containing two or three measures apiece. Jesus saith to them: Fill the water-pots with water. And they filled them, up to the brim. And Jesus saith to them: Draw out now, and carry to the chief steward of the feast. And they carried it. And when the chief steward had tasted the water made wine, and knew not whence it was, but the waiters knew who had drawn the water, the chief steward calleth the bridegroom, and saith to him: Every man at first setteth forth good wine, and when men have well drunk, then that which is worse. But thou hast kept the good wine until now. This beginning of miracles did Jesus in Cana of Galilee; and manifested His glory, and His disciples believed in Him.

HOMILY BY ST. AUGUSTINE
Ninth Tract on St. John

I. THE FACT THAT OUR LORD WAS PLEASED TO BE asked to, and to attend, the marriage, shows plainly even setting aside any mystical interpretation that He is the Author and Blesser of marriage. There were yet to arise those of whom the Apostle has warned us as *forbidding to marry* (1 Tim. 4: 3), and who say that marriage is a bad thing in itself and a work of the devil. Yet we read in the Gospel that when our Lord was asked: *Is it lawful for a* man to put away his wife for every cause? (Matt. 19: 3), He answered that it was not lawful, unless it were for fornication. In which answer you will remember that He used these words: *What God hath joined together, let no man put asunder* (ver. 6). They who are well instructed in the Catholic religion know that God is the Author of marriage and blessed it; and that, whilst the union of man and wife in marriage is from God, divorce is from the devil. But it is lawful for a man to put away his wife in case of fornication; for by not keeping her faith to her husband, the woman has first willed to be a wife no longer. But even those who have made a vow of their virginity to God, and have thereby attained to a higher degree of honour and holiness in the Church, are not unmarried; for they indeed pertain to that marriage with the whole Church, in which nuptials Christ is their Spouse. The Lord, then, being invited, went to the marriage, to strengthen the marriage-tie, and to shed light on the hidden meaning of matrimony. And in that marriage-feast the bridegroom, to whom it was said, *thou hast kept the good wine until now*, was a figure of the Lord, Who has kept until now the good wine, namely, the Gospel.

11. With the help and grace of God we will now fulfil our promise, and begin by explaining the mysteries hidden in this Gospel. We say, therefore, that in the earliest times God gave His revelation, and never ceased during the following generations, thereby to instruct the world. Should the Lord Jesus not be recognised in these revelations, then they may be compared with the water hiding in some degree the wine which was mixed with it. St. Paul conveys this meaning, when, speaking of the unbelieving Jews, he says: *Even until this day when Moses is read, the veil is upon their heart. But when they shall be converted to the Lord, this veil shall be taken away* (2 Cor. 3: 15). By this veil was meant the obscurity of the revelations, which prevented them from understanding their meaning. But this veil disappears when Jesus, the end of all prophecies, is known. Then the light dispels the darkness of our ignorance and false wisdom, and that, which like water was tasteless, is changed into precious wine; for, though we should read all the books containing the words of the prophets, yet, if

we had no knowledge of Jesus Christ, Who is the key of them, they would surely seem tasteless and meaningless. But when we read them in the knowledge of Jesus, they will impart to our heart real happiness; our soul will remain undefiled by sensuality; past things will be forgotten, and we shall think only of the great wonders spoken of by the ancient prophets.

III. Prophecy belongs to all times, yet it had not ceased to speak of Jesus Christ to the different generations following each other in the successive ages of the world, and its meaning was hidden to them. In order to show that the prophecies concerning the person of Jesus Christ continued to announce Him during all the ages preceding His coming, we need only mention the words that Jesus Christ Himself addressed to His disciples after His Resurrection. When He saw that, though they had followed Him during His life, yet for His sake were much troubled; that the hope of seeing Him rise from the dead had forsaken them, notwithstanding that the thief crucified with Him had, by his faith and confidence, deserved to be received by Christ into paradise on that day, and that His disciples were still uncertain and doubtful; yea, that they even reproached themselves for having perhaps been too credulous in believing Him to be the Messiah; then He said to one of the disciples going to Emmaus: *O foolish and slow of heart to believe in all things which the prophets have spoken! Ought not Christ to have suffered these things, and so to enter into His glory?* (Luke 24: 25). Then He expounded to them in all the Scriptures, beginning at Moses and all the prophets, the things that were concerning Him. Later on He ordered His disciples to see His hands and feet, and to feel Him with their hands, in order to be convinced that He was risen, and said to them: *These are the words which I spoke to you while I was yet with you, and all things must needs be fulfilled, which are written in the law of Moses, and in the prophets, and in the psalms, concerning Me* (Luke 24: 44). *Then He opened their understanding, that they might understand the Scriptures. And He said to them: Thus it is written, and thus it behoved Christ to suffer, and to rise again from the dead the third day; and that penance and the remission of sins should be preached in His name unto all nations, beginning at Jerusalem* (vers. 45, 46, 47).

IV. When these words, taken from Scripture — and their meaning is evident and clear — are well understood, then the mysteries, hidden under the miracle of our Gospel, are laid open to every Christian. Indeed, when we consider what our Lord said to His disciples, namely that all things must needs be fulfilled which were written concerning Him, we recognise that He spoke of the law, the prophets and the psalms, to show that He meant all the books of the Old Testament containing the prophecies concerning Him. But since all these sacred books, as we remarked, were represented by the water used for this miracle, our Lord called the disciples *foolish and slow of heart*, because they still considered Holy Scripture, which should have been to them a precious wine, as tasteless water. Yet, how does Christ change for His disciples the water into the choicest wine? *He opened their understanding, that they might understand the Scriptures,* and explained to them the prophets. And the disciples having drunk of this heavenly wine, said to one another: *Was not our heart burning within us, whilst He spoke in the way, and opened to us the Scriptures?* (Luke 24: 32).

Now the Apostles recognised Jesus Christ in these Sacred Books, wherein they had not perceived Him before, and understood the changing of the water into wine. For at that moment, what till then had seemed to them void of taste, became all at once agreeable food and precious drink, wherewith they were filled. We do not read that in working this miracle our Lord had the water contained in the water-pots poured out, to substitute for it wine. He could have done, on this occasion, what He did when feeding five thousand men, besides women and children, with five loaves, when He produced from the treasures of His infinite power the enormous quantity of bread required for the feeding of that vast multitude. The five loaves would not have been enough to fill the twelve baskets. How different His action in the miracle of which we are speaking! Instead of pouring it away, He changes the body of water into wine, in order to show us that the Old Testament, figured by the water, was also His work. But the Old Testament Scriptures, though from the Lord, are tasteless until Jesus Christ be recognised therein.

V. Let us return to the lesson indicated by the words of our Redeemer: *All things which are written in the law of Moses, and in the prophets, and in the psalms, concerning Me.* You know that the law began with the world, when God created heaven and earth. And since that beginning until the century in which we live, six different ages or epochs are counted. The first began with Adam, and lasted until Noah; the second extended from Noah to Abraham its order and succession are given by St. Matthew in his Gospel; the third from Abraham to David; the fourth from David to the time when the Jews were taken captive to Babylon; the fifth from the captivity of Babylon to St. John the Baptist; and the sixth, which began with St. John the Baptist, will last until the end of the world. In order to mark these six ages, God created man on the sixth day, and to His image and likeness. By this sixth day, on which God made man out of nothing, the Lord wished to indicate the sixth epoch of the world in which He came to restore the soul of man disfigured by sin, and to give back to it that likeness to God which it had received at the Creation. Jesus also changed water into wine, to teach us by this miracle to find real delight in the law and the prophets, who formerly seemed tasteless, for He revealed and manifested them to the world. Lastly, the six water-pots that He had filled, are a figure of the six ages of the world, which were not without their water of the prophecies. For these ages were like the vessels that would have remained empty, had not Jesus Christ filled them, thus teaching us that these epochs would have been useless, had not Jesus been announced to the world. They were, indeed, filled by the fulfilment of the prophecies; but the knowledge of Jesus is required to penetrate their incomparable meaning.

13. THIRD SUNDAY AFTER EPIPHANY

GOSPEL: Matt. 8: 1-13. *At that time*: When Jesus was come down from the mountain, great multitudes followed Him. And behold a leper came and adored Him, saying: Lord, if Thou wilt, Thou canst make me clean. And Jesus, stretching forth His hand, touched him, saying: I will; be thou made clean. And forthwith his leprosy was cleansed. And Jesus saith to him: See thou tell no man, but go, show thyself to the priest, and offer the gift which Moses commanded for a testimony unto them. And when He had entered into Capharnaum, there came to Him a centurion, beseeching Him and saying: Lord, my servant lieth at home sick of the palsy, and is grievously tormented. And Jesus saith to him: I will come and heal him. And the centurion making answer said: Lord, I am not worthy that Thou shouldst enter under my roof; but only say the word and my servant shall be healed. For I also am a man subject to authority, having under me soldiers, and I say to this, Go, and he goeth; and to another, Come, and he cometh; and to my servant, Do this, and he doeth it. And when Jesus heard this, He marvelled, and said to them that followed Him: Amen, I say to you, I have not found so great faith in Israel. And I say to you that many shall come from the east and the west, and shall sit down with Abraham and Isaac and Jacob, in the kingdom of heaven; but the children of the kingdom shall be cast out into the exterior darkness: there shall be weeping and gnashing of teeth. And Jesus said to the centurion: Go, and as thou hast believed, so be it done to thee. And the servant was healed at the same hour.

HOMILY BY ST. JEROME
Commentary on St. Matthew 8, Bk. I

I. WHEN JESUS CAME DOWN FROM THE MOUNTAIN, *great multitudes followed Him.* They had not been able to follow Him when He went up. And the first who now came was a leper. The disease of this poor creature had prevented him from hearing the Saviour's long sermon on the mount. Let it be noticed that he is the first person specially named as being cured. The second was the centurion's servant; the third, St. Peter's mother-in-law, who was sick of a fever at Capharnaum; the fourth were those brought to Christ as being troubled with evil spirits. By His word He cast out those evil spirits, and at the same time healed all them that were sick. *And behold a leper came and adored Him.* Properly after preaching and doctrine comes the occasion for a miracle, that the power of the sign might confirm in the hearers the truth of the teaching that had gone before.

II. And the leper said: *Lord, if Thou wilt, Thou canst make me clean.* The leper prayed the Lord to have the will, for he doubted not but that He had the power. *And Jesus, stretching forth His hand, touched him, saying: I will; be thou made clean.* And as soon as the Lord put forth His hand the leprosy departed. Let us remark how humble and unboasting is the Lord's language. The leper had said, *If thou wilt;* the Lord answered, *I will.* The leper, *Thou canst make me clean;* and the Lord, *Be thou made clean.* Most Latin readers, misled by the identity of form in that language, read Christ's answer as if it were: *I will to make thee clean.* This is wrong, for the sentences are separate. First comes the expression of volition, *I will,* then the command, *Be thou made clean.* And Jesus saith to him: *See thou tell no man.* Was there any need to tell what his body showed? *But go, show thyself to the priest.* There were divers reasons why Christ should send him to the priest. First for humility's sake, that he might show reverence to God's priest. Then there was a command of the law that they, who were cleansed from leprosy, should make an offering to the priests. Moreover, that when the priests saw the leper cleansed, they might either believe in the Saviour or refuse to believe; if they believed, that they might be saved, and if they believed not, that they might have no excuse. Lastly, that He might give no ground for the accusation too often brought against Him, that He was unobservant of the Law.

III. Then the centurion came to Jesus, beseeching Him and saying: *Lord, my servant lieth at home sick of the palsy, and is grievously tormented.* And Jesus saith to him: *I will come and heal him.* And the centurion making answer, said: *Lord, I am not worthy that Thou shouldst enter under my roof; but only say the word, and my servant shall be healed.* No one could accuse our Lord of an inordinate desire after honour, because He promised the centurion that He would go at once and heal the servant. It was on account of the faith, humility, and modesty which He saw in the centurion, that He at once and most generously granted his request. The centurion showed his faith in believing that He could heal a man sick of the palsy, who was still an unbeliever. He showed his humility, thinking himself unworthy to receive Jesus into his house; and his modesty was shown by his recognising the Divinity of Jesus hidden under the veil of His humanity. This centurion knew that it would be useless for him to follow the example of unbelievers, and to accept as true only what he could see with his bodily eyes, if he did not at the same time believe in the Divinity of Jesus, that he could not see. This prudence made him say: *I also am a man subject to authority, having under me soldiers; and I say to this, Go, and he goeth; and to another, Come, and he cometh; and to my servant, Do this, and he doeth it.* By these words he wished to express his belief that Jesus could convey His intentions to His angels, and through them perform whatsoever He would deign to fulfil Himself.

IV. When Jesus heard this He marvelled, and said to them that followed Him: *Amen, I say to you, I have not found so great faith in Israel.* Jesus marvelled, because the centurion recognised the majesty of the Son of God made man, and His power to heal the sick, and to deliver the possessed from the influence of the devil, either through His word only, or through the agency of His angels. He praised the centurion's faith as being greater than that of the Jews, His contemporaries, but did not speak of the patriarchs and prophets who had lived before Him. Under the figure of the centurion He wished perhaps to indicate the Gentiles, whose faith surpassed that of the children of Israel. *I say to you,* He added, *that many shall come from the east and the west, and shall sit down with Abraham and Isaac and Jacob in the kingdom of heaven.* Since the God of Abraham is the Creator of heaven, and the Father of Jesus Christ, it follows that Abraham and all the nations which with him believe in Jesus, the Son of the Creator, will sit in the kingdom of heaven. In this also is contained the meaning of what we have said, namely, that the faith of the centurion represented the Gentiles, who would believe with him were the Gospel preached to those who dwell in the east and the west. *But the children of the kingdom shall be cast out into the exterior darkness.* The Jews, who, until the conversion of the Gentiles, had God for their King, were the children of the kingdom. Their darkness was interior; yet we may say that, since they left the true Light and were rejected by God, they were also surrounded by exterior darkness.

14. FOURTH SUNDAY AFTER EPIPHANY

GOSPEL: Matt. 8: 23-27. *At that time*: When Jesus entered into a ship His disciples followed Him, and behold a great tempest arose in the sea, so that the ship was covered with waves; but He was asleep. And His disciples came to Him, and awakened Him, saying: Lord, save us; we perish. And Jesus saith to them Why are you fearful, O ye of little faith? Then rising up, He commanded the winds and the sea, and there came a great calm. But the men wondered, saying: What manner of man is this? for the winds and the sea obey Him.

I. HOMILY BY ST. JEROME
Commentary on St. Matthew 8, Bk. I

I. OUR LORD WORKED THE FIFTH MIRACLE WHEN He took ship at Capharnaum, and commanded the winds and the sea; the sixth, when, in the country of the Gerasens, He suffered the devils to enter into the swine; the seventh, when, coming into His own city, He cured the man sick of the palsy lying on a bed. The first man sick of the palsy, whom He cured, was the centurion's servant. *But He was asleep, and His disciples came to Him, and awakened Him, saying: Lord, save us; we perish.* A type of this is found in the history of Jonas, who was fast asleep when the storm arose, and whom the sailors woke up to help them. He saved the sailors by commanding them to throw him into the sea; this casting of Jonas into the sea being, as we know, a figure of Christ's Passion.

II. *Then, rising up, He commanded the winds and the sea.* The words give us to understand that all things, which have been made, recognise their Master; all things, which He rebukes or commands, hear His voice. This is not the error of the heretics, who pretend that everything is alive, but part of the majesty of the Creator, Who makes things to feel Him, which we cannot make to feel us. *But the men wondered, saying: What manner of man is this? for the winds and the sea obey Him.* It was not His disciples who wondered, but the sailors and others who were in the ship. If, however, anyone be willing to oppose this our interpretation, and to maintain that it was the disciples who wondered, we answer that those who knew not before the power of the Saviour deserve to be stripped of the title of disciples, and to be called simply *the men*.

II. HOMILY BY ST. AUGUSTINE
Commentary on Psalm 25

THIS SHIP, IN WHICH JESUS WAS ASLEEP, AND which was on the point of being swallowed up by the waves, is a figure of the dangers threatening man's life, compared to a sea continually agitated by winds and storms. The waves rising in the sea are the daily temptations of our life, assailing our fragile ship and threatening it with dismal wreck and destruction. And whence comes such impending danger, but because Jesus is asleep? Were not Jesus asleep within you, you would not be exposed to all these storms; but interior peace and perfect calm would be your happy lot, through Jesus watching with you. For what is the meaning of *Jesus is asleep*? Your faith in Jesus has fallen asleep. The tempests of the sea arise; you see evil men flourishing, good and just men in trouble and misery; your faith is shaken and tossed about as by furious waves. And in this temptation your soul says: 'Is this Thy justice, O God, that the wicked should flourish, whilst the just are in trouble and misery?' You say to God: 'Is this Thy justice?' And God says to you: 'Is this your faith? Have I promised you the perishable things of the world? Have I called you to be My followers, that is, Christians, that you should flourish in this life? Are you grieving because you see the wicked enjoying all earthly pleasures, who shall hereafter be tormented with the devil? But why all these complaints? Why are you disturbed by

14. FOURTH SUNDAY AFTER EPIPHANY

the waves of the sea and the storm?' Because Jesus is asleep; that is, because your faith in Jesus has been laid asleep in your hearts. How will you be delivered from this great danger? Awaken Jesus, and say to Him: *Lord, save us, we perish*; the waves of temptation rise against us and threaten our souls with impending death. And Jesus will awake, that is, your faith will return to you. And with His help you will recognise that the happiness the wicked enjoy will not abide with them. For, either it will be taken from them while they live, or they will be forced to leave it when they die. But the happiness promised to you will abide for ever and ever. What is granted to the wicked for a time, will soon be taken away; for they flourish like the flower of the grass. *All flesh is as grass; the grass is withered, and the flower thereof is fallen away; but the word of the Lord endureth for ever* (1 Pet. 1: 24, 25). Turn, therefore, your back upon that which falls and is perishable, and your face to that which abides to the end. Now that Jesus is awake, the storm shall no more shake your hearts, the waves shall not fill your barque. Your faith commands the winds and the waves, and the danger shall pass away, when a great calm will follow the storm. To all this, beloved brethren, belongs what the Apostle says about *putting off the old man. Be angry and sin not. Let not the sun go down upon your anger. Give not place to the devil* (Eph. 4: 26, 27). The old man did give place; let not the new man do the same. *He that stole, let him now steal no more* (ver. 28). The old man, then, did steal; not so the new. It is the same man, it is one man. It was Adam, let it be Christ; it was the old man, let it be the new man.

15. FIFTH SUNDAY AFTER EPIPHANY

GOSPEL: Matt. 13: 24-30. *At that time*: Jesus spoke this parable to the multitude, saying: The kingdom of heaven is likened to a man that sowed good seed in his field. But while men were asleep his enemy came and oversowed cockle among the wheat, and went his way. And when the blade was sprung up, and brought forth fruit, then appeared also the cockle. Then the servants of the good man of the house came and said to him: Sir, didst thou not sow good seed in thy field? From whence, then, hath it cockle? And he said to them: An enemy hath done this. And the servants said to him: Wilt thou that we go and gather it up? And he said: No, lest while you gather up the cockle, you root up the wheat also together with it. Let both grow until the harvest, and in the time of the harvest I will say to the reapers: Gather up first the cockle, and bind it in bundles to burn, but gather the wheat into my barn.

HOMILY BY ST. AUGUSTINE
Eighty-Eight Discourse on the Words of the Gospel

I. YOU WILL EASILY UNDERSTAND, BELOVED brethren, the hidden meaning of this Gospel, when you remember what we said about some other words of Holy Scripture comparing the just and the wicked in the Church of God to the wheat and the cockle. By this figure we are taught that the threshing-floor is not to be left before the time of the harvest, that the cockle may not be taken away without being separated from the wheat; for the floor would be deprived of its due, and the wheat thus taken off could not be preserved in the barn. A time will arrive when the Householder Himself will come with the fan in His hand, and separate the just from the wicked. There will be, in regard to the soul and in regard to the body, a separation of the just and the wicked; for, with your hearts and dispositions you must be separated from the wicked, though in a spirit of humility you are for a time associated with them by the bonds of the body. Let not this connection make you careless, for it is your duty to endeavour in every way to correct and convert those entrusted to your care, now teaching, then advising, or even threatening them as far as you are obliged or able to do so. Do not excuse your carelessness respecting this duty by quoting examples taken from the Old and New Testaments, or the lives of the saints, and thus endeavouring to show that, though living among the godless, they preserved their souls stainless. My answer will be: That these servants of God did not agree with the wickedness of sinners, but punished them. It is quite true that there can be no intimacy between ourselves and others as long as we are opposed to their opinions; but when we approve of the doings of the wicked and agree with them in their sinfulness, then we enter into mutual fellowship, forbidden by the Apostle, who says: *Have no fellowship with the unfruitful works of darkness* (Eph. 5: 11). However, since to refuse our consent to evil would not be enough, unless we apply the necessary remedies to cure it, the Apostle adds: *But rather reprove them (ibid.)*, giving us to understand that these two things must be united, namely, not to have any communication with sinners, and also to punish them. The first is observed, when the sinful act is neither praised nor approved of, nor consented to; and the second, when the sinner is reproved, punished, and prevented from doing wrong again.

11. However, when we reprove and punish sinners, let us not be puffed up on account of our own virtue; let us remember the words of the Apostle: *He that thinketh himself to stand, let him take heed lest he fall* (1 Cor. 10: 12). When you prevent others from committing sin, or fearlessly punish them, do not forget to make use of kindness and love at the same time, again remembering the teaching of the great Apostle: *If a man be overtaken by any fault, you, who are spiritual, instruct such a one in the spirit of meekness, considering thyself, lest thou also be tempted. Bear ye one another's burdens; and so you shall fulfil the law of Christ* (Gal. 6: 1,2). And in another epistle

the same Apostle says: *The servant of the Lord must not wrangle, but be mild towards all men; apt to teach, patient with modesty; admonishing them that resist the truth, if peradventure God may give them repentance to know the truth, and they may recover themselves from the snare of the devil, by whom they are held captive at his will* (2 Tim. 2: 24, *et seq.*). We conclude from all this that we must neither flatter nor praise the wicked, and that, when punishing them, we must be neither careless nor haughty, nor by proud and injudicious reproaches treat them with contempt.

III. He that forsakes the unity, that is, the union of the Christians belonging to the true Church, will infallibly suffer the loss of charity. And if he lose that virtue, he is nothing, even should he possess all other virtues in the highest degree. The great Apostle says: *If I speak the tongues of men and angels, and have not charity, I am become like a sounding brass and a tinkling cymbal. And if I should have prophecy, and should know all mysteries, and all knowledge, and if I should have all faith, so that I should remove mountains, and have not charity, I am nothing. And if I should distribute all my goods to feed the poor, and if I should deliver my body to be burned, and have not charity, it profiteth me nothing* (1 Cor. 13: 1-3). Thus will it be with the Christian who has not charity. He is deprived of that virtue which gives merits to all others, so that other virtues will be fruitless for heaven and dead before God. Let us, therefore, practise charity, and take great care to preserve the union of minds through the bond of peace. Let us not be deceived by the words of those who, being carnal, have left the communion of the faithful, and are thus separated, as through a spiritual sacrilege, from the true wheat of the Church sown all over the world. This precious seed was sown in the world by the good Sower, the Son of Man. For His will was not that this seed should be sown only in some countries, like Africa,* in which we live, but among all nations. The cockle, springing up among the wheat, was the work of the enemy. Yet the good man of the

---

* St. Augustine speaks against Donatus, who, coming from Numedia, was preaching his heretical doctrine in Africa. The great Doctor of the Church proves that neither scandals nor bad Christians afford a lawful and reasonable motive for leaving the true Church.

house would not allow his servants to gather it up, but told them to let both, the wheat and the cockle, grow until the harvest. Now, where is the good seed to grow up, unless in the field in which it was sown? Is Africa this special field? No. But which is this field? The words of our Lord are clear and explicit; for, when asked by His disciples to explain the parable, He said: *The field is the world. And the good seed are the children of the kingdom. And the cockle are the children of the wicked one. And the enemy that sowed them, is the devil. But the harvest is the end of the world. And the reapers are the angels* (Matt. 13: 38, 39). After these words shall we believe, according to heretics, that the field spoken of is not the world, but only Africa? That the harvest will not take place at the end of the world, but in the present time, and that Donatus, the chief of the heretics, is the reaper? Ah! far from accepting such doctrines against the teaching of Jesus Christ Himself, let us patiently await the harvest which will take place in the whole world. We let the good seed, spread out in the world, grow up until the time appointed by the householder, and we suffer the cockle, oversowed among the good seed and growing up everywhere, to remain until the time of the harvest. But let us take heed, lest we be deceived by the language of these wicked men who, being as light as chaff, will be cast out of the barn, even before the Householder comes to separate them. The application of this parable of the cockle, which we explained, ought to be sufficient to convince the heretics of the falsehood of their conclusions. But they will, perhaps, say, in order to excuse their errors and justify their conduct, that the Sacred Books were once handed over to the pagans by some Christians afraid of torments and tortures. But since these Christians being unknown, cannot be discovered, now this one and then another is accused of that crime. Yet, whatever may be the truth about these Christians, I ask whether their infidelity has destroyed the Faith which comes from God? Is it not the same Faith that God once promised Abraham, saying that all nations should be blessed in his seed? And what are we taught by this Faith? To let both, that is, the good seed and the cockle, the just and the wicked, grow up in the field of the Church, namely, the world, until the time of the harvest, the end of the world.

16. SIXTH SUNDAY AFTER EPIPHANY

GOSPEL: Matt. 13: 31-35 *At that time*: Jesus spoke to the multitude this parable: The kingdom of heaven is like to a grain of mustard-seed, which a man took and sowed in his field. Which, indeed, is the least of all seeds; but when it is grown up it is greater than all herbs, and becometh a tree, so that the birds of the air come and dwell in the branches thereof. Another parable He spoke to them: The kingdom of heaven is like to leaven, which a woman took and hid in three measures of meal, until the whole was leavened. All these things Jesus spoke in parables to the multitude, and without parables He did not speak to them; that the word might be fulfilled which was spoken by the prophet, saying: I will open My mouth in parables, I will utter things hidden from the foundation of the world.

HOMILY BY ST. JEROME
Commentary on St. Matthew 13, Bk. II

I. THE KINGDOM OF HEAVEN, HERE SPOKEN OF BY our Lord, is the propagation of the Gospel and the knowledge of the Scriptures, which are the way leading to life. Of this kingdom it was said to the Jews: *The kingdom of God shall be taken from you, and shall be given to a nation yielding the fruits thereof* (Matt. 21: 43). This kingdom, therefore, is like to a grain of mustard-seed, which a man took and sowed in his field. Our Saviour is understood by many to be that man who sowed the seed in his field, for He is the Sower who sows in the souls of believers. Others understand every man who sows good seed in his own field, that is, in himself, in his own heart. Now, who is he that sows, but our own mind and soul, which take the good grain from preaching, and by nourishing it in the soil, cause it to spring up in the field of our own heart? The preaching of the Gospel is the beginning of all doctrines, He that preaches, for his first lesson, a God made man, Christ's death, and the stumbling-block of the Cross, receives at first but little credit. Compare such teaching as this with the doctrines of philosophers, with their books, their splendid eloquence and their rounded sentences, and you will see that the grain of the Gospel, when it is sown, is the humblest of all seeds. But when the doctrines of men grow up, there is nothing piercing, nothing healthy, nothing life-giving therein; the plant is drooping, weak and withered. There are herbs and grass of which it may truly be said that *the grass is withered and the flower is fallen* (Isa. 40: 8). But the grain of the Gospel-seed, though, when it is sown, seems to be the least of all seeds, when once it is rooted in the soul of man or in the whole world, grows, not into a herb, but becomes a tree, so that the birds of the air—whereby we may understand either the souls of the believers or the powers bound to the service of God—come and dwell in the branches thereof. I consider that the branches of the Gospel-tree, growing from the grain of the mustard-seed, are the divers developments of doctrine, on which the mysterious birds mentioned above find resting-places. Our duty, therefore, is to take the wings of the dove and, in a quick flight, to soar up to the most sublime things, so that we may make our dwelling in the branches of this mysterious tree, where we shall rest in the shadow of the doctrine of salvation, be separated from earthly things, and thus be nearer to heaven. There are many who, reading in the Gospel that the mustard-seed is the least of all seeds, heard that the disciples said to their Master: *Lord, increase our faith*; and that He answered: *If you have faith as a grain of mustard-seed, you shall say to this mountain: Remove from hence, and it shall remove, and nothing shall be impossible to you* (Matt. 17: 19). Such people imagine that the Apostles asked for a little faith only, or that our Lord doubted their faith. But if they considered the words of St. Paul, they would recognise that the faith, compared by our Saviour with a grain of mustard-seed, was in His eyes a very great faith; for the Apostle says: *If I should have all faith, so that I could remove mountains, and have not charity, I am nothing* (1 Cor. 13: 2). Thus we are taught that, what we can do

16. SIXTH SUNDAY AFTER EPIPHANY

with faith like a grain of mustard-seed, according to our Lord, is done, as St. Paul explains, with the most perfect faith.

II. And our Lord spoke another parable to the multitude: *The kingdom of heaven is like to leaven, which a woman took and hid in three measures of meal, until the whole was leavened.* Jesus, to accommodate Himself to the different classes of His hearers, made use of different parables, all meant to be the means for curing divers spiritual ailments. The woman, who in the parable takes the leaven, seems to me to signify the preaching of the Apostles, or the Church formed of different nations. The leaven taken by the woman means the knowledge of the Holy Scriptures; whereas the three measures of meal, in which the leaven is hidden, represent our intellect, soul and body, united in perfect agreement and harmony. They are like two or three persons gathered together in prayer, and receiving from the Heavenly Father whatsoever they ask for. Yet, another meaning may also be found in these words of the parable. We read in the writings of Plato and this is the general opinion of philosophers, that there are in our soul three passions called *the reasonable, the irascible and the concupiscent*. The same pagan philosopher also speaks of the different parts of our body wherein each passion resides. Take, therefore, the *leaven* mentioned in the Gospel, that is, the wisdom of Holy Scripture, and you will keep these passions in check; you will even make them serve as means to attain your desired object, that is, reason will help you to practise prudence, anger will inspire you with hatred against sin, and concupiscence will give you a longing for Christian virtues. And you will succeed in all this through the doctrine given to us by the true Church of Christ.

III. I will also mention some opinions held by different learned men concerning this parable, so that the reader may accept what pleases him best. Some think that the woman of the Gospel is the figure of the Church founding the belief of the faithful upon the doctrine of the three Divine Persons, the Father, the Son, and the Holy Ghost, represented under the image of the three measures of meal. These, they say, are of the same substance, and consequently speak to us of the same Divine Nature of the three

Persons, being one and the same God. However, this is only a pious opinion which, like other comparisons, cannot be used to prove the fundamental truths of our holy religion, revealed to us by an infallible Authority. Other interpretations of the words of this parable cannot be mentioned here without going beyond the limits assigned to this commentary.

IV. *All these things Jesus spoke in parables,* says the Gospel, *to the multitude,* not to the Apostles. The same language is even now used by zealous preachers addressing large assemblies; but the disciples wished to learn from the very source, that is, from the Master Himself, the true doctrine which they were to preach to others. Again the Gospel says: *That the word might be fulfilled which was spoken by the prophets, saying: I will open my mouth in parables, I will utter things hidden from the foundation of the world* (Ps. 77: 2). The prophet, relating the events that took place at the departure of the Israelites from Egypt, and the miracles wrought by God in their favour, announces that all these things are not to be taken in a literal sense, for they contain comparisons and hidden mysteries which will one day be explained by the Saviour of the world Himself.

17. SEPTUAGESIMA SUNDAY

GOSPEL: Matt. 20: 1-16. *At that time*: Jesus spoke to His disciples this parable: The kingdom of heaven is like to a householder who went out early in the morning to hire labourers into his vineyard. And having agreed with the labourers for a penny a day, he sent them into his vineyard. And going out about the third hour, he saw others standing in the market-place idle. And he said to them: Go you also into my vineyard, and I will give you what shall be just. And they went their way. And again he went out about the sixth and the ninth hour, and did in like manner. But about the eleventh hour he went out and found others standing, and he saith to them: Why stand you here all the day idle? They say to him: Because no man hath hired us. He saith to them: Go you also into my vineyard. And when evening was come, the lord of the vineyard said to his steward: Call the labourers, and pay them their hire, beginning from the last even to the first. When, therefore, they were come that came about the eleventh hour, they received every man a penny. But when the first also came, they thought that they should have received more; and they also received every man a penny. And receiving it, they murmured against the master of the house, saying: These last have worked but one hour, and thou hast made them equal to us that have borne the burden of the day and the heats. But he answering, said to one of them: Friend, I do thee no wrong; didst thou not agree with me for a penny? Take what is thine, and go thy way. I will also give to this last even as to thee. Or, is it not lawful for me to do what I will? Is thy eye evil because I am good? So shall the last be the first, and the first last. For many are called, but few chosen.

HOMILY BY POPE ST. GREGORY, PREACHED IN THE CHURCH OF ST. LAWRENCE ON SEPTUAGESIMA SUNDAY
Nineteenth Homily on the Gospels

I. THIS GOSPEL CONTAINING MANY THINGS which need explaining, I will try as far as possible to shorten my explanation, that it may not become tedious to you. *The kingdom of heaven,* so we are told by our Lord, *is like to a householder, who went out early in the morning to hire labourers into his vineyard.* Who, indeed, is more justly to be likened to a householder than our Creator, Who is the Head of the household of faith, ruling over those He has made, and being Master of His chosen ones in the world, as a master of those in his house? He it is that has the Church as His vineyard, a vineyard that ceases not to bring forth branches of the true Vine, from just Abel to the last of the elect that shall be born in the world. This householder, then, for the cultivation of his vineyard, goes out early in the morning, and at the third hour, the sixth, the ninth, and the eleventh, to hire labourers into his vineyard. Thus the Lord, from the beginning to the end of the world, never ceases to gather together preachers for the instruction of His faithful people. The early morning of the world was from Adam until Noah; the third hour from Noah until Abraham; the sixth from Abraham until Moses; the ninth from Moses until the coming of the Lord; the eleventh from the coming of the Lord to the end of the world. At this eleventh hour were sent forth as preachers the Apostles, who received full wages, though they came in late. For the cultivation of His vineyard— that is, the instruction of His people,—the Lord has never ceased to send labourers into it. First by the patriarchs, then by the prophets and teachers of the law, and lastly by the Apostles, He dressed and tended the lives of His people, as the owner of a vineyard dresses and tends it by means of workmen. Whoever, in whatever degree, joined to a right faith the teaching of justice, was so far one of God's labourers in God's vineyard. By the labourers at early morning, at the third, the sixth, and the ninth hour, may be understood God's ancient people, the Hebrews, who, striving to worship Him with a right faith, in company with His chosen ones from the beginning of the world, continually laboured in His vineyard. And now, at the eleventh hour, it was said to the Gentiles: *Why stand you here all the day idle?* The Lord speaks of their carelessness and indifference concerning their salvation, for they had not yet done anything to be assured of it; yet, if you ponder upon their answer to the householder sending them to his vineyard, you will have cause of being ashamed. Their answer to the householder's question, why they stood all the day idle, was: *Because no man hath hired us.* Indeed, they, unlike others, had neither patriarchs nor prophets to instruct them. No one had hired them, for no one had shown them the way leading to salvation. As to us, who neglect the practice of good works, and lead an idle life, what shall we answer for our justification? For we received the true faith, so to speak, in the womb of our mother; we heard the words of life when still in the cradle, and we drank the milk of Christian doctrine, given by our holy Church at the time when, for the life of our bodies, we were sucking the breasts of our natural mothers.

II. The different hours of the parable may also be compared to the different periods of man's life. Childhood, on account of the small sphere of knowledge, is the early hour of morning; youth may be compared to the third hour, when the sun rises and the heat of years increases; the sixth hour represents manhood, the virility, when the sun has reached the zenith of his course; by the ninth hour, showing the sun slowly retreating from his height, we recognise the elderly age of man, when he loses the strength and power of younger years; whereas old age is figured by the eleventh hour. Now, consider how some are called, already in their childhood, to lead a perfect and holy life; others in their youth; these in their manly age; some others in advanced years; and lastly others in their old age. Do you understand that all of us are labourers, who may at any time be sent into the vineyard of the

Lord? Again, beloved brethren, consider your own lives, and ask yourselves whether you are worthy labourers of the Lord, whether you are mindful of the work you are doing, and lastly whether you labour indeed in the Lord's vineyard. Be sure that those who work for their own interests only, have not entered the vineyard of the Lord; for those only are accounted as His labourers, who prefer the glory of God to their own profit and interest. Such worthy Christians endeavour to serve God with ardent love and sincere devotion; they strive to win souls to God, and exert themselves to take others along with them to the habitation of the Saints; whereas those who live for themselves and try to satisfy their vices and concupiscences, are condemned as idle labourers, making no effort to work in, or care for, the Lord's vineyard.

III. What shall we say of those who put off their conversion to the end of their life? Are they not like those labourers standing in the market-place until the eleventh hour, to whom the householder said: *Why stand you here all the day idle?* Our Saviour wishes them to understand that, having spent their childhood and youth in the service of the world and far from God, they are called upon to begin to turn to God, at least, now at the extreme limits of life, and with greater courage to walk on the road of justice, that leads to perfection and eternal life; for the work they are bid to do cannot last very long, since they came so late. Thus this good Householder invites them to come back to Him, and often rewards them before those who had been called from their childhood, since very often the last comers are called away the first. Remember the good Thief (Luke 23). He came at the eleventh hour; but by the capital punishment he suffered, he obtained a reward certainly not deserved by his former sinful life. He recognised Jesus to be the Redeemer of the world, confessed Him publicly, and almost at the same moment gave up the ghost. We see thereby that the Householder, giving the promised penny, began with the last; for the good Thief was received into Paradise before St. Peter. The same happened to many good and pious souls living before the Law and under the Law. They had to wait for their reward, whilst those called after the coming of the Messiah, at once went to

Paradise. We may also say, in all truth, that the same reward that is, a penny, was given to them that had worked one hour only, as to the others who had been working the whole day and had *borne the burden of the day and the heats*. For the eternal happiness, that reward given to them that worked well, will be common to all of them, both to those who came at the beginning and to those who arrived with the Redeemer. This very equality was the cause of complaints: *These last have worked but one hour, and thou hast made them equal to us that have borne the burden of the day and the heats.* Indeed, the first comers can say that they have borne the burden of the day and the heats, since their life was longer than ours. They came at the beginning, when the life of man was very long, and they had to fight against their own self for many years. We also feel in us the fire of concupiscence, against which we contend, and which we try to extinguish; and this continual fighting may be compared to the *burden of the day and the heats*.

IV. Besides all this, I ask, what is the meaning of the murmurs of those who received the reward in heaven very late? Also in what sense can we say that they murmured, since heaven will not be given to those who murmur, and since those who have entered heaven neither murmur nor complain? I answer: If I consider that the patriarchs, though leading a good and holy life, could not enter Paradise before the coming of the Son of God, Who by His death reopened the gates of heaven, we find therein, that is, in the delay preventing them to receive the reward for which they worked so hard, the real motive of their murmuring. After fighting for justice' sake, and thus deserving the crown of glory, their souls went to limbo, a place of rest and peace. To them, therefore, we may attribute the murmurs of the labourers after their day's work. However, after this presupposed murmuring, the souls of the just, leaving their prison, that is limbo, wherein they had been detained for a long time, receive the promised penny, namely, the happiness of the eternal kingdom, of which they take possession. As to us who, though arriving at the end of the day, receive a penny, we do not murmur like those who arrived the first. Since the coming of the Redeemer into this world, we enter into the kingdom of heaven as soon as we leave this life, and we receive without any delay the crown of glory granted to the patriarchs after their very long waiting.* On this occasion the master of the house said to one of the labourers: *I will also give to this last even as to thee.* And, as the place in heaven assigned to a soul is an effect of His generous will, He adds: *Or, is it not lawful for me to do what I will?* It would be man's greatest folly to criticise the manner in which God's goodness deigns to act. Indeed, we could murmur against God, were He to refuse that which He is bound to give, but not when He refuses to grant what He is not in justice obliged to give. He, therefore, that murmurs, deserves this rebuke: *Is thy eye evil because I am good?* Hence we conclude that nobody is to boast of his work or of the time spent in doing it, for the Eternal Truth tells us: *The last shall be first, and the first last.* Though we be aware of our good works, we know not how strictly they will be scrutinized by the great Judge; yea, each of us ought to feel exceedingly happy to receive even the last place in the kingdom of God.

V. The following words of this Gospel, *many are called, but few are chosen*, cannot but inspire us with terror; for many receive the light of faith, but to a few only is granted the happiness of heaven. On account of the festival there are now a great many gathered together here, and there is hardly room for all within the walls of this temple. Yet, who can tell how many of them will one day be found among the number of the elect? All voices are loud in confessing Jesus, but the lives of those who confess Him do not agree with their exterior acts of faith. The greater number of those here present think it sufficient to follow Jesus in words, whilst by their acts they are separated from Him. St. Paul points them out to us, saying: *They profess that they know God, but in their works they deny Him* (Tit. 1: 16). This is confirmed by St. James: *Faith without works is dead* (Jas. 2: 26). And the Psalmist repeats the words of

---

* It would be a mistake to infer from these words that St. Gregory did not believe in Purgatory. Their meaning is that a soul, leaving the body and having nothing to atone for, will be at once received into Paradise, unlike the just souls of the patriarchs which, before the coming of Christ, descended into limbo.

17. SEPTUAGESIMA SUNDAY

God: *I have declared and I have spoken; they are multiplied above number* (Ps. 39: 6). By these words we understand that, when the Lord calls men through His prophets, the number of believers greatly increases. However, not all those who by the gift of faith obtain the knowledge of the truth will be numbered among the elect. It is certain that when a great number of wicked Christians are gathered together with true servants of God, because of the same faith that they profess, they nevertheless do not deserve to be numbered with the faithful on account of their unchristian lives. For it cannot be denied that, though the holy Church includes in the same fold the sheep and the goats, the Eternal Judge will one day separate the just from the wicked, *as the shepherd separates the sheep from the goats* (Matt. 25: 32). Know ye, therefore, and recognise that none of those now given up to the pleasures of the world will be received among the elect; that the Judge will exclude them from the happy fate of the humble, since in this world they were lifted up on the wings of pride. They had received the gift of heavenly faith, but they clung to the earth, and heaven will not be opened to them.

VI. Meanwhile, though a great many people, whose lives are unchristian, may be found in the Church of God, I beseech you, beloved brethren, neither to imitate them nor to think them to be lost. We are aware of the unhappy condition of these people today, but we know not what they will be tomorrow. It often happens that those whom we see behind us on the road to holiness, soon precede us on account of their progress in spirituality; then it is with great difficulty that we follow those whom at some time we seemed to precede. When St. Stephen shed his blood for Christ, his murderers *laid their garments at the feet of a young man whose name was Saul* (Acts 7: 57), and who may be accused of having also stoned St. Stephen by assisting the murderers; yet, by his great labours undertaken for the Church, Saul has gone before the holy martyr, to whose death he contributed. Let us, therefore, consider these two things greatly deserving our attention. First, knowing that many are called but few are chosen, no one can help himself without the grace of God, and, though being called by faith, no one is sure of his eternal salvation. Secondly, when we see our neighbour in the clutches of sin and vice, let us not presumptuously think that he will be lost, for God's infinite mercy is unknown to us.

18. SEXAGESIMA SUNDAY

GOSPEL: Luke 8: 4-15. *At that time:* When a very great multitude was gathered together, and hastened out of the cities to meet Jesus, He spoke by a similitude. A sower went out to sow his seed; and as he sowed, some fell by the wayside; and it was trodden down, and the fowls of the air devoured it. And other some fell upon a rock; and as soon as it was sprung up, it withered away, because it had no moisture. And other some fell among thorns; and the thorns growing up with it choked it. And other some fell upon good ground, and sprung up, and yielded fruit a hundredfold. Saying these things, He cried out: He that hath ears to hear, let him hear. And His disciples asked Him what this parable might be. To whom He said: To you it is given to know the mystery of the kingdom of God, but to the rest in parables; that seeing they may not see, and hearing they may not understand. Now the parable is this: The seed is the Word of God. And they by the wayside, are they that hear; then the devil cometh, and taketh the word out of their hearts, lest believing they should be saved. Now, they upon the rock are they who, when they hear, receive the word with joy; and these have no roots, for they believe for a while, and in time of temptation fall away. And that which fell among thorns are they who have heard, and going their way, are choked with the cares and the riches and pleasures of this life, and yield no fruit. But that on the good ground are they, who, in a good and perfect heart, hearing the word, keep it, and bring forth fruit in patience.

HOMILY BY POPE ST. GREGORY, PREACHED IN THE CHURCH OF ST. PETER ON SEXAGESIMA SUNDAY
Fifteenth Homily on the Gospels

I. THE EXTRACT FROM THE HOLY GOSPEL WHICH you have just heard, beloved brethren, needs not so much that it should be explained as that its lesson should be impressed on your minds. The Truth Himself has explained it, and after that, it is not becoming man's frailty to discuss His exposition as if not reliable. But there is, in that very explanation of our Lord, somewhat which it behoves us well to weigh. For, if we asked you to believe that by the seed is signified the word, by the field, the world, by the birds, the devils, and by the thorns, riches, you would perhaps doubt the truth of our exposition. Therefore, the Lord Himself deigned to give this explanation, and that, not for this parable only, but that you may know in what manner to interpret others, the meaning of which He has not given. Beginning His explanation, the Lord says that He is speaking in parables; and thereby He assures us when our weakness would unveil to you the hidden meaning of His words. For who would believe me were I to say that riches are thorns? Thorns prick, but riches afford us delight. And yet riches are thorns, indeed, for the anxiety they bring is a ceaseless pricking in the minds of their owners, and, if they lead to sin, they are thorns which tear the soul to bleed. But we understand from another Evangelist (Matt. 13: 28), that in this place our Lord speaks not of the riches themselves, but of the deceitfulness of riches. Those riches are deceitful, which can be ours for a little while only; those riches are deceitful, which cannot relieve the poverty of our souls. If, then, you seek to be rich, beloved brethren, earnestly desire the true riches; if you would be truly honourable, strive after the kingdom of heaven; if you love to reach the summit of titles and dignities, hasten to have your names written in Court above, where angels are.

11. Take to heart the Lord's words which your ears hear. The food of the soul is the word of God. When the stomach is sick it rejects again the food that is put into it; and so is the soul sick when a man hears and digests not in his memory the word of God. And if any man cannot retain his food, that man's life is in a desperate case. Thus we ought to fear for our soul, lest it should be lost, when receiving the food of holy admonition, we do not keep in our memory the words of life which would preserve in us true Christian justice. Further, consider that, whatsoever you are

doing now, will in time pass away, and that every day you come nearer the moment of the strict account to be given to God. Are you convinced of this truth? Then why do you love such goods as you must leave, and why are you careless about that end which you will soon reach, and by which your fate in eternity will be decided? Do remember the words of your Redeemer: *He that hath ears to hear let him hear.* Not all of those who were present and heard these words, understood them; for our Lord wished them to be heard with the ears of the heart and mind, and not with the ears of the body only, so that His doctrine may be understood and *accepted*. Be careful, therefore, that the Divine word you receive be not taken from your heart and memory; be careful that this word fall not by the wayside, that is, watch, lest through your carelessness and distraction the devil take the word out of your hearts. Be careful that this precious seed fall not into your souls as upon rocks, that is, that for want of perseverance on your part, it cannot take root, and will, therefore, wither away. Many are seen receiving the words of salvation with joy; some also are noticed beginning to practise virtues, but they fall away in time of temptation. By their inconstancy and the fickleness of their mind they are like the dry and rocky ground, where the seed springs up and withers away, because it has no moisture. Such Christians perhaps hear a sermon against avarice, and at once they feel for that vice the aversion it deserves, and they praise those who despise the goods of this world. But as soon as an opportunity is at hand to gratify their own concupiscence and covetousness, the praises given to the contempt of riches disappear from their memory. When a sermon against impurity is preached, there are many who, at the terrible picture drawn of this shameful vice, not only resolve never to commit such heinous sins, but are also deeply ashamed of their past offences where with they are reproached by their own conscience. Yet, should a dangerous object be presented, they long for it with the same eagerness, as if they had not made the resolution to avoid such objects. They relapse into the same sins which they had previously committed and execrated. It sometimes happens that they shed tears over their debaucheries, and yet they return to them as soon as they cease to bewail them. Thus Balaam shed tears of contrition, seeing the camp of the Israelites, and wished to be in death like this people beloved by God. *Let my soul die the death of the just, he said, and my last end be like to them* (Num. 23: 10). But these feelings of contrition were hardly expressed, when the desires of this impious man were again inflamed by avarice. At the sight of the presents offered to him, he gave the most abominable advice, so as to bring about the destruction of the very people to whom he had wished to be like. His sorrow and contrition were forgotten, for he had not entirely extinguished the flames of avarice burning in his soul.

III. Explaining His parable, our Redeemer says that the cares, the riches and the pleasures of this life choke the seed of the Divine word. Indeed, they choke it through the continual thoughts awakened in the mind, preventing this word of life from taking root. Then, since these useless thoughts shut the door of the heart to good desires, they also prevent the heart from receiving the inspirations of the Holy Ghost, Who preserves the life of the soul. Let us also note that, in the parable of the Lord, both the cares and the pleasures of this life are connected with the possession of riches, because the troubles about riches oppress the mind; then, by their superabundance, they deliver us up to sinful pleasures. For it is certain that rich people have many cares and troubles on account of their love for the things of this world; and it is also certain that they indulge in sensual pleasures, though it seems that these two statements do not agree. Yet, we may say, that if at one time they feel uneasy about their riches, at another they are mollified by the allurements of lust, to which they are attracted by their wealth.

IV. The good seed, falling upon good ground, yields fruit a hundredfold, yet brings forth that fruit in patience. For our good works would be of no avail to us, did we not patiently and generously bear the trials inflicted on us by our neighbour. The more we advance in virtue, the heavier become the crosses wherewith our Father in heaven allows us to be burdened, in order to try those who serve Him. How is this? Because the more a soul endeavours to be separated from the love of the world, the more it finds this same world contemptible and loathsome. Indeed, we see that the greater number of virtuous people doing good works are nevertheless overwhelmed with troubles and trials. The stronger they fight against sensual temptations, the more bitter are their sufferings. Yet it is just in this manner that, according to the Redeemer's words, the just bring forth fruit in patience. They humbly submit to the scourges wherewith they are smitten by God in this world, and afterwards rise to enjoy the eternal rest prepared for them in heaven. We may compare them with grapes, which, being trodden under feet, yield a delicious wine. They are also like the fruit of the olive-tree, which yields in the press a frothy liquid, that becomes the precious oil. Lastly, the just are like to the wheat, which, being thrashed on the floor and separated from the chaff, is preserved in the barn. Those, therefore, who wish their sins and passions to be destroyed, ought to submit willingly, for their spiritual progress, to the stripes wherewith Divine Providence chastises them. Then they will appear before the judgment-seat of God so much the purer, the more they were cleansed from the rust of sin by the fire of suffering.

V. My assertions will be proved by the example of Servulus, which I now place before you. He was begging at the door of the Church of St. Clement, and many among you have known this poor man as well as I did. Deprived of all earthly riches, yet rich in spiritual goods, he was for years afflicted with a terrible disease. From his youth to the very end of his life, he was on his sick-bed, without being able to rise or even to sit up. Palsy, which reduced him to this sad condition, had deprived him of the use of his limbs; he could neither raise his hand to his mouth, nor turn over on his bed. The mother and brother of this poor man waited on him, and gave to other poor people the remainder of the alms he received. Though he had never learnt how to read, he had a copy of the Holy Scripture bought, and pious people, whom he most hospitably received, read it out to him. Thus he acquired a thorough knowledge of the Holy Writ, according to his intellect, which, as I said, had not been cultivated. Amidst his sufferings, his principal object was to thank and praise God day and night with psalms and spiritual canticles. But when the hour came that heaven was to reward such heroic virtue, the acute pains of the palsy reached the heart, and, feeling himself at the point of death, he summoned his own people and others, and asked them to stand up and sing psalms until he died. Whilst he himself was singing with others, he suddenly stopped, and said in a strong and extraordinary voice: 'Do you hear the songs of praise resounding in heaven?' And while listening to that melodious heavenly harmony, his innocent soul left his body. A delicious fragrance was noticed by the assistants, and recognised by them as a sign that his soul had been taken up to heaven. A monk belonging to a monastery, where I stayed for some time, witnessed these facts, the remembrance of which made him shed tears of joy. I was assured by him that, until the burial of the body, the same delicious odour was perceived by all those present. Beloved brethren, do think of the precious death of one who, whilst on earth, bore all the troubles and trials of life with patience and resignation. By his invincible courage, he became like to the good ground, which, according to our Redeemer, brings forth fruit in patience, and, after suffering the plough of tribulations, yields fruit a hundred-fold. Now, I ask you and entreat you to consider what answer we shall give at the terrible judgment? In spite of the graces wherewith we were enriched by Divine Providence; in spite of the hands given to us for useful work, we languish in idleness and neglect good works. Does not the example of that poor and sick man condemn our carelessness? He had in this life neither the goods of this world nor the use of his limbs, yet he strictly observed the Lord's precepts. What shall we say for our justification, when the example of the Apostles, surrounded by the innumerable nations converted by their labours and preaching, will be placed before us by the Judge; when we shall see so many praiseworthy martyrs who, making the sacrifice of their lives, bought heaven with their blood shed for Jesus Christ? What shall we answer, when blessed Servulus stands before us he who constantly laboured and did good works, though his arms, paralyzed by disease, were of no use to him? Do think of all this, beloved brethren, in order to encourage yourselves to do good works; place before your eyes the beautiful models of virtue proposed to your imitation, and one day you will share with them the eternal beatitude in heaven.

19. QUINQUAGESIMA SUNDAY

GOSPEL: Luke 18: 31-43. *At that time*: Jesus took unto Him the twelve, and said to them: Behold, we go up to Jerusalem, and all things shall be accomplished which were written by the prophets concerning the Son of Man. For He shall be delivered to the Gentiles, and shall be mocked, and scourged, and spit upon; and after they have scourged Him, they will put Him to death, and the third day He shall rise again. And they understood none of these things. And this word was hid from them and they understood not the things that were said, it came to pass, that when He drew nigh to Jericho, a certain blind man sat by the wayside begging. And when he heard the multitude passing by, he asked what this meant. And they told him that Jesus of Nazareth was passing by. And he cried out, saying: Jesus, Son of David, have mercy on me. And they that went before rebuked him, that he should hold his peace; but he cried out much the more: Son of David, have mercy on me. And Jesus, standing, commanded him to be brought unto Him. And when he was come near He asked Him, saying: What wilt thou that I do to thee? But he said: Lord, that I may see. And Jesus said to him: Receive thy sight; thy faith hath made thee whole. And immediately he saw, and followed Him, glorifying God. And all the people when they saw it, gave praise to God.

HOMILY BY POPE ST. GREGORY, PREACHED IN THE CHURCH OF ST. PETER ON QUINQUAGESIMA SUNDAY
Second Homily on the Gospels

I. FORESEEING THAT THE MINDS OF HIS APOSTLES would be troubled by the thought of His suffering, our Redeemer told them long before, both of the pains of that suffering and of the glory of His rising again; to this end that, when they should see Him die, as He had prophesied, they might not doubt that He was likewise to rise again. But, since His disciples were as yet carnal, and could not understand His words, telling of this mystery, He wrought a miracle before them. A blind man received his sight before their eyes, that, if they could not comprehend heavenly things by words, they might be convinced of heavenly things by deeds. But we must so take the miracles of our Lord and Saviour, as believing, both that they were actually wrought, and that they have some mystic meaning for our instruction. For in His works power speaks one thing, and mystery again another. Behold, for instance: we know not historically who this blind man was, but we know of what he was mystically a figure. Mankind is blind, driven out of Paradise in the persons of our first parents, knowing not the light of heaven, and suffering the darkness of condemnation. Nevertheless, by the coming of his Redeemer man is enlightened, so that he sees by hope already the gladness of interior light, and walks by good works in the path of life.

II. Note also, beloved brethren, that, as Jesus drew nigh to Jericho, a blind man received his sight. Now, this name *Jericho*, being interpreted, signifies *the city of the moon*, and in Holy Scripture the moon is used as a figure of our imperfect flesh, of whose gradual corruption her monthly waning is a type. Therefore, as our Creator draws nigh to Jericho, a blind man receives his sight. Whilst God takes unto Himself our weak human nature, man receives again the light which he had lost. By God's suffering in the Manhood, man is raised up towards God. This blind man is also well described as sitting by the wayside begging; for the Truth says: *I am the way* (John 14: 6). He that knows not Him Who is eternal light, is blind. But as soon as he believes in Jesus, the Redeemer, then he is sitting on the road leading to salvation. When man has faith, but is not continually asking to be enlightened by *Divine* light, he may, like the blind man, sit on the road, but he is not begging alms. But when by means of faith he begins to believe, when he recognises the blindness of his heart, and unceasingly asks to be delivered from it and to receive the light of truth, then he is like to the poor and unhappy blind man who, sitting by the wayside, was begging.

Let him, therefore, who recognises his darkness, and the need of eternal light, cry out with all the desires of his heart and all the fervour of his soul: *Jesus, Son of David, have mercy on me!* This was the prayer of the blind man to the Redeemer, whilst those who *went before rebuked him,* and asked him to *hold his peace.*

III. And what do we understand by those who went before, but the crowd of bad desires and the restlessness of our passions disturbing our mind and troubling our heart, when we cry to our Saviour? We experience this only too often, that, when after a sinful life we wish to return to God; when we ask Him for strength to pray well, and to renounce the sins enslaving us, the image of our former sins is pictured in our memory, the light of our intellect is darkened, our courage is weakened, and we remain insensible to the voice of God's minister preaching the truth. Thus, those who went before our Lord rebuked the blind man of Jericho, that he should hold his peace; and we learn therefrom the important lesson that, before Jesus comes into our hearts, the awful image of our sensual pleasures rises in our memory, so as to prevent the effects of our prayers.

IV. However, the blind man, waiting to be cured, is our teacher. Though he was rebuked, he cried out much more: *Son of David, have mercy on me!* Thus our prayer must be the more ardent and assiduous, the stronger the noise of wicked thoughts that rise in our mind and endeavour to prevent it. When the stormy crowd of temptations call back the remembrance of our sins, and assail us from all sides, trying to make us neglect, if possible, our prayers, then our powerful and repeated cry towards heaven will render all these phantoms useless and powerless. However, the things I say now, may be learned by you, through your own experience. For when we begin to tear our thoughts and desires away from the world, and to turn them to God; when we give up our mind to prayer, then the worldly thoughts and sinful pleasures of our former life return to attack and distract us. And this assault of our former thoughts is so strong that, in spite of good desires and even tears of repentance, it is only by the greatest care and watchfulness that we succeed in keeping our hearts in safety.

V. Meanwhile, we may be sure that, if we persevere in our prayers, Jesus will remain with us, as He stayed for some time with the blind man. *And Jesus, standing, commanded him to be brought unto Him.* And the words of the Gospel tell us, not without a special motive, that Jesus was first passing by, then was standing. We learn from this that, when powerless phantoms endeavour to disturb us in our prayers, Jesus seems to be passing by; but that when, in spite of their attacks, we persevere in these prayers, Jesus remains standing by us, and delivers us from blindness. For when God takes His abode in our heart, He dispels darkness by His Divine light.

VI. There is yet another lesson taught by our Lord in that miraculous cure of the blind man, that is, the manifestation both of the marks of His Divinity and of the signs of His humanity. For when the Man-God heard the blind man cry out to Him, He did not cure him until standing still, showing us that He was man, because He passed by, and that He was also God, because He remained standing. Was not our Redeemer, as man, to be born among us, to increase in years, to die, to rise from the dead, and to move about from one place to another? But, being at the same time God, He gives us to understand that He is immovable, and that all changes noticed in Him, came from His humanity; whilst, as God, He is always the same, without any change, present everywhere, without shifting His dwellings. Again, our Redeemer heard the voice of the blind man whilst passing by, and granted him light whilst standing still, thus teaching us that His humanity called His attention and love to the blindness of which we suffered, and His Divine power enlightened us with the light of His grace.

VII. For our further instruction we hear Jesus, as soon as He saw the blind man, say to him: *What wilt thou that I do to thee?* Our Saviour, having the power to restore the sight to the blind man, was certainly not ignorant of that which he was going to ask. But He wished to teach us that it was His will we should ask Him, though He knows our desires and is willing to grant them. He, therefore, very often exhorts us to pray to Him, though He assures us that His Father in heaven knows all our needs before we ask. He wishes to encourage us to trust in Him, and to awaken in our hearts real love for prayer. We hear the blind man at once uttering his request, and asking to receive the light. He was asking neither for gold nor for riches of any kind, but for light, since, without this gift, all other goods could not satisfy him. Let us, then, beloved brethren, imitate this man in his prayer, for he received therewith the health both of soul and body. Let us beseech the Lord not for the riches of this world, nor for the perishable blessings of honour and fame, but for the *true light*, and not for the limited light, which for a moment only interrupts the long night, and is common to us with the unreasonable animals. Let us ask for the uncreated light to be seen in the company of the elect, that light having no beginning and being eternal in its duration. Faith will lead us to this light, according to the words of Jesus to the blind man: *Receive thy sight; thy faith hath made thee whole.* Should the sensual man object and say that this light, being invisible, cannot be reached, that nobody can be sure of a thing which cannot be seen, he will soon be convinced of his error, when told that his interior feelings do not arise from his body, but from his thinking soul. Though nobody can see his soul, yet there cannot be any doubt about our having an invisible soul, ruling our visible body. For, when this invisible soul is separated from our visible body, the latter is immediately destroyed, being deprived of the essence of its existence. Therefore, since it is certain that we live by means of this invisible being, namely, the soul, not perceived by our senses, why should we doubt the Truth teaching us that there will be another life which we cannot see now?

VIII. When we perceive the good result of the blind man's prayer, we recognise from the words of the Gospel why this man at once saw the light and followed our Redeemer. He that recognises what is good and at the same time endeavours to do it, imitates the blind man who, seeing Jesus, followed Him. Whereas he who sees Jesus and does not follow Him, acknowledges what is good, but does not consider it his duty to do it. Beloved brethren, when we are aware of the blindness in which we are weeping in this vale of tears; when, by the help of faith telling us of the mystery of Redemption, we sit on the road leading to life; when daily we ask the Author of salvation to enlighten us; when, lastly, we enjoy that heavenly light, taking us out of the darkness in which we were wandering, then nothing remains to us but to follow by our good works the Saviour, Whom we see by the light of faith. Let us carefully examine the place He passes through, then follow His steps by imitating His example; for it is by imitation that we follow Him, as He Himself teaches, saying to one of His disciples: *Follow Me, and let the dead bury the dead* (Matt. 8: 22). And to show that the words *follow Me* mean imitate Me, our Lord says in another place of the Gospels: *If any man minister to Me, let him follow Me* (John 12: 26). To be worthy of Him, we must follow His steps and examine the way in which He walked. And first we see that He, the Creator of all heavenly and reasonable beings, deigned to descend into the womb of a virgin, there to assume the human nature, which He Himself had created out of nothing. We see that He did not choose to be born of rich parents, when taking our human nature, but chose poor parents, who were not even able to offer for Him in the temple a lamb, but only a pair of turtle-doves or two young pigeons. Thus our Redeemer did not seek happiness in this world; He endured insults, scorn, and blasphemies; He allowed Himself to be spit upon, to be buffeted, scourged, crowned with thorns, and nailed to a cross. He would give us to understand that the pleasures we derived from corporeal things, robbed us of the eternal happiness, of which we can again take possession only by drinking the bitter chalice of suffering. Yet, since God suffered so much for man, what suffering will the sinful man be ready to endure? When after all this a Christian, believing in Jesus Christ, is still ruled and led by avarice or ambition; when he is still devoured by the fire of envy or carnal pleasures; when he is eagerly rushing after the happiness of this world, then we can truly say that, instead of following Jesus, he is despising Him, because he is walking on quite a different road, and not on the road taken by the Son of God during His mortal life of bitter suffering. Let us, therefore, recall to our mind our own wickedness; let us remember that the eternal Judge will punish our sins most severely; then, let us endeavour to destroy them by sorrowful repentance. Now, let us do severe penance, and thus escape in eternity the terrible wrath of an offended God. The tears shed in this life will take us to the joys of heaven, for our Lord said: *Blessed are they that mourn, for they shall be comforted* (Matt. 5: 5); whereas the pleasures of this world will, according to the same Saviour, bring us to the eternal dwelling of tears and sorrow. *Woe to you that now laugh, for you shall mourn and weep* (Luke 6: 25). If we wish to obtain the highest felicity, let us now walk in the path of penance, and our penitential life will not only gain for us great merits with God, but will be to His greater glory; for, according to the words of the Gospel, others will be encouraged by our good example: *And all the people, when they say it, gave praise to God.*

20. ASH-WEDNESDAY

GOSPEL: Matt. 6: 16-21. *At that time*: Jesus said to His disciples: When you fast, be not as the hypocrites, sad. For they disfigure their faces, that they may appear to men to fast. Amen, I say to you, they have received their reward. But thou, when thou fastest, anoint thy head, and wash thy face, that thou appear not to men to fast, but to thy Father, Who is in secret; and thy Father, Who seeth in secret, will repay thee. Lay not up for yourselves treasures on earth, where the rust and moth consume, and where thieves break through and steal; but lay up for yourselves treasures in heaven, where neither rust nor moth doth consume, and where thieves do not break through nor steal. For where thy treasure is, there is thy heart also.

HOMILY BY ST. AUGUSTINE
Bk. II, On the Lord's Sermon on the Mount, Chapter 12

I. BY THESE PRECEPTS, AS IT IS EVIDENT, WE ARE bidden to seek for interior gladness, lest, by running after that reward which is without, we should become conformed to the ways of this world, and should so lose the promise of that blessing which is all the truer and more solid as it is inward; that blessing wherein God chose us to be conformed to the likeness of His Son. In this chapter we will principally consider that vain-glory finds a ground for action in sordid poverty as much as in worldly distinction and display; and this development is the more dangerous, since it deceives under the pretence of serving God. He that is marked out by his unbridled indulgence in dress or luxury, or any other display, is by these very things recognised to be a follower of worldly vanities, and deceives no one by putting on a hypocritical mask of holiness. But those professing true Christianity, who draw all eyes on themselves by an eccentric show of filthiness and dirtiness, not suffered by necessity, but by their own will, we must judge of them by their other works, whether their conduct really proceeds from the desire of mortification, giving up unnecessary comfort, or is only the means of some ambitious design. The Lord tells us to beware of wolves in sheep's clothing, but, *by their fruits you shall know them*, He says (Matt. 7: 20). We test them, when by some trials such persons lose the very things which, under the cover of pretended unworldliness, they either gained or sought to gain. Then it will appear whether they be wolves in sheep's clothing, or, indeed, sheep in their own. But, that hypocrites do such contrary things, does not entitle the true Christian to think it his duty to shine before the eyes of men by the display of needless luxury; for the sheep need not lay aside their own clothing, because wolves sometimes falsely assume it.

II. Let us note that Jesus combines fasting with prayers and alms, spoken of in this Gospel, as one of the best means to resist the devil. Though our Lord attacks the vain-glory attending the false virtues of the Pharisees, and making them hypocrites in the eyes of God, He does not condemn the sadness of a sinful, humbled, and contrite heart. On the contrary, this sadness accompanying our fasting, is agreeable to God. But He condemns the voluntary forced sadness, that comes not from a heart penetrated with the love of God, but is only exterior. It is a pretended sadness that tries to obtain the esteem of the multitude, who praise the severe penance of such people, whom God, seeing their hearts, justly condemns. The words of the Gospel: *When thou fastest, anoint thy Head and wash thy face*, must not be taken in a literal sense, for we should certainly be found guilty if observing them. The real meaning of these words is this: As the ancients anointed their heads and washed their faces in days of joy, so we, in the days of fasting, ought to show holy joy. It is evident that, in all these commandments, our Redeemer had in view one object only, that is, to make us enter into our own heart, there to find the interior joy of the Holy Ghost. There may be as much vanity in the neglected exterior appearance of some people and their mournful looks, as in fine garments and exterior cheerfulness. And this kind of vanity is to be feared the more, since it is the more deceitful under the appearance of piety and godliness. He, fasting, anoints his head, when subject to Jesus, his Divine Head, he refers to Him all the merits of fasting, and feels an interior joy when, avoiding the pleasures of the world for His sake, he takes no notice of the praise of the people. He washes his face, who is carefully purifying his heart, knowing that the sight of the countenance of the Lord is promised to a pure heart.

III. You wish to fast well; then humble your soul, especially at the approaching of that day, when the Teacher of humility humbled Himself and was obedient unto death, even to the death on the cross. Let us imitate Him in His sufferings by subduing our desires with salutary abstinence. Let us chastise our body in order to keep it into subjection, and, that our perverse flesh may not tempt us to commit unlawful deeds, let us refuse to it, at least for a time, the lawful enjoyment of some things. Drunkenness and intemperance can never be allowed; but in these holy days meals which may be permitted at other times, should be restricted. Your body will feel more obedient and subservient, the more it is separated from things lawful, and is accustomed to abstain from rightful pleasures. And you will continue in holy cheerfulness to retrench the expenses of your table, the excesses of meals, and even avoid whatsoever flatters the palate.

21. FIRST SUNDAY IN LENT

GOSPEL: Matt. 4: 1-11. *At that time*: Jesus was led by the Spirit into the desert, to be tempted by the devil. And when He had fasted forty days and forty nights, He was afterwards hungry. And the tempter coming, said to Him: If thou be the Son of God, command that these stones be made bread. Who answered and said: It is written, 'Not by bread alone doth man live, but by every word that proceedeth out of the mouth of God.' Then the devil took Him into the holy city, and set Him upon a pinnacle of the temple, and said to Him: If Thou be the Son of God, cast Thyself down; for it is written: He hath given His angels charge over Thee, and in their hands shall they bear Thee up, lest perhaps Thou dash Thy foot against a stone. Jesus said to Him: It is written, 'Thou shalt not tempt the Lord thy God.' Again the devil took Him up into a very high mountain, and showed Him all the kingdoms of the world, and the glory of them, and said to Him: All these will I give Thee, if Thou wilt fall down and adore me. Then Jesus said to him: 'Begone, Satan; for it is written, The Lord thy God shalt thou adore, and Him only shalt thou serve.' Then the devil left Him, and, behold, angels came and ministered unto Him.

HOMILY BY POPE ST. GREGORY, PREACHED IN THE CHURCH OF ST. JOHN LATERAN
Sixteenth Homily on the Gospels

I. IT IS OFTEN ASKED BY SOME PEOPLE WHAT spirit it was by which Jesus was led into the wilderness, on account of the words a little further on: *Then the devil took Him into the holy city*; and again: *The devil took Him up into a very high mountain*. But in truth, and without any further searching, we may believe it was the Holy Ghost who led Him up into the wilderness. His own Spirit led Him where the evil spirit found Him to tempt Him.

However, when it is said that He, God and Man, was taken up by the devil, either into a very high mountain or into the holy city, the mind shrinks from believing, and the ears of man tingle when hearing it. Yet we know these things are not incredible, when we consider certain other things concerning Him. Indeed, the devil is the head of all the wicked, and every wicked man is a member of that body, of which the devil is the head. Was not Pilate a limb of Satan? Were not the Jews who persecuted, and the soldiers who crucified Christ, likewise limbs of Satan? Is it then strange that He should allow Himself to be led up into a mountain by the head, Who allowed Himself to be crucified by the members? Therefore it is not unworthy of our Redeemer, Who came to be slain, that He should be willing to be tempted. It was meet that He should thus overcome our temptations by His own, even as He came to overcome our death by His own. We ought to know that temptation works under three forms. There is first the suggestion, then the delectation, or pleasure, and, lastly, the consent. When we are tempted, it often happens that we fall into delectation, and even into consent, because in the sinful flesh of which we are begotten, we carry in ourselves matter to favour the attack. But God, when He took flesh in the womb of the Virgin, and came into the world without sin, did so without having in Himself anything of this lusting of the flesh against the spirit. It was possible, therefore, for Him to be tempted in the first stage, namely, suggestion; but there was nothing in His mind, in which delectation could fix its teeth. Thus all the temptation He endured from the devil was without, and none within Him.

II. If, now, we consider the order of the temptations attacking the Redeemer of the world, we see with what power our Saviour delivered us from the snares prepared for us by the enemy of our salvation. For, when the old Serpent rose against the first man, the father of the human race, he attacked him with three kinds of temptations, namely, intemperance, vain-glory and avarice. And being thus tempted, he was overcome by the devil, for he gave his consent. When Satan showed to man the forbidden fruit, and persuaded him to eat of it, he attacked him with the weapon of intemperance; then he tempted him with vain-glory, saying that he would be like to God; lastly, avarice was his weapon, since he assured him that he would possess the knowledge of good and evil. For avarice consists not only in the inordinate love of riches, but also in the desire of exaltation; and we are in reality avaricious, when in an ambitious manner we desire to obtain dignities to which we cannot lay claim. This is also the teaching of St. Paul, who, speaking of Jesus Christ, says: *Who, being in the form of God, thought it not robbery to be equal to God; but emptied Himself, taking the form of a servant* (Phil. 2: 6, 7). The devil, therefore, attacked our first parent with the arrows of avarice, for he awakened in him the desire of exalting himself.

III. But this tempter, the old dragon, who by his artifice had overcome the first man, was in his turn overcome by another Man, with the very same weapons he had used in former times. For our Redeemer, the Man-God, was assailed by the devil in the same manner as our first parent; first, with the sensual appetite, since he said to Him: *If thou be the Son of God, command that these stones be made bread.* Then he tempted Him with vain-glory, asking Him to cast Himself down from a pinnacle of the temple, and so to show that He was the Son of God, saving His life by a miracle. Lastly, he tempted Him with avarice, when he showed Him all the kingdoms of the world, and promised to give them to Him, if falling down He would adore him. But our Saviour overcame this enemy by the same means that He had employed to tempt the father of the human race. And after this defeat he was enchained by our Lord, and forced by Him to go out of our heart by the same door by which he had entered to enslave us. Yet, beloved brethren, there is another lesson contained in this temptation of our Lord. He could cast His tempter into the eternal abyss by one single word, He being the Eternal Word. But He only answered with the commandments contained in Holy Scripture, so as to give us an example of His patience and moderation, instead of a brilliant sign of His almighty power. By this He teaches us that, when our sufferings are caused by the wicked, we should make good use of such persecutions, and be instructed by them, rather than take revenge. But are we not ashamed, when we consider, on one side God's patience, and on the other our own impatience, when suffering injustice? It often happens, when we are unjustly treated or despised, that anger fills our heart at once. We try to take revenge, as far as lies in our power, and even threaten with a revenge of which we are powerless. Our Lord overcame the temptations of the devil through His patience and meek words. He bore an enemy who deserved the arrows of His justice, and He is thus the more worthy of our admiration and praise, since He was victorious over that enemy by His moderation rather than by the stripes of His anger.

IV. Take notice of the fact that, as soon as the devil left Jesus, *Angels came and ministered unto Him.* Thereby we are given to understand that there are two natures in Jesus Christ. By the temptation of the devil we know that He was true Man, whilst the coming of the Angels and their ministering to Him, teach us that He is also true God. Let us, then, recognise our own nature in our Saviour, for the devil would not have dared to tempt Him, had he not perceived in Him our humanity. At the same time we bring Him our adorations, for the Angels would not have considered it their duty to minister unto Him, were He not as God exalted over them and all creatures.

V. This Gospel, calling to our mind the forty days and forty nights of fasting spent by our Lord in the desert, entirely agrees with the fast we observe during this holy season. But why was this number of forty days fasting sanctified? We read in the history of the Israelites that Moses prepared himself for the reception of the Law by fasting forty days; that Elias observed the same fast; that Jesus, before beginning His public life, abstained from food for forty days and forty nights; and lastly, that we also, as far as lies in us, observe this abstinence and fasting during the time of Lent. Though several motives may be set forth to explain this law of the Church, we can say in all truth that, by observing this commandment, we offer to God the tenth part of the year granted to us for satisfying our corporeal necessities. After living solely for ourselves during the course of the year, we now in Lent live

21. FIRST SUNDAY IN LENT

for God, offering Him by our abstinence a part of that year. Now, after deducting from the six weeks of Lent the Sundays on which we do not fast, we find that there remain thirty-six days, so to speak, the tenth part of the year that we offer to God. The Lord God, beloved brethen, commands you in the Old Law to offer to Him the tithe (tenth part) of your possessions; it is, therefore, just that you should give Him the tithe of your days. For this reason it is everybody's duty to mortify his body, according to his strength, to crucify his desires and subdue his sinful passions, that he may be, as St. Paul says, a *living sacrifice* (Rom. 12: 1). For we are a living sacrifice when, as long as we live, we mortify the desires of the flesh. Just as the lust of the flesh led us to commit sin, true penance must bring us back to God. Consider, again, that since by the eating of the forbidden fruit we were shut out of heaven, so we must endeavour to re-enter these gates by that temperance and abstinence which will atone for all the offences against God committed by our intemperance.

VI. Yet, let us not think that our fasting will be sufficient to appease God, if it is not accompanied by the merits of almsgiving; for He said to us: *Is not this rather the fast that I have chosen? Loose the bonds of wickedness, undo the bundles that oppress, let them that are broken go free, and break asunder every burden. Deal thy bread to the hungry, and bring the needy and harbourless into thy house; when thou shalt see one naked, cover him, and despise not thy own flesh* (Isa. 58: 6, 7). This testimony teaches us that the fasting most pleasing to God is the one accompanied by alms offered by our hands, that is, by the love for our neighbour, perfected through works of mercy. Of whatsoever you deprive yourselves, give it to your poor neighbour, to relieve him; and these goods, of which you deprive yourselves by mortifying your appetite, will rejoice your neighbour who is in need. Hear the Lord's complaint: *When you fasted and mourned, did you keep a fast unto Me? And when you did eat and drink, did you not eat for yourselves, and drink for yourselves?* (Zach. 7: 5, 6). Now, we eat for ourselves when the needy has no share in the food we are taking, which, being a gift of God, has been created for all men. And he keeps a fast for himself, who, depriving himself for a time of the food he used to take, preserves it to satisfy his desires later on, instead of giving it to the poor. The prophet Joel exhorts us *to sanctify a fast* (Joel 1: 14), teaching us, if we wish to make our abstinence worthy of God the Almighty, to unite the mortification of our flesh with the practice of other virtues; to refrain from anger and banish hatred from our heart. In vain do we chastise our body, if the mind is not subdued by our victory over sinful passions. God Himself declares this through His prophet: *Behold, in the day of your fast your own will is found, and you exact of all your debtors. Behold, you fast for debates and strife, and strike with the fist wickedly* (Isa. 58: 3, 4). No injustice is committed when you ask your debtors to pay what they owe you. Yet you easily understand that he, who practises penance, will even abstain from exacting that which is owed to him in justice. When he mortifies himself in this manner and feels real sorrow for his sins, then God will be ready to forgive the debts due to His justice, seeing that for His sake the sinner forgives to others what they owe him in justice.

22. SECOND SUNDAY IN LENT

GOSPEL: Matt. 17: 1-13. *At that time*: Jesus taketh unto Him Peter and James, and John his brother, and bringeth them up into a high mountain apart; and He was transfigured before them. And His face did shine as the sun; and His garments became as white as snow. And behold, there appeared to them Moses and Elias talking with Him. Then Peter answering, said to Jesus: Lord, it is good for us to be here; if Thou wilt, let us make here three tabernacles, one for Thee, and one for Moses, and one for Elias. And as he was yet speaking, behold a white cloud overshadowed them. And lo, a voice out of the cloud, saying: This is My beloved Son, in Whom I am well pleased; hear ye Him. And the disciples hearing, fell upon their faces, and were very much afraid. And Jesus came and touched them, and said unto them: Arise, and fear not. And when they lifted up their eyes, they saw no one, but only Jesus. And as they came down from the mountain, Jesus charged them, saying: Tell the vision to no man, till the Son of Man shall be risen from the dead.

HOMILY BY POPE ST. LEO THE GREAT
Homily on the Transfiguration of Jesus

I. THE GOSPEL YOU HAVE JUST HEARD, AND WHICH demands your whole attention, invites you to the knowledge of a great mystery. We shall attain this purpose more surely and with less trouble, if we consider what is written in Holy Scripture just before this event (Matt. 16). Indeed, our Lord, the Redeemer of all men, when He began to introduce His doctrine into the world, namely, His Divine doctrine, which gives life to the dead and leads the wicked to justice, instructed His disciples no less by the wonders of His Almighty power than by the words of His eternal wisdom and truth. He wished to convince them that He was both the Son of God and the Son of Man; for one without the other of these prerogatives could not save the world. It would have been as dangerous to believe that Jesus was only God, as to think that He was only man. It was necessary to believe that He was at the same time the one and the other, since the real humanity was in God, as the real Divinity was in man. Therefore, in order to confirm His disciples in the necessary knowledge of and faith in this mystery, our Lord asked them what they thought of Him, and what were the opinions of men concerning Him. St. Peter, one of the Apostles, enlightened by God the Almighty, rose above all that which was human and sensual, and recognised in Jesus *the Son of the living God*. With a loud voice he confessed the glory of His Divinity, revealed to the eyes of his soul, whilst the eyes of his body only saw the corporeal presence of his Divine Redeemer. And this testimony of the Apostle to truth was so pleasing to our Saviour, that, to reward his faith, He called him *blessed*, and at the same time appointed him a firm rock, upon which He would build His Church, against which the gates of hell should never prevail. Jesus Christ even promised Peter that, whatever sentence he pronounced on earth, it would be ratified in heaven.

II. This sublime knowledge of the Divinity of Jesus was also to be united with that of the mystery of His humanity, so that the Apostles, after confessing their belief in the Divinity of the Saviour, should not think it unbecoming to God, unable to suffer, to unite Himself with our weak human nature. Again, they should not cherish the belief that His humanity was so glorified, as to be unable either to be subject to death or even to suffer torments. Indeed, we know that our Lord said to *His disciples that He must go to Jerusalem, and suffer many things from the ancients and scribes and chief priests, and be put to death, and the third day rise again* (Matt. 16: 21). We see also that Peter, filled with love after proclaiming the Divinity of Jesus Christ, and certainly animated by a true zeal for the honour of his Divine Teacher, rebuked Him, saying: *Lord, be it far from Thee; this shall not be unto Thee* (Matt. 16: 22). But our Lord, by a gentle reproof, changed the aversion of the Apostle to the ignominy of His sufferings, into a generous desire to take part in these very sufferings. This was also the motive and the effect of

22. SECOND SUNDAY IN LENT

the advice given by Jesus to all of His disciples: *If any man will come after Me, let him deny himself, and take up his cross, and follow Me.* And He continued: *He that will save his life, shall lose it, and he that shall lose his life for My sake, shall find it* (Matt. 16: 24, 25). And the more to strengthen them in this unmovable firmness, by which they were prompted to embrace without fear even the sharpest crosses; to prevent them from being ashamed of the capital sentence He was to undergo; and lastly, to instruct them not to be scandalized at the patience He was going to show during His Passion, when the brilliant signs of His almighty power would be hidden, He took Peter and James, and John his brother, and brought them up into an exceeding high mountain apart, and there made manifest the brightness of His glory. Hitherto, though they understood that there was in Him the majesty of God, they knew not the power of that body which veiled the Godhead; and therefore He had individually and expressly promised to some of His disciples, who had stood with Him, that they should *not taste death, till they saw the Son of Man coming in His kingdom* (Matt. 16: 28); that is, in the kingly splendour which is the right of the humanity taken into God, and which He desired to make visible to those three men. This is what they saw, for the unspeakable and inaccessible vision of the Godhead Himself, which will be the everlasting life of the pure of heart (Matt. 5: 8), no man, who is still burdened with a mortal body, can see and live. Our Lord, therefore, manifested His glory before the witnesses He had chosen, and allowed His body, which is like to ours, to appear in such brilliant light, that *His face did shine as the sun, and His garments became as white as snow.* However, the principal reason for this transfiguration was to banish the scandal of the cross from the hearts and minds of His disciples; also, after showing them the perfection and dignity hidden in His person, He wished to prevent their faith from being weakened by the sight of the humiliations He would so willingly endure. This mystery was also to be the foundation of His Church. For the Church, being the mystic body of Jesus Christ, recognised in this glory surrounding Him, the promise of that glory which she expects to be adorned with when, united to the Head in the happy dwellings, she will participate in His own everlasting felicity. Our Lord Himself said so, when speaking of His coming: *Then shall the just shine as the sun in the kingdom of their Father* (Matt. 13: 43). And this is confirmed by St. Paul, saying: *I reckon that the sufferings of this time are not worthy to be compared with the glory to come, that shall be revealed in us* (Rom. 8: 18). And again: *You are dead, and your life is hid with Christ in God. When Christ shall appear, Who is your life, then you also shall appear with Him in glory* (Col. 3: 3, 4).

III. Now, the more to strengthen the faith of His Apostles, and to instruct them in a more perfect manner, our Lord, at the miracle of the Transfiguration, let Moses and Elias appear, talking with Him and representing the Law and the Prophets respectively. The presence of these two personalities was to justify what is prescribed by the law: *In the mouth of two or three witnesses every word shall stand* (Deut. 19: 15). Can there be anything more certain and credible than the word of truth confirmed by the testimony of both the Old and the New Testament? The doctrine of the Gospel, preached by Jesus Christ, perfectly agrees with the prophecies of the old law, and He, Who was foreshadowed by the types and figures of the Old Testament, is manifested in the glory of His Transfiguration. *The law was given by Moses; grace and truth came by Jesus Christ* (John 1: 17). By His coming He fulfilled all promises made by the Almighty to His people, and in His person were verified the commands and legal ceremonies by which He was announced. Lastly, He gave us to understand by His coming into this world that the prophecies concerning Him were true, and, by means of the grace He gives us, He makes the fulfilling of the commandments very easy to us. Through the knowledge of this truth St. Peter felt in himself new life, and began to despise the things of this world; he was disgusted with earthly things, and all his desires were then directed to heaven. In the excess of his joy at this beatific vision of our Redeemer's glory, he cried out: *Lord, it is good for us to be here. If Thou wilt, let us make here three tabernacles, one for Thee, and one for Moses, and one for Elias.* Our Lord did not answer these words; He wished the Apostle to understand that his request, though not sinful in itself, was untimely, since

22. SECOND SUNDAY IN LENT 119

the world was to be redeemed by the death of the Saviour. Again, our Redeemer wished to teach all the faithful that, though it be unlawful to doubt the promise of eternal happiness, they should ask Him for the necessary patience to bear the trials of this life, rather than for the happiness that is to be their reward; for the time of reigning with Him in heaven cannot precede the time of fighting and suffering.

IV. Peter was *yet speaking, when a bright cloud over-shadowed them. And lo, a voice out of the cloud, saying: This is My beloved Son, in Whom I am well pleased; hear ye Him.* They plainly heard Him say: *This is My Son,* Whose it is to be of Me, and with Me without all time. For neither is He that begets before Him that is begotten, nor He that is begotten after Him that begets. *This is My Son,* between Whom and Me, to be God is not a point of difference, to be Almighty, a point of separation, nor to be Eternal, a point of distinction. *This is My Son,* not by adoption, but My very own; not created from, or of another substance, or out of nothing, but begotten of Me; not of another nature, and made like to Me, but of My own Being, born of Me, equal to Me. *This is My Son,* by Whom all things are made, and without Whom was made nothing that was made; Who makes likewise all things whatsoever I make; and whatsoever things I do He does likewise, inseparably and indifferently. *This is My Son,* Who thought it not robbery, nor took it by violence, to be equal with Me, but, abiding still in the form of My glory, that He may fulfil the common decree for the restoration of mankind, bowed the unchangeable Godhead even to the form of a servant (Phil. 2: 6, 7).

V. Instantly, therefore, *hear ye Him,* in Whom I am in all things well pleased, by Whose preaching I am manifested, and by Whose lowliness I am glorified. For He is the Truth and the Life (John 14: 6), My Power and My Wisdom (1 Cor. 1: 24). *Hear ye Him,* Whom the Law prefigured, Whom the prophets constantly announced; Him, Who redeemed the world by the merit of His Blood, Who subdued the power of the devils, and rendered their efforts and assaults useless; Who destroyed the sentence pronounced against man, who by his disobedience was truly guilty. *Hear ye Him,* Who opened to you the road to heaven, and Who by the punishment on the Cross erected the steps leading you up to Me. Why are you afraid of Him, since He offers you salvation? Why do you distrust Him? See, He offers Himself to deliver you from your miseries! Do, then, the will of My Anointed, which agrees with My own. Get rid of that fear, with which the weakened nature fills you, and arm yourselves with that courage, which ought to be awakened in you by faith. For it would be unbecoming in you to feel depressed at the sight of our Redeemer's sufferings, which, by His help, you will share one day, when it will be necessary to give your life for His sake.

VI. It was not only for the benefit of the witnesses of these events that these truths were declared, but the whole Church received them in the person of the three disciples, to whom they were revealed by God. We must, therefore, ground our faith upon the teaching of the Gospel, so that no one may be scandalized by the Cross on which Jesus deigned to redeem the world. Let no one among you be afraid of suffering for justice' sake; let no one doubt the revelations promising an eternal reward; for through labour we are made sure of rest, and through death we come to life. Since our Saviour willed to take upon Himself our weakness, we, on our side, being faithful to Him, and persevering in His love, shall surely overcome our enemies, and infallibly receive the crown prepared for us, specially if we listen to the voice of the Father, Who, to arm us against all adversities, and encourage us to observe His commandments, says: *This is My beloved Son, in Whom I am well pleased; hear ye Him.* The same He is Who with the Father and the Holy Ghost reigneth for ever and ever. Amen.

23. THIRD SUNDAY IN LENT

GOSPEL: Luke 11: 14-28. *At that time*: Jesus was casting out a devil, and the same was dumb; and when He had cast out the devil, the dumb spoke, and the multitude were in admiration at it. But some of them said: He casteth out devils by Beelzebub, the prince of the devils. And others tempting, asked of Him a sign from heaven. But He, seeing their thoughts, said to them: Every kingdom divided against itself shall be brought to desolation, and house upon house shall fall. And if Satan also be divided against himself, how shall his kingdom stand? because you say, that through Beelzebub I cast out devils. Now, if I cast out devils by Beelzebub, by whom do your children cast them out? Therefore they shall be your judges. But if I by the finger of God cast out devils, doubtless the kingdom of God is come upon you. When a strong man armed keepeth his court, those things are in peace which he possesseth. But if a stronger than he come upon him, and overcome him, he will take away all his armour wherein he trusted, and will distribute his spoils. He that is not with Me is against Me; and he that gathereth not with Me, scattereth. When the unclean spirit is gone out of a man, he walketh through places without water, seeking rest; and not finding, sayeth: I will return into my house whence I came out. And when he come he findeth it swept and garnished. Then he goeth and taketh with him seven other spirits more wicked than himself, and entering in they dwell there; and the last state of that man becometh worse than the first. And it came to pass, as He spoke these things, a certain woman from the crowd, lifting up her voice, said to Him: Blessed is the womb that bore Thee, and the breasts that gave Thee suck. But He said: Yea, rather, blessed are they who hear the word of God and keep it.

HOMILY BY THE VENERABLE BEDE
Bk. IV, Chapter 48, On St. Luke 11

I. IN MATTHEW (12: 22) WE READ THAT THE DEVIL by whom this poor creature was possessed, was, not only dumb, but also blind; and that, when he was healed by our Lord, he saw as well as he spoke. Three miracles, therefore, were performed on this one man: the blind saw, the dumb spoke, and the possessed was delivered. This mighty work was then wrought carnally indeed; but it is still wrought spiritually in the conversion of believers, when the devil is cast out of them, so that their eyes see the light of faith, and the lips, which before were dumb, are opened that their mouth may utter the praise of God. *But some of them said: He casteth out devils by Beelzebub, the prince of devils.* These some were not of the multitude, but were liars among the Pharisees and Scribes, as we are told by the other Evangelist (Matt. 12: 24). While the multitude, who seemed to be less instructed, wondered at the work of the Lord, the Pharisees and Scribes, on the other hand, denied the facts when they could, and, when they were not able to do so, twisted them by an evil interpretation, and asserted that the works of God were the works of an unclean spirit.

II. *And others, tempting, asked of Him a sign from heaven.* They wished Jesus either to call down fire from heaven, like Elias (4 Kings 1: 10), or, like Samuel (1 Kings 7: 10), to make thunder roll, and lightning flash, and rain fall at mid-summer. Yet, had He done so, they would have tried to explain away these signs also, as being the natural result of some unusual, though till then unremarked, state of the atmosphere. O thou, who stubbornly deniest what thy eye sees, thy hand holds, and thy sense perceives, what wilt thou say to a sign from heaven? Perhaps thou wilt say that the magicians in Egypt also wrought many signs from heaven (Exod. 7: 8) *But He, seeing their thoughts, said to them: Every kingdom divided against itself shall be brought to desolation, and house upon house shall fall.* He answered not their words, but their thoughts, as though He would compel them to believe in His power, since He sees the secrets of the heart. But if every kingdom divided against itself is brought to desolation, then the kingdom of the Father, and the Son, and the Holy Ghost, is not divided, since His is a kingdom that, without all contradiction, shall never be brought to desolation by any shock, but shall abide unchanged and unchangeable for ever. *And if Satan also be divided against himself, how shall his kingdom stand? because you say, that through Beelzebub I cast out devils.* Saying this, He sought to draw from their own mouth a confession that they had chosen for themselves to be part of the devil's kingdom, which, if divided against itself, cannot stand. It was, therefore, the duty of the Pharisees to answer our Redeemer; for should they say that Satan has not the power to cast out devils, they must confess that they have not anything to say against Jesus. On the other hand, should they pretend that the devil has that power, then, in order to secure their own safety, they will be forced to leave a kingdom which, being divided against itself, will be brought to desolation. However, should the Pharisees wish to know by what power our Lord casts out devils, and to be convinced that this is not done by the power of Beelzebub, let them listen to the words He added, saying: *Now, if I cast out devils by Beelzebub, by whom do your children cast them out? Therefore they shall be your judges.* Here our Lord is speaking of His disciples by saying to the Pharisees that their children would be their judges; for the disciples of Jesus, being their posterity, knew for certain that in the school of so perfect a Teacher they had not learnt the detestable art of casting out devils by the power of the devil. Just as if our Lord had said: You will be judged by these simple men, whom you despise, in whom there is no guile, who are free from all cunning artifice, whose faces bear the mark of virtues and holiness, which they discover in Me. Or should you wish to explain these words in another sense, then say that our Lord wished to give to the Pharisees and Scribes this other lesson: If your children cast out devils from the bodies of the possessed by the power of the Holy Ghost, what reason have you to attribute the works I perform to any other than to God the Almighty? Therefore, these children will be the judges of their fathers and will condemn them, for the children refer to God the power they possess to cast out devils, whereas their fathers referred that power to Beelzebub, the prince of devils.

III. Then, to confirm this truth, and to justify the great wonders He performed, our Saviour continued His discourse with these words: *But if I by the finger of God cast out devils, doubtless the kingdom of God is come upon you.* It was the finger of God, which was recognised by the magicians of Pharaoh, when they played their tricks or enchantments before Moses; for, seeing the unheard-of wonders of this man sent by God, they exclaimed: *This is the finger of God* (Exod. 8: 19). By this finger of God the Commandments were written on the tables of stone on Mount Sinai. All this teaches us that the Holy Ghost is that finger of God proceeding, as it were, from the hand of the Son, Who is the arm of the Almighty Father, whilst the Father has one and the same nature with the Son and the Holy Ghost. Should you be scandalized by this comparison of the members which seem unequal, the unity of the body formed by them will edify and even encourage you. It may also be said that the Holy Ghost is called the finger of God, on account of the special graces bestowed by Him to angels and men; for no other limb points like the finger at the different parts composing the Body. When our Lord said: *The kingdom of God is come upon you*, He meant by this kingdom the happy dispositions of those who now do penance for their sins, and are, even in this life, separated from the wicked condemned by them. *When the strong man armed keepeth his court, those things are in peace which he possesseth.* This strong man is the devil; his court is the world, which he continually guards, which is thoroughly corrupted through his wickedness, and over which this unclean spirit ruled powerfully before the coming of the Saviour; for he reigned without opposition over the idolatrous nations, his worshippers. Holy Scripture therefore calls him *the prince of this world*, and our Lord says of him to His disciples: *The prince of this world shall be cast out* (John 12: 31). And the better to describe the defeat and flight of this prince of darkness, our Lord added these words: *But if a stronger than he come upon him, and overcome him, he will take away all his armour wherein he trusted, and will distribute the spoils.* We are thus taught by our Lord that He is the stronger One, more powerful than the devil, whose dominion was overcome, from whose tyranny He delivered mankind by the strength of His almighty arm, and not by a deceiving or with Beelzebub-concerted deliverance, as by their calumnies the Jews tried to make the multitude believe. The cunning artifices of this wicked spirit are the armour wherein the enemy of our salvation trusted, and men deceived by him, are the spoils taken from him and distributed by Jesus after His victory. For, according to the prophet, He will take with Him, on the day of His triumph, a multitude of prisoners up to heaven, where He grants His gifts in abundance, setting up in the Church, some as Apostles, others as prophets, and choosing some as shepherds or as teachers.

IV. *He that is not with Me, is against Me, and he that gathereth not with Me, scattereth.* Though these words may be applied to heretics and apostates, they specially refer to the devil; for, according to the words following, our Lord wished the multitude to understand that there cannot be any comparison between His works and those of hell. What does the devil desire but to keep souls in his slavery? whilst Jesus offers them freedom. The devil presents idols and false gods for our adoration; Jesus teaches us to adore the one and true God. The devil praises sin and vice, and Jesus encourages us to practise virtue, therefore, there cannot be anything in common between Jesus and Satan, for their works are in direct opposition. The Redeemer of the world says that, *when the unclean spirit is gone out of a man, he walketh through places without water,* and thus teaches us the difference between His works and those of the devil. This latter endeavours to defile that which is clean, whereas the Redeemer cleanses what is defiled. Nevertheless, by these words may also be understood heretics and apostates, and even wicked Christians who, after receiving the grace of Baptism, making profession of the true Catholic faith, and renouncing the pomps and vanities of the world, banished the devil from their hearts. And to this unclean spirit, who finds his former house swept and garnished, and the dwelling of the Holy Ghost, one place only remains a dry and barren land, to the approaches to which he goes, trying to take the soul by surprise, and to re-enter his former home. It may be said in all truth that this infernal spirit is seeking rest therein, and cannot find it. For this unclean spirit, who shuns the proximity of pure and innocent souls, can only make his abode in the souls of the wicked and godless, offering him an agreeable refuge and a place of rest. This enemy of the human race, according to Holy Scripture, *sleeps in the shadow, in the covert of the reed, and in moist places* (Job 40: 16). This shadow, hiding him, represents the darkness of a sinful soul; by the reed, smooth outwardly, yet inwardly hollow, are meant the hypocrites, who cover the emptiness of their merits with the appearance of virtue; lastly, sensual and lascivious souls are represented by the moist places into which the devil retires. *He sayeth: I will return into my house whence I came out.* Such resolution on the part of our enemy must make us fear lest our passions and vices, which we thought destroyed, return with greater force to overthrow and take possession of us at the very moment when we but carelessly resist them. Though the enemy on his return will find our soul sanctified by the grace of Baptism and adorned with the gifts of the Holy Ghost, he will also find in it a dry and desolate place, as the Gospel says, when we do not endeavour to increase these graces and merits by practising virtues and good works, or when we do not try to obtain the spiritual goods of which we were at one time deprived. And should our soul only seem to be adorned with virtues, these will be but apparent virtues, brought forth by our hypocrisy.

V. *And the devil goeth and taketh with him seven other spirits more wicked than himself, and, entering in, they dwell there.* By these wicked spirits, seven in number, are meant all sins and vices. For those who, after being sanctified in Baptism, let their faith be perverted by error and heresy, or give themselves up to the sinful desires of the children of the world, will soon, by the blandishments of Satan, be thrown into the abyss of all wickedness. These other devils, taking possession of the souls, are justly called more wicked than the first, not only because they introduce into them the seven capital sins, opposed to the seven gifts of the Holy Ghost, but also because these souls, by their hypocrisy, preserve the exterior appearance of virtues, which they no longer possess. In all truth we can say with the Gospel, that *the last state becometh worse than the first*, since it would be better, had these souls never known the way of justice, than to forsake it when once recognised. This happened to Judas, the traitor, to Simon, the magician, and to many others mentioned in Holy Scripture. Moreover, our Lord had also another object in view when He spoke this parable, namely, to apply it in a special manner to the Jews, and to teach them that, what He said about one man would be fulfilled in the whole nation. For in St. Matthew He concludes the same parable with these words: *So shall, it be also to this wicked generation* (Matt. 12: 45). This truth is confirmed in a most astonishing manner, when we bear in mind that the Jews, accepting the Divine law, forced the devil to go out of their hearts. This unclean spirit, driven out of his house, took refuge among the pagans, as in a desert, and there he found rest. But when these idolatrous nations began to believe in the Saviour of the world, then the devil, again driven out of this house, purposed to return to the Jews, where he had formerly taken up his abode. He returned into the house he had left, and found it again deserted, for Jesus, Who had foretold the Jews that their house would be desolate, no longer dwelt in their temple. This, however, still seemed to be adorned; but these ornaments were but exterior and meaningless observances, introduced by the Pharisees. This house was deprived of the assistance both of God and of the angels, and the enemy, accompanied by seven other spirits, entered without difficulty, and secured to himself the conquest of this nation, whose unfortunate end was worse than its beginning. For, since this unbelieving people has been blaspheming Jesus Christ, it is possessed by devils in a more cruel manner than it was in Egypt before the promulgation of the Law. At the time, when the Jews did not believe in the coming Messiah, they were less guilty than when, after His coming, they refused to acknowledge and to receive Him.

24. FOURTH SUNDAY IN LENT

GOSPEL: John 6: 1-15. *At that time*: Jesus went over the sea to Galilee, which is that of Tiberias; and a great multitude followed Him, because they saw the miracles which He did on them that were diseased. Jesus therefore went up into a mountain, and there He sat with His disciples. Now the Pasch, the festival day of the Jews, was near at hand. When Jesus, therefore, had lifted up His eyes, and seen that a very great multitude cometh to Him, He said to Philip: Whence shall we buy bread that these may eat? And this He said to try him, for He Himself knew what He would do. Philip answered Him: Two hundred pennyworth of bread is not sufficient for them, that every one may take a little. One of His disciples, Andrew, the brother of Simon Peter, saith to Him: There is a boy here that hath five barley loaves and two fishes; but what are they among so many? Then Jesus said: Make the men sit down. Now there was much grass in the place. The men, therefore, sat down, in number above five thousand. And Jesus took the loaves, and when He had given thanks, He distributed to them that were sat down. In like manner also of the fishes, as much as they would; and when they were filled, He saith to His disciples: Gather up the fragments that remain, lest they be lost. They gathered up, therefore, and filled twelve baskets with the fragments of the five barley loaves which remained over and above to them that had eaten. Now these men, when they had seen what a miracle Jesus had done, said: This is of a truth the Prophet that is to come into the world. Jesus, therefore, when He knew that they would come to take Him by force and make Him King, fled again into the mountain Himself alone.

HOMILY BY ST. AUGUSTINE
Twenty-Fourth Tract on St. John

I. THE MIRACLES DONE BY OUR LORD JESUS Christ were the very works announcing His Divinity, and inviting men to recognise God in the visible work of His almighty power. God Himself is of such a nature as the human eye cannot see, and the miracles, by which He continually rules the whole world, and satisfies the needs of all His creatures, do not excite our admiration; for we always see them, and hardly take any notice of the wonderful fertility given by Him to the little grain of grass trodden under our feet. According to His mercy, He kept some special works to be done in due season, but out of the common order of nature, so that men might see them and wonder, not because they are greater, but because they are not so common as those they but lightly esteem, since they see them every day. For it is a greater miracle to govern the whole universe than to feed 5,000 men with five loaves of bread. Yet no man marvels at it, though everyone wonders at the feeding of 5,000 men, not because it is a greater miracle than the other, but because it is rarer. For is it not the same God Who feeds the whole world, and Who, from a little grain that is sown, makes the fulness of the harvest? God works in both cases in one and the same manner; He makes the harvest to come of a few grains that are sown, and in His hands five barley loaves are multiplied for the feeding of 5,000 men. In Christ's hands is this power. He that multiplies the grains of corn, also multiplied the loaves, though not committing them to the earth created by Him. This miracle, therefore, is brought to bear upon our senses, that our mind may thereby be enlightened. It is shown to our eyes, to give food to our intellect; so that, through His works which we see, we may marvel at God, Whom we cannot see, and, being roused up to believe, and being purified by believing, we may be longing to see and to know, by the things we can see, Him Who is unseen.

11. However, it is not sufficient for us to see this meaning only in the miracles of Christ. We must ask the miracles themselves what they have to tell us concerning Jesus Christ. Indeed, they have a tongue of their own, if only we will understand it. Since Christ is the Word of God, the work of this Word is a word for us. Let us, therefore, endeavour to understand the miracle before us, and to discover the mystery contained in it.

Our Lord went up into a mountain, and this was done that His voice might be better heard, and the miracle He was going to perform, might be seen more clearly, the higher the place and the easier He could be seen. From this place He perceived the multitude, recognised that they were hungry, and fed them. Yet, the compassion of our Lord for all these people would have been of no avail to satisfy them, had He not had at the same time the power to do so. For the disciples of Jesus, being themselves tormented by hunger, felt great sympathy with the multitude, and wished to help them; yet they had neither the means nor the power. Our Lord, seeing the great multitude, said to Philip: *Whence shall we buy bread that these may eat? And this He said to try him, for He Himself knew what He would do.* By this question He intended the ignorance of His disciple to be shown; and, since this was manifested, He, without doubt, wished to teach us a truth that shall be seen afterwards.

III. In order briefly to explain the profound meaning contained in the story and circumstances of this wonderful multiplication of bread, let us first say that the five loaves represent the five Books of Moses, which, belonging to the Old Testament, may be compared with barley rather than with wheat. For you know that the former is, by its nature, covered with chaff, from which it is removed with some difficulty. And it is the same with the writings of the Old Testament: they are hidden under thick veils, and the meaning of them cannot be discovered but with difficulty, though they yield rich food as soon as the shadow of the types, covering this meaning, has been sufficiently removed. The boy mentioned here, who brought *five loaves and two fishes*, probably means the Jewish people, among whom the Scriptures — of which they made no real use to recognise the truth — were deposited. The two fishes seem to be the figure of the two powers established by God in the old covenant to govern and sanctify the nation, one being the priesthood and the other the royal dignity. However, since both these dignities were united in the person of Jesus Christ, Whose types they were, He perfectly fulfilled their duties by sacrificing Himself for us as High

Priest, and reigning over us as King. And thus the mysteries of the Old Testament, announcing Jesus Christ, and seeming unintelligible, were made clear and intelligible by the coming of this Divine Saviour. He broke the loaves and multiplied them, thus showing that the five Books of Moses, typifying these five loaves, are by their fruitfulness infinitely multiplied when they are by interpretation opened, or, so to speak, broken. The ignorance of the people living under the Old Law, is signified by the barley of which the loaves were made; for it is said of the Jews that even now, when they read Moses, they are covered with a veil, which the coming, the passion and the death of the Messiah were not able to remove or to tear asunder. Our Lord makes us perceive this ignorance of the Jews by the ignorance of His disciple whom He addressed, when on the point of working the great miracle.

IV. All the different circumstances of this great miracle, perfectly well connected, instruct us if only we know how to draw the right conclusions. The number of 5,000 men fed by our Lord clearly represents the Israelites living under the Law, which is explained by the five Books of Moses. The same may be said of the pool of Bethsaida, in Jerusalem, surrounded by five porches to shelter the sick. It represents the weak and languid state of that people, who could only be cured by the power of the Saviour, Who restored health to the man for many years sick of the palsy. Lastly, the multitude sitting on the grass are a figure of the bestial dispositions of this carnal people, who only loved what flatters the senses; for, according to the Scripture, *all flesh is as grass* (Isa. 40: 6). By the fragments of the bread not eaten by the multitude we are taught that there are certain truths which are above the intellect of common people, and the understanding of which is given only to those able to teach others, like the Apostles, represented by the twelve baskets filled with the remaining fragments. The multitude, witnessing this great miracle, never tired of admiring it. As for us, beloved brethren, who hear it related, and know that it was performed for our instruction, we ought not to admire it solely, like the Jews witnessing it. Our faith, by which we believe what we have not seen, raises us up far above the Jews, since our Lord calls blessed those who *have not seen and have believed*, especially as we have the privilege to understand what the multitude could not perhaps perceive in this great miracle. Let us be convinced that, as soon as we are able to penetrate the mystery of this miracle, we shall find therein a far more useful food than that received by this multitude.

V. Those witnessing this miracle said of our Lord: *This is of a truth the Prophet that is come into the world.* They probably spoke thus, because they only consulted their own senses witnessing the circumstances of the miracle. But the light of faith shows us Jesus as the Teacher of the prophets, a Teacher by Whom they were sanctified, and in Whom their prophecies were fulfilled. Jesus was a true Prophet; for the Almighty said to Moses: *The Lord thy God will raise up to thee a Prophet of thy nation* (Deut. 18: 15); that is, Who will be like Moses in the flesh, but Who will be exceedingly higher than Moses, on account of His Divine Majesty. The truth of this promise was confirmed by our Lord, Who, speaking of Himself, said: *Amen, I say to you that no prophet is accepted in his own country* (Luke 4: 24). Finally, the proof that He is truly a prophet lies in the fact that He is the Divine Word, by which all prophets, whom we may call the word of God, were inspired. And if the world has in olden times wonderingly gazed at prophets inspired by God and filled by the Holy Ghost to bring His words to the world, we have the happiness of seeing that Prophet, Who is the all-powerful and uncreated Word of God. Since Jesus Christ is called a Prophet, though superior to all other prophets, we also, using the words of Holy Scripture, call Him an Angel, though He is the Prince of all heavenly spirits. When the prophet calls Him *the Angel of the great counsel* (Isa. 9: 6; Septuagint), he does not contradict himself, since he says elsewhere: Not an angel, nor an ambassador, but *God Himself will come and save them*; that is, to save them He will not send an angel, will not send an ambassador, but will come Himself. Who will come? The Angel Himself. Certainly not by an angel, except as He is an Angel, so as to be also the Lord of angels. For angels, in our tongue, are *messengers*. If Christ brought no message, He would not be called an Angel; and if Christ prophesied nothing, He would not be called a Prophet. Since He exhorted us to accept the faith, and to walk on the road leading to eternal life, He fulfilled the duties of an Angel sent by God, for He announced these truths whilst with us. In the same manner He fulfilled the duties of a Prophet by His prophecies concerning the future. That He was the Word of God made flesh, He was the Lord both of angels and prophets.

VI. But why did He again ascend into the mountain when He perceived that they wished to take Him by force and make Him a King? Did He not know that He was a King, since He feared to be made a King? Indeed, He was a King; not such a King as could be made by men, but such as should give a kingdom to men. May we not suppose that by this action Jesus signifies something special to us, since His deeds are words? Therefore, their wishing to take Him by force and make Him a King, and His retiring into the mountain Himself alone, does this speak nothing and signify nothing? It may be that their wish to take Him by force meant they wanted to forestall the time of His kingdom. For He came into this world not to reign now, as He shall reign in that kingdom for which we pray when we say, *Thy kingdom come.* For being the Son of God, the Word of God—Word by which all things were created—He forever reigns with the Father. The prophets foretold His kingdom, according to that wherein He is Christ, made man, and has made His believers Christians. There shall, therefore, be a kingdom of Christians, which is now gathering and getting together, and which is bought by the Blood of Jesus Christ. But there shall be also, at some future time, a glorious kingdom of Christ, at the time when the glory of His saints shall be revealed, after the judgment executed by Him, which, as He said above, the Son of Man will execute. Of this kingdom the Apostle says: *When He shall have delivered up the kingdom to God and the Father* (1 Cor. 15: 24). Jesus Christ Himself speaks of this kingdom: *Come, ye blessed of My Father; possess you the kingdom prepared for you from the foundation of the world* (Matt. 25: 34). But the disciples and the multitude, believing in Him, thought He had come to reign now; hence they wanted to take Him by force and make Him a King, not knowing that the time had not yet come. Therefore, our Lord, fleeing into the mountain, shows that He wished to hide this knowledge within Himself, and bring it forth in due season, that is, at the end of the world.

25. FIFTH SUNDAY IN LENT, OR PASSION SUNDAY

GOSPEL: John 8: 46-59. *At that time*: Jesus said to the multitude of the Jews: Which of you shall convince Me of sin? If I say the truth to you, why do you not believe Me? He that is of God heareth the words of God. Therefore you hear them not, because you are not of God. The Jews therefore answered and said to Him: Do not we say well that Thou art a Samaritan, and hast a devil? Jesus answered: I have not a devil; but I honour My Father, and you have dishonoured Me. But I seek not Mine own glory; there is One that seeketh and judgeth. Amen, amen, I say to you: If any man keep My word, he shall not see death for ever. The Jews therefore said: Now we know that Thou hast a devil. Abraham is dead, and the prophets; and Thou sayest: If any man keep My word, he shall not taste death for ever. Art Thou greater than our father Abraham, who is dead? And the prophets are dead? Whom dost Thou make Thyself? Jesus answered: If I glorify Myself, My glory is nothing. It is My Father that glorifieth Me, of Whom you say that He is your God; and you have not known Him, but I know Him. And if I shall say that I know Him not, I shall be like to you, a liar. But I do know Him, and do keep His word. Abraham, your father, rejoiced that he might see My day. He saw it and was glad. The Jews therefore said to Him: Thou art not yet fifty years old, and Thou hast seen Abraham? Jesus said to them: Amen, amen, I say to you, before Abraham was made, I AM. They took up stones, therefore, to cast at Him. But Jesus hid Himself, and went out of the temple.

HOMILY BY POPE ST. GREGORY, PREACHED IN THE CHURCH OF ST. PETER ON PASSION SUNDAY
Eighteenth Homily on the Gospels

I. LET US CONSIDER HERE, BELOVED BRETHREN, the great goodness and meekness of the Son of God. He came into this world to take away sins, and He says to the Jews: *Which of you shall convince Me of sin?* He was able, through the power of His Divinity, to justify sinners, and was contented to show by argument that He was not Himself a sinner. But the words He added, *He that is of God, heareth the words of God,* must fill us with fear and fright; for *you hear them not, because you are not of God,* He at once added. If, then, whosoever is of God hears God's words, and whosoever is not of God cannot hear Him, let everyone ask himself, whether in the ear of his heart he hears God's words, and understands whose words they are. The Truth commands us to be longing for a home in heaven, to bridle the lusts of the flesh, to turn away from the glory of the world, not to seek any man's goods and to give away our own. Let, therefore, every one of you think within himself, if this voice of God be heard in the ear of his heart, and if he already know that he is of God. For there are some, who do not deign to hear the commandments of God, not even with their bodily ears. And there are some who do not mind hearing them with their bodily ears, but whose heart is far from them. And there are some, who hear the words of God with joy, and even are thereby moved to tears, but who turn again to iniquity as soon as the fit of weeping is past. Those who despise to do the words of God, do not hear them. Therefore, beloved brethren, carefully recall to your mind your own life; then with fear and trembling ponder on those awful words spoken by the mouth of the Eternal Truth: *Therefore you hear them not, because you are not of God.* And what the Lord here speaks about the reprobate, they themselves make the same thing concerning them manifest by their evil deeds. These words follow immediately: *The Jews therefore answered and said to Him: Do not we say well that Thou art a Samaritan, and hast a devil?*

II. Now let us hear what the Lord answered to such an insult. *I have not a devil, but I honour My Father, and you have dishonoured Me.* The Lord said, I have not a devil; but He did not say, *I am not a Samaritan*, for in one sense He was a *Samaritan*, because the word Samaritan in the Hebrew language signifies 'a watcher.' And the Lord is that Watcher of Whom the Psalmist says: *Unless the Lord keep the city, he watcheth in vain that keepeth it* (Ps. 128: 2). He also is the Watchman to Whom Isaias says: *Watchman, what of the night? Watchman, what of the night?* (Isa. 21: 11) Therefore the Lord said, *I have not a devil*, but not, *I am not a Samaritan*. Of the two things brought against Him He denied one, but by His silence admitted the other. Indeed, our Saviour came into this world to watch over the whole human race, therefore He said nothing when accused of being a Samaritan, but defended Himself against and denied the unjust and wicked imputation of having a devil. By the extraordinary meekness shown by our Lord towards His enemies He puts to shame our pride and haughtiness; for, when we receive the slightest injustice, we often accuse our opponents of greater crimes than those imputed to us. We do to them whatever injury we are able to, and even threaten them with punishments that are not in our power. Now consider the example of patience given by our Lord: the blackest calumnies are invented against Him and He is not angry; when justifying Himself He never makes use of an offensive word. In truth He could have answered the Jews, who in such improper manner calumniated Him, that they were themselves possessed by the devil, since they could not blaspheme God without being animated by the evil spirit. Yet He, Who is Truth itself, did not on this occasion make use of the truth to defend Himself. His words were spoken solely for giving testimony to the truth, and not for revenging Himself on His enemies. By this action of the Son of God we are taught that, when we are attacked by our brethren with false accusations, we are not to publish the faults they are themselves guilty of, so that passion should not give to our hands weapons wherewith to satisfy our anger, instead of punishing them in a lawful manner. And since it is well known that those, who most zealously exert themselves to work for the glory and intentions of God, are very often calumniated by the wicked and freethinkers, our Lord wished to give us in His own person an example of patience, saying to the Jews, by whom He was unjustly accused: *I honour My Father, but you have dishonoured Me*. And in order perfectly to instruct us concerning the dispositions of our mind when we suffer for justice sake He added: *I seek not Mine own glory. There is One that seeketh and judgeth.* Now the Gospel tells us that *the Father hath given all judgment to the Son* (John 5: 22); therefore, when the Son, overwhelmed with insults and accusations, and without vindicating His own honour, leaves the duty of revenge to His Father, He wishes us to understand that we are calmly to bear any detractions or calumnies coming from our brethren. For we see that He, Who received from His Father the power to judge, did not make use of it then, to administer justice. However, should, in spite of our moderation, the malice of the wicked against us increase from day to day, let us not withhold from them the teachings of the Divine doctrine. On the contrary, let us persevere in our instructing them according to our Lord's example, Who, in spite of the insulting reproaches of His enemies, saying that He had a devil, continued even with greater zeal His kind and patient teaching. For immediately after He added: *Amen, amen, I say to you: If any man keep My word, he shall not see death for ever.* As it is certain that the just become more perfect by the injuries done to them, so it is also true that the wicked grow worse through the kindness shown to them. We see, that after the kind exhortations and admonitions addressed to them by Jesus, the Jews were still more angry, and had the wickedness to say to His face: *Now we know that Thou hast a devil.* They were spiritually blind, and could not perceive the deadly state in which they were through their sins. But since they considered temporal death as the greatest of all evils, they said to our Saviour: *Abraham is dead, and the prophets, and Thou sayest: If any man keep My word, he shall not taste death for ever.* By their words these Jews seem to have believed in the Scriptures, since they recognised Abraham and the prophets, and honoured their memory; yet the honour given to His servants by those who do not recognise God is neither real nor true.

III. Though our Lord saw that the Jews tried their utmost to oppose His doctrine, He never ceased to preach the truth, and continued His teaching, for He said to them: *Abraham your father rejoiced that he might see My day; he saw it and was glad.* That day of the Lord, which Abraham really saw, was that on which he received into his house three Angels under the appearance of travellers. For these three Angels, appearing under a human form, represented to the faith of Abraham the adorable mystery of the Blessed Trinity which he recognised. He addressed the Three present before him, as if speaking only to one, so as to show that in the three Persons of the Holy Trinity, whom he adored, there was the Unity of the Divine Nature. As to those who keep their souls bowed down to the earth, it is in vain they hear the doctrine of heaven; their eyes never look upwards to gaze at it. Thus we see that the Jews, with their carnal thoughts, had in view only the years of our Saviour's mortal life, and said to Him: *Thou art not yet fifty years old, and Thou hast seen Abraham?* Thereon our Lord, to raise them up to the comprehension of His Divinity, and to shut the eyes of their bodies, wherewith alone they looked at Him, answered: *Amen, amen, I say to you, before Abraham was made, I AM.* You will notice that our Lord did not say, I was before Abraham, but before Abraham was made, I AM, in order to show by this expression that His Divine Nature, which is eternal, knows neither the past nor the future, but is ALWAYS PRESENT. For this reason God the Almighty, speaking to Moses, said: I AM WHO AM; then added: *Then shalt thou say to the children of Israel: He who is, hath sent Me to you* (Exod. 3: 14). As man Jesus Christ was by His birth to come either before or after the time of Abraham. But, being the Eternal Truth, and not subject to any time, He could have neither beginning nor end. Yet, as the unbelieving Jews were not able to understand these eternal truths, announced to them by the Redeemer, *They took up stones to cast at Him*, and tried to kill Him Whom they were unable to understand.

IV. To avoid the fury of the Jews, who were on the point of stoning Him, *Jesus, as the Gospel says, hid Himself and went out of the temple.* What ought to be to you, beloved brethren, a motive of astonishment, is the fact that our Saviour is seen escaping the persecution of His enemies, whose hands He could have bound by His mere will, and whose lives He could have taken, had He made use of His almighty power. Yet, this infinitely good God, Who had come into this world to suffer and to die, would not show the severity of a judge. This was again proved at the time of His Passion, when He said to the soldiers, who had come with Judas to apprehend Him: *I am He* (John 18: 5), and *they went backwards and fell to the ground.* Yet, He allowed them to take hold of His Sacred Person, and He willingly submitted to all the tortures they inflicted on Him. Now, if we ask why our Lord hid Himself, since, without escaping from the presence of His enemies, He could have rendered all their efforts powerless, we shall see that this Redeemer of the world wished to teach us an important lesson both by His example and His words. His action tells us that even when we are able to scorn the attacks of our enemies, and the injuries they try to inflict on us, we are, after His example, to avoid by timely retirement, the wrath of their excited passions. St. Paul, in his Epistle to the Romans (Ch. 12) repeats the same exhortation. Let us therefore carefully avoid the fury of our brethren whom we see angry with us; let us not rise against those by whom we are calumniated, nor render evil for evil; but let us be convinced by the example given by God Himself, that it is more honourable to overcome all insults and persecutions by flight and silence, than by taking revenge.

V. Yet the spirit of pride whispers into our ears: Silence brings shame, when we are attacked and do not resist. When those, witnessing the affronts put upon us, notice that we are silent, they will not be convinced of our patience, but will imagine that in the depth of our conscience we confess ourselves guilty of the sins imputed to us. Thus speaks pride. However, such thoughts arising in our mind, and trying to stifle the feelings of moderation inspired by patience, come from our human opinion, and our inclination to think more of the false honour of the world and people's opinions, than of the esteem and approval of God, Who from the heights of heaven witnesses our doings. This is not the way of following Jesus, for He says: *I seek not Mine own glory; then is One that seeketh and judgeth.*

The words of the Evangelist, *Jesus hid Himself and went out of the temple,* may have yet another meaning, namely, that our Saviour was forsaking the Jews, who despised the word of salvation announced to them, and of which they made no other use than to become more wicked, and even to wish to stone Him. He hid the truth before them, since by their pride and their contempt for it, they had become unworthy of His heavenly doctrine. For proud and vain souls, not knowing the value of humility, are abandoned by the Truth. Yet, are there not many Christians, perhaps among us, who, detesting the obduracy of the Jews who were deaf to the Lord's teaching, are just as guilty by refusing to put into practice this same doctrine of Jesus? Many hear what our Redeemer commands us to practise; they recognise the Divine power in His miracles, but they refuse to change their lives and thus to be converted. Jesus calls us, and we do not return to Him; He bears with us in our sinful life, and we abuse His patience. Oh, my beloved brethren! let us not hesitate to renounce our sinful ways whilst there is yet time; let us take care lest God be tired of waiting for us, and, after despising His infinite mercy, we fall into the hands of His infinite justice.

26. SIXTH SUNDAY IN LENT, OR PALM SUNDAY

GOSPEL: Matt. 21: 1-17. And when they drew nigh to Jerusalem, and were come to Bethphage, unto Mount Olivet, then Jesus sent two disciples, saying to them: Go ye into the village that is over against you, and immediately you shall find an ass tied, and a colt with her; loose *them* and bring *them* to Me. And if any man shall say anything to you, say ye that the Lord hath need of them, and forthwith he will let them go. Now, all this was done that it might be fulfilled which was spoken by the Prophet, saying: 'Tell ye the daughter of Sion: Behold thy king cometh to thee, meek, and sitting upon an ass, and a colt the foal of her that is used to the yoke.' And the disciples going, did as Jesus commanded them. And they brought the ass and the colt, and laid their garments upon them, and made Him sit thereon. And a very great multitude spread their garments in the way; and others cut boughs from the trees, and strewed them in the way; and the multitudes that went before and that followed, cried, saying: 'Hosanna to the Son of David: Blessed is He that cometh in the Name of the Lord. Hosanna in the highest.' And when He was come to Jerusalem, the whole city was moved, saying: 'Who is this?' And the people said: 'This is Jesus, the Prophet, from Nazareth of Galilee.' And Jesus went into the Temple of God, and cast out all them that sold and bought in the Temple, and overthrew the tables of the money-changers, and the chairs of them that sold doves. And He saith to them: 'My house shall be called the house of prayer; but you have made it a den of thieves.' And there came to Him the blind and the lame in the Temple, and He healed them. And the chief priests and scribes, seeing the wonderful things that He did, and the children crying in the Temple, and saying: 'Hosanna to the Son of David,' were moved with indignation, and said to Him: 'Hearest Thou what they say?' And Jesus said to them: 'Yea, have you never read: "Out of the mouth of infants and of sucklings thou hast perfected praise"?' And leaving them, He went out of the city into Bethania, and remained there.

HOMILY BY ST. AMBROSE
Bk. IX, On St. Luke

I. WHAT A BEAUTIFUL TYPE IS BEFORE OUR EYES! Our Lord, on the point of forsaking the Jews, and of taking His abode in the hearts of the Gentiles, goes up into the Temple, thus indicating that He would be adored by them in spirit and in truth; that the temple they were to consecrate to Him, would not be a building erected by the hands of men, but the real Temple of the true God, laid upon the foundation of faith. Thus our Lord prefers the Gentiles, who would love Him, to the Jews, who had only hatred for Him. Therefore He goes up to the Mount of Olives, that upon the heights of grace He may plant those young olive-branches whose mother is the Jerusalem which is above. And the heavenly Husbandman stands upon this holy mount, so that all those whom He planted in the House of God may be able truthfully to say: *But I am as a fruitful olive-tree in the house of God* (Ps. 51: 10). Perhaps that mountain signifies Jesus Christ Himself. For what other mount could bring forth such fruitful olive-trees, not bending under the weight of their own fruit, but spiritually fruitful with the fulness of the Gentiles? He also it is by Whom and unto Whom we go up; for He is the Way in which we walk; He is the Door at which we knock, and which opens to let us enter into the sanctuary after being made worthy to worship Him.

II. The Gospel also says that the disciples went into a village, and that there they found an ass tied and a colt with her. Neither could be loosed but by the command of the Lord; and it was the hand of His Apostles that loosed them. This was done to indicate the great grace imparted by our Lord to His servants, giving them power to loose from sin; and also to teach His ministers to imitate the holiness of the Apostles, since they also have received the same power to loose them that are bound. Now, if we consider the great misfortune of our first parents who, after their fall, were banished from their home in Paradise into a village, we shall find that those who had been cast out by death, were again called back by the Giver of Life. For this reason we read in Matthew that there were tied both an ass and her colt, to give us to understand that, as man was banished from Paradise in a member of either sex, so is his recall by the Redeemer figured in animals of both sexes. The she-ass is a type of our sinful mother, Eve, and the colt of the multitude of the Gentiles; and it was upon the colt that Jesus took His seat. And it is well said that on that colt *no man ever hath sitten* (Luke 19: 30), because before Jesus Christ no man ever called the Gentiles into the Church. And when St. Mark (11: 2) repeats the statement, *You shall find a colt, upon which no man yet hath sat*, it is to teach us that though the idolatrous nations had been until then kept in the darkness of error by an unjust authority, no ruler had any lawful right over them, because they were free by nature, though slaves by sin. For this reason our Lord commanded His disciples to say: *The Lord hath need of them*; to give us to understand that, though there are many rulers and masters in the world, there is only one God and Lord, Who is the absolute Ruler of all His creatures.

III. St. Mark also says in his Gospel, that the colt was *tied before the gate without, in the meeting of two ways* (11: 4), to indicate that everyone who is not Christ's, is without the gate of salvation. Whereas he that is Christ's, is not without, and is not, like this animal, standing in the meeting of two ways, exposed to the gaze of passers-by, and having neither stable nor fodder. This colt belonged to no special owner, and its condition was most pitiable, because it was ready to bear the yoke of the first comer, and to be the slave of many, having no special master. Consider also the difference between Jesus and the rulers of the world. These latter make use of fetters and chains to secure their possessions, whilst Jesus Christ, as seen by the command given to His Apostles, looses and delivers those who serve Him. His blessings and gifts are more powerful to attach us to Him than the chains by which we are bound. We also notice that the disciples sent by our Lord to bring to Him the ass and the colt, spoke not by their own authority, but answered the owner in the manner commanded by our Lord Himself. By this also we understand that the Apostles announced the true faith to the pagan nations not by their own words, but by the Word of God; not in their own name, but in the name of Jesus Christ; and also that the powers of darkness, keeping the nations in idolatry, were forced to restore them by the command of God announced to them by His ambassadors. When, lastly, we see the Apostles spread their garments in the way under the feet of Jesus, we learn thereby that practice of edifying works must needs precede the preaching of the Gospel. Garments, according to Holy Scripture, often signify virtues, which are powerful means to soften the hearts of unbelievers to whom the tenets of faith are preached. These virtues also make straight the path leading to the minds of those whom the apostolic labourers endeavour to convert. Let us not think that the King of the whole world had any other object in view at His triumphal entry into Jerusalem, than to announce, by the exterior decorations covering the way, His wish to enrich our souls with His gifts, and to erect His throne in our hearts. It was a sign of His triumph, and of the loving dominion He would establish in all these souls, after overcoming their passions and winning for Himself their affections. Happy, therefore, the Christian who receives into his heart this great and peaceful Conqueror! Happy also he whose tongue is ruled by this Divine Word.

IV. However, beloved brethren, what bridle will be able to keep our tongue in check, or to loose it for speaking at the opportune moment? St. Paul gives the answer; for he asked the Ephesians to continue their prayers and supplications to God, *and for me, that speech may be given to me, that I may open my mouth with confidence, to make known the mystery of the Gospel* (Eph. 6: 19). The word of the Lord, that is heard in the innermost of our heart, is the bridle governing us, and the goad exciting our souls, and against which it is hard to kick, as Jesus said to His Apostle. After learning from this Apostle to obey the grace of God, to accept the goad and bear His yoke, let us also learn from the Prophet how to bridle our tongue; for the science of keeping silent is a virtue rarer than that of speaking at the right time. No one will be more able to teach us this science than the Prophet himself, who set a guard to his mouth, when sinners stood against him; who was dumb, and was humbled, and ready for the scourges sent by Providence (Ps. 38). Learn, therefore, to imitate the example given by the Man-God; learn to bear Jesus Christ, Who has borne you, carrying you back to the fold, when you had gone astray; learn gladly to submit to the yoke of the Redeemer, that you may become the rulers of the world. But no one can boast of bearing Jesus Christ, unless he be able to say with the Prophet: *I am become miserable, and I am bound down even to the end; I am afflicted and humbled exceedingly; I roared with the groaning of my heart* (Ps. 37: 7, 9). In order never to leave the right and straight path, you must step upon the garments spread by the disciples on the way of the Redeemer; you must be careful not to soil your feet — that is, your works, with the filth of the world; and you must follow the road made straight for you by the Prophets. Thus, those who went before our Lord on His entry into the city, spread their garments in the way, to point out to the Gentiles the road to be taken by them. Thus, also, the Apostles reddened this road of salvation with their own blood, to guide you and make your steps sure on that road. However, the meaning we give to these words does not hinder us from saying that the Gentiles, typified by the colt stepping upon the garments of the Jewish people, have already begun to take possession of the inheritance destined by God for them, and of which the Jews made themselves unworthy.

V. It would, perhaps, be a useless question to inquire about the meaning of the branches cut off the trees and strewed in the way, since they would hinder the progress of the passers-by rather than smooth their path. But we are told by the Lord of the whole world, whose Providence governs the universe, that the axe was already laid to the root of the trees, to cut down every tree not yielding good fruit. We see this fulfilled at the coming of the Saviour of the world, by Whom the pride of the Gentiles was trodden under foot by being subjected to the yoke of His Gospel. On the knowledge of the Gospel these converted pagans founded their glory, and, treading on their pride, followed Him. These once idolatrous nations, now renewed and animated by the Spirit, are, so to speak, new branches bringing forth the fruit of life on a stem that formerly seemed unfruitful. St. Luke justly remarks that, *when He was now coming near the descent of Mount Olivet the whole multitude of His disciples began with joy to praise God with a loud voice, for all the mighty works they had seen* (Luke xix. 37), thus testifying that the great mystery of salvation was going to be fulfilled by this Redeemer sent from heaven. These people acknowledged in the Person of Jesus Christ their God and King; they recalled to mind the words of the Prophet glorifying the Son of God, and they recognised Him as the Saviour of the House of Israel, for Whom they had been waiting so long. But, since the ungrateful nation of the Jews, who were soon to crucify Him, gave beforehand testimony to His Divinity, they pronounced against themselves the sentence of damnation, because exteriorly they recognised the God of truth, and yet in their hearts they betrayed and condemned Him.

27. GOOD FRIDAY

THE PASSION OF OUR LORD JESUS CHRIST, ACCORDING TO ST. JOHN 18 AND 19

At that time: Jesus went forth with His disciples over the brook Cedron, where there was a garden, into which He entered with His disciples. Now Judas also, who betrayed Him, knew the place, because Jesus had often resorted thither, together with His disciples. Judas, therefore, having received a band of soldiers and servants from the chief priests and the Pharisees, cometh thither with lanterns and torches and weapons. Jesus, therefore, knowing all things that should come upon Him, went forth and said to them: 'Whom seek ye?' They answered Him: 'Jesus of Nazareth.' Jesus saith to them: 'I am He.' And Judas also, who betrayed Him, stood with them. As soon, therefore, as He had said to them, I am He, they went backward, and fell to the ground. Again, therefore, He asked them: 'Whom seek ye?' And they said: 'Jesus of Nazareth.' Jesus answered: 'I have told you that I am He; if, therefore, you seek Me, let these go their way, that the word might be fulfilled, which He said: "Of them whom Thou hast given Me I have not lost anyone."' Then Simon Peter, having a sword, drew it, and struck the servant of the high priest, and cut off his right ear. And the name of the servant was Malchus. Jesus therefore said to Peter: 'Put up thy sword into the scabbard. The chalice which My Father hath given me, shall I not drink it?' Then the band and the tribune and the servants of the Jews took Jesus, and bound Him, and led Him away to Annas first, for he was father-in-law to Caiphas, who was the high priest of that year. Now, Caiphas was he who had given the counsel to the Jews, that it was expedient that one man should die for the people. And Simon Peter followed Jesus, and so did another disciple, and that disciple was known to the high priest, and went in with Jesus into the court of the high priest. But Peter stood at the door without. The other disciple, therefore, who was known to the high priest, went out and spoke to the portress, and brought in Peter. The maid, therefore, that was portress, saith to Peter: 'Art not thou also one of this Man's disciples?' He saith: 'I am not.' Now, the servants and ministers stood at a fire of coals, because it was cold, and warmed themselves, and with them was Peter also standing, and warming himself. The high priest, therefore, asked Jesus of His disciples, and of His doctrine. Jesus answered him: 'I have spoken openly to the world; I have always taught in the synagogue and in the temple, whither all the Jews resort, and in secret I have spoken nothing. Why askest thou Me? Ask them who have heard what I have spoken to them. Behold, they know what things I have said.' And when He had said these things, one of the officers standing by gave Jesus a blow, saying: 'Answerest Thou the high priest so?' Jesus answered him: 'If I have spoken evil, give testimony of the evil, but if well, why strikest thou Me?' And Annas sent Him bound to Caiphas, the high priest. And Simon Peter was standing, and warming himself. They said, therefore, to him: 'Art not thou also one of His disciples?' He denied it, and said: 'I am not.' One of the servants of the high priest (a kinsman to him whose ear Peter cut off) saith to him: 'Did not I see thee in the garden with Him?' Then Peter again denied, and immediately the cock crew. Then they led Jesus from Caiphas to the governor's hall. And it was morning, and they went not into the hall, that they might not be denied, but that they might eat the pasch. Pilate therefore went out to them, and said: 'What accusation bring you against this Man?' They answered and said to him: 'If He were not a malefactor, we would not have delivered Him up to thee.' Pilate then said to them: 'Take Him you, and judge Him according to your law.' The Jews therefore said to him: 'It is not lawful for us to put any man to death.' That the word of Jesus might be fulfilled, which He said, signifying what manner of death He should die. Pilate therefore went into the hall again, and called Jesus, and said to Him: 'Art Thou the King of the Jews?' Jesus answered: 'Sayest thou this thing of thyself, or have others told it thee of Me?' Pilate answered: 'Am I a Jew? Thy own nation and the chief priests have delivered Thee up to me. What hast Thou done?' Jesus answered: 'My kingdom is not of this world. If my kingdom were of this world My servants would certainly strive that I should not be delivered to the Jews: but now My kingdom is not from hence.' Pilate therefore said to Him: 'Art Thou a King, then?' Jesus answered: 'Thou sayest that I am a King. For this was I born, and for this came I into

27. GOOD FRIDAY

the world, that I should give testimony to the truth. Everyone that is of the truth heareth My voice.' Pilate saith to Him: 'What is truth?' And when he had said this, he went out again to the Jews, and said to them: 'I find no cause in Him; but you have a custom that I should release one unto you at the pasch: will you, therefore, that I release unto you the King of the Jews?' Then cried they all, saying: 'Not this man, but Barabbas.' Now Barabbas was a robber. Then, therefore, Pilate took Jesus and scourged Him, and the soldiers, platting a crown of thorns, put it upon His head, and they put on Him a purple garment. And they came to Him, and said: 'Hail, King of the Jews!' And they gave Him blows. Pilate therefore went forth again, and saith to them: 'Behold, I bring Him forth unto you, that ye may know that I find no cause in Him.' Jesus therefore came forth bearing the crown of thorns and the purple garment. And he saith to them: 'Behold the Man.' When the chief priests, therefore, and the servants had seen Him, they cried out, saying: 'Crucify Him! crucify Him!' Pilate saith to them: 'Take Him you, and crucify Him, for I find no cause in Him.' The Jews answered him: 'We have a law, and according to the law He ought to die, because He made Himself the Son of God.' When Pilate, therefore, had heard this saying, he feared the more. And he entered into the hall again, and he said to Jesus: 'Whence art Thou?' But Jesus gave him no answer. Pilate therefore saith to Him: 'Speakest Thou not to me? Knowest Thou not that I have the power to crucify Thee, and I have the power to release Thee? Jesus answered: 'Thou should'st not have any power against Me unless it were given thee from above. Therefore, he that hath delivered Me to thee hath the greater sin.' And from thenceforth Pilate sought to release Him. But the Jews cried out, saying: 'If thou release this Man thou art not Caesar's friend. For whosoever makes himself a King, speaketh against Caesar.' Now, when Pilate had heard these words, he brought Jesus forth, and sat down in the judgment-seat, in the place that is called Lithostrotos, and in Hebrew, Gabbatha. And it was the parasceve of the pasch, about the sixth hour. And he saith to the Jews: 'Behold your King.' But they cried out: 'Away with Him; away with Him! Crucify Him!' Pilate saith to them: 'Shall I crucify your King?' The chief priests answered: 'We have no King but Caesar.' Then, therefore, he delivered Him to them to be crucified. And they took Jesus, and led Him forth; and bearing His own cross, He went forth to that place which is called Calvary, but in Hebrew, Golgotha: where they crucified Him, and with Him two others, one on each side, and Jesus in the midst. And Pilate wrote a title also, and he put it upon the cross, and the writing was: 'JESUS OF NAZARETH, THE KING OF THE JEWS.' This title, therefore, many of the Jews did read, because the place where Jesus was crucified was nigh to the city; and it was written in Hebrew, in Greek, and in Latin. Then the chief priests of the Jews said to Pilate: 'Write not, "The King of the Jews," but that He said: "I am the King of the Jews."' Pilate answered: 'What I have written, I have written.' Then the soldiers, when they had crucified Him, took His garments (and they made four parts, to every soldier a part), and also His coat. Now, the coat was without seam, woven from the top throughout. They said then one to another: 'Let us not cut it, but let us cast lots for it, whose it shall be;' that the Scripture might be fulfilled, saying: 'They have parted My garments among them, and upon My vesture they have cast lots.' And the soldiers indeed did these things.

Now, there stood by the cross of Jesus His mother and His mother's sister, Mary of Cleophas and Mary Magdalene. When Jesus, therefore, had seen His mother and the disciple standing, whom He loved, He saith to His mother: 'Woman, behold thy son.' After that, He saith to the disciple: 'Behold thy mother.' And from that hour, the disciple took her to his own. Afterwards, Jesus knowing that all things were now accomplished, that the Scripture might be fulfilled, said: 'I thirst.' Now there was a vessel set there full of vinegar, and they, putting a sponge full of vinegar about hyssop, put it to His mouth. Jesus therefore, when He had taken the vinegar, said: 'It is consummated.' And, bowing His head, He gave up the ghost. **(Here all kneel and pause.)** Then the Jews, because it was parasceve, that the bodies might not remain upon the cross on the Sabbath-day (for that was a great Sabbath-day), besought Pilate that their legs might be broken, and that they might be taken away. The soldiers therefore came, and they broke the legs of the first and of the other that was crucified with Him. But after they were come to Jesus, when they saw that He was already dead, they did not break His legs, but one of the soldiers opened His side with a spear, and immediately there came out blood and water. And he that saw it gave testimony, and his testimony is true, that you also may believe. For these things were done that the Scripture might be fulfilled: 'You shall not break a bone of Him.' And again another Scripture sayeth: 'They shall look on Him they pierced.' And after these things, Joseph of Arimathea (because he was a disciple of Jesus, but secretly, for fear of the Jews) besought Pilate that he might take away the body of Jesus. And Nicodemus also came, he who at first came to Jesus by night, bringing a mixture of myrrh and aloes, about a hundred pounds weight. They took, therefore, the body of Jesus, and bound it in linen cloths, with the spices, as the manner of the Jews is to bury. Now there was a garden in the place where He was crucified, and in the garden a new sepulchre, wherein no man yet had been laid. There, therefore, because of the parasceve of the Jews, they laid Jesus, because the sepulchre was nigh at hand.

HOMILY BY ST. AUGUSTINE
Tract 118, 119 etc.

I. WHEN PILATE HAD JUDGED AND CONDEMNED the Lord Jesus Christ at his judgment seat, *they took Him* about the sixth hour, and *led Him forth; and bearing His own cross, He went forth to that place which is called Calvary, but in Hebrew Golgotha, where they crucified, Him.* He was going, therefore, to the place where He was to be crucified. Jesus *bearing His own cross.* A great spectacle! But then to impiety a great sport to look upon, to piety an exceedingly great mystery! Impiety sees in it a great display of ignominy, piety a great strengthening of faith. Impiety looks on, and laughs at a king bearing, instead of the sceptre of sovereignty, the wood of the punishment; piety looks on, and sees the King bearing that cross for Himself, to be fixed thereon, which He would thereafter fix even on the brows of kings. An object of contempt in the eyes of the impious, yet the same thing in which later on the hearts of the Saints will glory. Thus to St. Paul, who one day will say, *God forbid that I should glory but in the cross of our Lord Jesus Christ* (Gal. 6: 14), the Lord commanded that very cross by bearing it on His shoulders; and for that candle, which was to be lighted and not to be put under a bushel, the Lord bore the candlestick.

II. The human race was lost by sin; for all men, coming from

Adam, had sinned in him. One alone was born without sin, and He delivered from the yoke of sin. He was made man in order to heal our wounds inflicted by sin. The Jews were as sick as all other men in the world, yet their pride made them believe that they were not in need of the physician; and their disease was so much the more incurable, as their pride, by which it was caused, led them to despise Him who had come to cure it. But they were not contented with despising Him; they even put Him to death. Yet at the very time they took His life He fulfilled for them the duties of a Physician. They struck Him, and He cured them. He felt the effects of their madness, but He abandoned not the sick. The Jews surrounded Jesus Christ; they bound Him with ropes, buffeted Him, struck Him with a reed, overwhelmed Him with insults and blasphemies; lastly, they asked Him juridical questions, condemned Him, and nailed Him to the cross; yet He still remained their Physician. You have seen the character of the Jews in their madness, now consider the character of their Physician. *Father*, He cried out, *forgive them, for they know not what they do* (Luke 23: 34). Blinded by their rage and envy, they shed the blood of their Physician, and the Physician shed His own blood to cure them of their blindness and fury; and in that intention that His blood might flow for them, He cried out: *Father, forgive them, for they know not what they do.*

III. And Jesus, knowing that all things were now accomplished, that the Scripture might be fulfilled, said: *I thirst*. The Divinity of Jesus Christ was hidden under the veil of His humanity. This humanity suffered all the insults and mockery of the Jews, whilst His Divinity allowed free scope to their fury. He saw, then, that all things were finished; that no more required to be done before He should receive the vinegar and give up the ghost; and that this also might be accomplished what was foretold in the Scripture: *And in My thirst they gave Me vinegar to drink* (Ps. 68: 22). He said, *I thirst*, as if it were, One thing you have left undone; give what you are. For the Jews were themselves the vinegar, degenerated as they were from the wine of the Patriarchs and Prophets, and filled like a full vessel with the wickedness of this world. This godless people did all these things, and a compassionate Christ suffered them. This blinded people knew not what they were doing; but Jesus knew what was done, and why it was done; and He wrought what was good through those who were doing what was evil. *When Jesus, therefore, had taken the vinegar, He said: It is consummated.* What was finished, save all that the prophecies had foretold so long before? Then, because nothing remained that yet was to be done before He died, as He had the power to lay down His life, and the power to take it up again; now that all was accomplished, for the accomplishment of which He was waiting, *He bowed His head and gave up the ghost.* Who so sleeps when he will, as Jesus died when He pleased? Who so lays aside his garment when he will, as He put off His flesh when He would? What traveller departs from a place when he pleases, as He departed this life when He pleased? Therefore, what must we hope or fear to find His power as a Judge, if it was so great when He died?

28. EASTER SUNDAY

GOSPEL: Mark 16: 1-7. *At that time:* Mary Magdalen and Mary, the mother of James, and Salome brought sweet spices, that coming, they might anoint Jesus. And very early in the morning, the first day of the week, they come to the sepulchre, the sun being now risen. And they said one to another: Who shall roll us back the stone from the door of the sepulchre? And looking, they saw the stone rolled back. For it was very great. And entering into the sepulchre, they saw a young man sitting on the right side, clothed with a white robe; and they were astonished. Who saith to them: Be not affrighted; you seek Jesus of Nazareth, Who was crucified; He is risen, He is not here; behold the place where they laid Him. But go, tell His disciples and Peter that He goeth before you into Galilee; there you shall see Him, as He told you.

HOMILY BY POPE ST. GREGORY, PREACHED IN THE CHURCH OF THE BLESSED VIRGIN MARY ON EASTER SUNDAY
Twenty-First Homily on the Gospels

I. YOU HAVE HEARD, BELOVED BRETHREN, THE deed of the holy women who followed our Lord, how they brought sweet spices to His sepulchre, and, having loved Him while He was still alive, they still followed Him with careful tenderness now that He was dead. But, what these holy women did, points to something which is to be done in the holy Church. And it behoves us well to give ear to what they did, that we may afterwards consider with ourselves what we must do after their example. We also, believing in Him Who is dead, we come to His sepulchre bearing sweet spices, if we seek Him with the savour of pious living and the fragrant odour of good works. These women, when they brought spices, saw a vision of angels, and those souls who are moved by the pious desire to seek the Lord with the good odour of holy lives, will see the countrymen of our Fatherland that is above.

II. If we inquire about the mystery contained in the fact of the Angel who, appearing to the holy women, sat on the *right side*, we shall find that by the left side is meant the life which now is, and life everlasting by the right side. For in the Book of the Canticles it is said of the Bridegroom: *His left hand is under my head, and His right hand shall embrace me* (Cant. 2: 6). Since, therefore, our Redeemer had passed from the corruption of this life, the Angel, who told that His eternal life was come, sat becomingly on the right side. They saw him clothed with a white robe, for he announced the joy of this our great solemnity, and the shining whiteness of his raiment told of the brightness of this our holy festival. Of ours, did I say? or of his? But, if we speak the truth, we must acknowledge that it is both his and ours. The Resurrection of our Lord is a festival of gladness for us, since we now know that we shall not die for ever; and for the angels also it is a festival of joy, for they now know that we are called to complete their number in heaven.

III. Therefore, on this glad festival, which is both his and ours, the Angel appeared in a white robe. For as the Lord, rising again from the dead, leads us to the eternal dwellings above, He repairs the breaches or gaps of the heavenly Fatherland. But what is the meaning of these words spoken by the Angel to the women who had come to the sepulchre: *Be not affrighted?* Is it not as though he had said openly: Let them fear who love not the coming of the heavenly citizens; let them be affrighted who are so burdened by fleshly lusts, that they despair ever to be joined to their company. But as to you, why do ye fear, since seeing us you only see your fellow-citizens? Thus also St. Matthew, describing the appearance of the Angel, says: *His countenance was as lightning, and his raiment as snow* (Matt. 28: 3). The lightning speaks of fear and terror, the snow of the brilliant whiteness of rejoicing. Since God the Almighty shows Himself terrible to sinners, but at the same time well pleased with good and pious souls, it was but right that the Angel, who had been sent by Him to give testimony to His

Resurrection, should inspire some with fear and terror by the lightning, and others with confidence and hope by His garment. God Himself wished to convey to us this meaning, for He guided the Israelites through the desert by a pillar of fire in the night and a cloud during the day (Exod. 13). For the life of the just may be compared to daylight, and that of the sinner to a dark night. Thus the pillar of fire is to inspire sinners with fear, whilst the just, wandering in the light of the day, see a cloud which fills them with hope and security. St. Paul, writing to converted sinners, says: *You were heretofore darkness, but now light in the Lord* (Eph. 5: 8). Lastly, all this will be accomplished by the Lord on the day of His wrath, when His loving countenance will shine on the just, while the terror of His justice will crush the wicked.

IV. *You seek Jesus of Nazareth, Who was crucified?* said the Angel, to prevent any mistake about Him, since there were several others bearing the same name of Jesus. Yet, this holy Name belongs in reality only to the Redeemer of the world, Who was crucified. As the Angel said: *He is risen, He is not here.* He is no longer here in His humanity, though His Divinity is present everywhere. *But go,* the Angel continued, *tell His disciples and Peter that He goeth before you into Galilee.* You will perhaps ask why the Angel, after speaking of the disciples, specially mentioned Peter. But when we consider that Peter, after the great misfortune of denying his Master, would probably not have dared to accompany the other disciples to seek and meet Jesus, you will easily understand why he was specially invited and his name mentioned that is, that he should have no motive to doubt that his faithlessness was forgiven him. Acknowledge the infinite goodness of God! He had permitted that disciple, chosen by Him to be the visible head of His Church, to be so frightened by the words of a maid servant, as to deny his Redeemer, so that the remembrance of his own weakness and sin might teach him patience and forbearance with other people's misery, and with the failings of the great flock that was to be entrusted to him.

V. Not without a special reason did our Lord send word to His disciples that He expected them in Galilee, where they would find Him. The word 'Galilee' means 'change;' and this was entirely conformable with the state of our Saviour, for He had passed from suffering to the glory of the resurrection, from death to life, from a state of corruption to incorruptibility. He showed Himself in Galilee, glorious and risen from the dead, to manifest Himself to them by the place He had chosen, and to give us to understand that one day we shall have the joy and happiness of seeing Him in the glory of His resurrection, if now we pass from the state of sin to the heights of Christian virtues. Notice also that our Redeemer had Himself announced to the disciples near the place of His sepulchre, yet appeared to them only after changing His dwelling-place, because, according to His example, the mortification of the flesh must precede in this life if we wish for the beatific contemplation in the next. These few words, beloved brethren, I wished to address to you on the Gospel of this great festival; yet, just on account of this great day, I will add a few more remarks.

VI. It is certain that there are two kinds of life: the one we now lead in this world, the other of which we have no knowledge. The life we now know is mortal, the other is immortal; by the one we are subject to corruption, by the other we obtain incorruptibility. Death will be the end of the first, and our resurrection will be the beginning of the second. Jesus Christ, Who came as the Mediator between God and man, lived the one and the other life; for He suffered the death of the first, and He rose from the dead to give us some knowledge of the second. Had He only promised that one day we shall rise again, without giving us in His own flesh an example of that resurrection, no one perhaps would have referred to His testimony. But by taking our human nature, and becoming like ourselves, He willingly gave up His body to death; then, by His infinite power, He rose again, and gave us in His own Person a pledge of the resurrection He had promised. Should anyone say that it was easy for God to rise from the dead, since He could not be overcome by death, he will consider that, to enlighten our ignorance and strengthen our faith in a future resurrection, our Lord wished us to be convinced not by the example of His resurrection only. For notice, though He was the only one who

28. EASTER SUNDAY

died at that moment, yet Holy Scripture tells us (Matt, 27), that many bodies of the saints, that had slept, arose *At that time*, thus destroying any doubts still remaining in the minds of unbelievers. Therefore, should anybody, seeing that a Man-God rose from the dead, still doubt about his own resurrection, he being only a mere man, he must remember that Providence willed people of the same nature as ours to rise with Jesus Christ. Being members of the Redeemer, we have no doubt but that what is seen in the Head will be fulfilled in the members; that what happened to those who, as the first members of the Saviour, rose from the dead, will also happen to us though the last.

VII. The Jews blasphemed the crucified Redeemer, and said: *If He be the King of Israel, let Him now come down from the cross, and we will believe in Him* (Matt, 27: 42). Had Jesus yielded to these insults and mockery, He would not have given us the beautiful example of His astonishing patience. However, He waited; He accepted and bore insults and blasphemies; He persevered in that wonderful patience, and put off the time for giving a sign of His almighty power, that would then have caused a momentary amazement only, in order to show a greater miracle, namely, the glory of His resurrection. It was a more glorious triumph to leave the sepulchre, full of renewed life, than to come down from the cross. By His resurrection He triumphed over death, whilst by descending from the cross He would only have saved His life. Meanwhile, the Jews were jubilant, for, in spite of their insults, our Lord was still hanging on the cross; and they presumed that, after His death, His name would be forgotten for ever. Yet, out of the bosom of the earth, His Name was spread abroad all over the world, and with such glory that this perfidious nation, so eager to punish Him with an ignominious death, was quite confounded, when seeing that the torments inflicted on Him had become the cause of His triumph. It was thought of Samson by the Philistines that, being enclosed within the walls of the city of Gaza, and surrounded by guards, he would soon be overcome and bound with the chains they had prepared; but during the night He took the doors of the gate, and, laying them on His shoulders, carried them up to the top of the hill (Judg. 16: 2, 3). Thus the all-powerful Saviour, the strong God typified by Samson, burst the bonds of the sepulchre, surrounded by the Jews with guards, whilst they fancied that the Author of life, Whom they had killed and enclosed in the grave, would be for ever buried therein. And this all-powerful God, more terrible after His death than Samson in his life, came out, after descending into Limbo, and, triumphing over His enemies, ascended into heaven. Let us abide by this glorious resurrection, which, announced by the Prophets, was so happily accomplished. Let us desire to die, that we may be partakers of that resurrection. And since we heard that the angels who announced the resurrection of our Lord, are inhabitants of the eternal dwelling for which we are longing, let us endeavour to reach them, and thus celebrate this festival with them. Though we are not just now able to enjoy a glorious resurrection with these heavenly spirits, we will, nevertheless, join them with the ardour of our desires. Let us forsake sin and practise virtue, and by this change be able to see the face of our Redeemer. Ask God the Father, Who for the sake of our salvation delivered His only-begotten Son to a cruel death, to strengthen our desires, so that we may for ever praise Him, the Father, and the Son, and the Holy Ghost. Amen.

29. EASTER MONDAY

GOSPEL: Luke 24: 13-35. *At that time*: Two of the disciples went the same day to a town, which was sixty furlongs from Jerusalem, named Emmaus. And they talked together of all these things which had happened. And it came to pass, that while they talked and reasoned with themselves, Jesus Himself also drawing near, went with them. But their eyes were held, that they should not know Him. And He said to them: What are these discourses that you hold one with another as you walk and are sad? And the one of them, whose name was Cleophas, answering, said to Him: Art Thou only a stranger in Jerusalem, and hast not known the things that have been done there in these days? To whom He said: What things? And they said: Concerning Jesus of Nazareth, Who was a prophet, mighty in work and word before God and all the people. And how our chief priests and princes delivered Him to be condemned to death, and crucified Him. But we hoped that it was He that should have redeemed Israel; and now besides all this, today is the third day since these things were done. Yea, and certain women also of our company affrighted us, who before it was light, were at the sepulchre, and, not finding His body, came saying that they had also seen a vision of angels, who say that He is alive. And some of our people went to the sepulchre, and found it so as the women had said, but Him they found not. Then He said to them: Oh, foolish and slow of heart to believe in all things which the Prophets have spoken! Ought not Christ to have suffered these things, and so to enter into His glory? And beginning at Moses and all the Prophets, He explained to them in all the Scriptures, the things that were concerning Him. And they drew nigh to the town, whither they were going, and He made as though He would go farther. But they constrained Him, saying: Stay with us, because it is towards evening, and the day is now far spent. And He went in with them. And it came to pass, whilst He was at table with them, He took bread, and blessed, and brake, and gave to them. And their eyes were opened, and they knew Him: and He vanished out of their sight. And they said one to the other: Was not our heart burning within us, whilst

He spoke in the way, and opened to us the Scriptures? And, rising up the same hour, they went back to Jerusalem; and they found the eleven gathered together, and those that were with them. And they told what things were done in the way, and how they knew Him in the breaking of bread.

HOMILY BY POPE ST. GREGORY, PREACHED IN THE CHURCH OF ST. PETER ON EASTER MONDAY
Twenty-Third Homily on the Gospels

I. YOU HAVE HEARD, BELOVED BRETHREN, HOW two of the Lord's disciples went together to Emmaus, and were talking about Him. They did not believe in His resurrection, yet talked about it, when the Lord Himself appeared to them, but held their eyes so that they should not recognise Him. And this holding of their corporal eyes was a figure of the spiritual veil by which the eyes of their hearts were still covered. In their hearts they loved, yet they doubted; and the Lord drew nigh to them outwardly, though He did not show Himself to their soul. He revealed His immediate presence to them that talked of Him, and He hid from them who doubted the knowledge of His Person. By words He associated with them, and rebuked their heart-hardness: *He expounded to them in all the Scriptures, the things that were concerning Him*; nevertheless, seeing that He was still a stranger to faith in their hearts, *He made as though He would go farther*. These words, *He made as though*, would seem to mean, *He feigned*; but He, who is Truth itself, has nothing to do with feigning. He showed Himself to them in bodily manners, as He was to them spiritually; but they were put to the proof whether they could love Him, at least, as a wanderer, though they loved Him not yet as their God.

II. However, since it was impossible that they, with whom the Truth was walking, should be without love, they invited Him as a wanderer to accept their hospitality. Why do we say they invited Him, since it is written: *But they constrained Him?* Their example teaches us not only to bid, but even to compel wanderers, to accept our hospitality. These disciples, therefore, laid a table, and set before Him bread and meat; and they knew in the breaking of the bread *that* God, Whom they had not known in the expounding of the Holy Scripture. They were not enlightened in hearing the Commandments of God, but they were enlightened in doing them, as it is written: *Not the hearers of the law are just before God, but the doers of the law are justified* (Rom. 2: 13). Whosoever will understand that which he hears, let him make haste to practise in his works what he was able to hear. Behold, the Lord was not known while He spoke, but deigned to be known when breaking the bread.

III. I say this to you, beloved brethren, that you might willingly practise hospitality and all other works of charity. Remember St. Paul's words: *Let the charity of the brotherhood abide in you; and hospitality do not forget; for by this some, being not aware of it, have entertained angels* (Heb. 13: 1,2). And St. Peter says: *Using hospitality one towards another without murmuring* (1 Pet. 4: 9). Lastly, Truth Himself says to you: *I was a stranger, and you took Me in* (Matt. 25: 35). An authentic history, related in the writings of our forefathers, tells us of a father of a family who, with all the members of his household, zealously practised the virtue of hospitality. Every day he received poor strangers at his table, and waited on them. One day, among the poor strangers there was one who suddenly disappeared out of the room, at the moment when the humble and charitable man presented him, as was his custom, with water to wash his hands therewith. His surprise was great; but during the night he had a vision. Our Lord appeared, and said to him: 'On other days you received Me in My members, but yesterday you received Me in Person.' At the last judgment our Lord will say: *Amen, I say to you, as long as you did it to one of these My least brethren, you did it to Me* (Matt. 25: 40). All this teaches us that, before the time of the last judgment, Jesus Christ is received by us in the person of poor strangers, and that those, who receive them, are considered by Jesus as receiving Him. Yet we neglect the blessings and merits acquired by true hospitality. Consider the excellence of this virtue, and receive Jesus at your table, that one day He may receive you at His eternal banquet. Take into your house, in the persons of strangers, the Lord Jesus, that on the day of the judgment He treat you not as strangers whom He knows not, but take you as friends into His kingdom, there to enjoy His glory, Who liveth and reigneth for ever and ever. Amen.

30. FIRST SUNDAY AFTER EASTER, OR LOW SUNDAY

GOSPEL: John 20: 19-31. *At that time*: When it was late that same day, being the first day of the week, and the doors were shut, where the disciples were gathered together for fear of the Jews, Jesus came and stood in the midst, and said to them: Peace be to you. And when He had said this, He showed them His hands and His side. The disciples therefore were glad when they saw the Lord. He said, therefore, to them again: Peace be to you. As the Father hath sent Me, I also send you. When He had said this, He breathed on them, and He said to them: Receive ye the Holy Ghost; whose sins you shall forgive, they are forgiven them; and whose sins you shall retain, they are retained. Now Thomas, one of the twelve, who is called Didymus, was not with them when Jesus came. The other disciples, therefore, said to him: We have seen the Lord. But he said to them: Except I shall see in His hands the print of the nails, and put my finger into the place of the nails, and put my hands into His side, I will not believe. And after eight days, again the disciples were within, and Thomas with them. Jesus cometh, the doors being shut, and stood in the midst, and said: Peace be to you. Then He said to Thomas: Put in thy finger hither, and see My hands, and bring hither thy hand, and put it into My side; and be not faithless, but believing. Thomas answered and said to Him: My Lord and my God. Jesus said to him: Because thou hast seen Me, Thomas, thou hast believed: blessed are they that have not seen, and have believed. Many other signs also did Jesus in the sight of His disciples, which are not written in this book. But these are written that you may believe that Jesus is the Christ, the Son of God; and that, believing, you may have life in His Name.

HOMILY BY POPE ST. GREGORY, PREACHED IN THE CHURCH OF ST. JOHN LATERAN ON THE FIRST SUNDAY AFTER EASTER.
Twenty-Sixth Homily on the Gospels

I. WHEN WE HEAR THIS GOSPEL, OUR HUMAN mind can hardly understand how it was that the Body of the risen Lord, being a real Body, could pass through closed doors into the room where the disciples were assembled. But this will not surprise us when we consider that the works of God would no longer be wonderful, were they understood by man's reason, and that our faith would be destitute of all merit, were the human intellect able to demonstrate how these works of God are done. However, these very works of our Redeemer, which we are unable to understand, must be taken in connection with some others of His works, so that we may be led to believe in wonderful things by means of others still more wonderful. For that Body of our Lord, which came into the assembly of the disciples, the doors being shut, was the same which at His birth was manifested to the eyes of men, by passing out of the Virgin's womb without breaking the seal of her virginity. What wonder, then, is it that Jesus Christ, after His Resurrection, enjoyed a glorious and immortal life, showed Himself to His disciples, the doors being shut, since as a weak and mortal child He came out of a Virgin's womb in an incomprehensible manner? But since the Body of our Lord, after His resurrection, though real and visible, could raise doubts in the minds of the beholders, *He showed them His hands and His side,* and allowed them to touch that same flesh which had just passed through closed doors. In this event two strange things which, according to our understanding, are contrary the one to the other, were manifested, namely, that His Body was incorruptible and yet palpable. For, whatsoever can be touched must needs be corruptible; and whatsoever is not subject to corruption cannot be touched. But, in a way altogether wonderful and incomprehensible, our Redeemer appeared after His resurrection in a Body at the same time palpable and incorruptible. He appeared in an incorruptible Body, inviting us to seek the same glorification; and in a palpable Body to strengthen our faith. He showed Himself both incorruptible and palpable, to make manifest this fact, that His risen Body was the same in nature, though transfigured in glory.

II. *He said therefore to them again: Peace be to you. As the Father hath sent Me, I also send you.* The Father, Who is God, sent Me Who am God; and I Who am also man, send you who are men. The Father sent the Son, Whom He appointed to be made man for the redemption of man. He willed to send the Son into the world to suffer, though He loved that Son Who was sent to suffer. And our Lord sent His chosen Apostles into the world, not to be happy in the world, but to suffer, as He Himself had been sent. For, as the Father loves the Son, and yet sent Him to suffer, so does the Lord love His Apostles, though sending them into the world to suffer therein. Therefore it is well said: *As the Father hath sent Me, I also send you*; meaning, while I send you into storms and persecutions, I love you all the same with a love like that wherewith My Father loves Me, Who yet sent me into the world to suffer. This sending of the Son may also be understood of His Eternal and Divine generation, for the Holy Ghost, equal to the Father and to the Son, and Who has not assumed our human nature, was to be sent according to the promise of our Redeemer: *When the Paraclete cometh, Whom I will send you from the Father* (John 15: 26). For should the word *send* only mean to become man, then the Holy Ghost could not be said to have been *sent*, since He did not become man. We call Him, therefore, *sent*, in that sense that He proceeds from the Father and the Son, and, as His sending refers to His Divine procession, so may the sending of the Son be referred to His Divine generation.

III. When Jesus, standing in the midst of His disciples, had said: *Peace be to you*, He breathed on them and said: *Receive ye the Holy Ghost.* Let me remark that Holy Scripture speaks of two occasions only on which the Holy Ghost was given by our Redeemer:

the first, when He was still on earth, and the second when He was already reigning in heaven. On the first occasion, as it is seen in this Gospel, He breathed on His disciples, and on the second the Holy Ghost came down from heaven upon them in the form of fiery tongues. Now, should we wish to know the reason why the Holy Ghost was imparted at two different times, and under different circumstances, we must consider that charity contains two commandments, namely, the love of God and the love of our neighbour. It seems, therefore, that the Holy Ghost was given on earth to move us to fulfil the duty of loving our neighbour; whereas He was sent from heaven to inflame our hearts with true love for God. But, since the two commandments spring forth from charity, which is one and the same, so was the one and the same Holy Ghost given by our Redeemer on two occasions to wit, the first time when He was still on earth, and the second after His Ascension into heaven, giving us to understand that the love for our neighbour serves like steps leading us up to the love for God, according to the words of His beloved disciple: *If anyone say, I love God, and hateth his brother, he is a liar. For he that loveth not his brother, whom he seeth, how can he love God, Whom he seeth not* (1 John 4: 20). Yet let us not conclude that the Apostles had not received the Holy Ghost before, since they possessed Him by faith. But after the Resurrection the Holy Ghost was given to them in a special and visible manner; and we understand in this sense the words, *As yet the Holy Ghost was not given, because Jesus was not yet glorified* (John 7: 39). Hence Moses said: *He set him that he might suck honey out of the rock, and oil out of the hardest stone* (Deut. 32: 13). For, perusing the Books of the Old Testament, we find that these words cannot be applied to the Israelites, since we do not see anywhere that they ever sucked honey and oil out of stones. We conclude, therefore, according to the testimony of St. Paul, that this rock was Christ. Indeed, seeing the acts and wonders of Jesus, the disciples sucked honey out of this Stone, and oil out of this Rock; for, after His Resurrection, they received the anointing of the Holy Ghost. We may also compare our Saviour with a soft stone, that, through the sweetness of His miracles, in His earthly life, He offered honey to the disciples. But since, after His Resurrection He cannot suffer any more, and has become like a hard rock, He sent them the anointing of the Holy Ghost.

IV. This is the supernatural oil spoken of by the prophets: *The yoke shall putrefy at the presence of the oil* (Isa. 10: 27). We were under the yoke of the cruel slavery of Satan; but having received the anointing of the Holy Ghost, and the grace to be set at liberty, the tyrannical yoke, under which we were groaning, has disappeared. This truth is confirmed by St. Paul, saying *Where the Spirit of the Lord is, there is liberty* (2 Cor. 3: 17). However, take notice that these very disciples, who had already received the Holy Ghost, so as to lead a holy life with His assistance, and by their preaching to be useful to others, again received the Holy Ghost after the Resurrection, and in a most striking manner, for the benefit of the nations they were to instruct in the course of time. Hence our Lord, giving them the Holy Ghost, says: *Whose sins you shall forgive, they are forgiven them; and whose sins you shall retain, they are retained*. Let us wonder at the high degree of honour to which the disciples were raised at a time when destined to suffer the deepest humiliations. They were promised that not only their own sins were forgiven, but that they had power to absolve others from their sins that is, power to sit on God's judgment-seat, and, like God Himself, to forgive or retain sins committed against His Divine justice. It was meet that those who, for the love of God, were ready to accept every humiliation and contempt, should be honoured in this way, and that their fear of being condemned by the severe Judge Whom they adored should be the motive prompting God to set them up as judges of souls, which were to be condemned or to be absolved.

V. Consider again, beloved brethren, this important truth, and carefully endeavour to be preserved from the eternal perdition. These Easter-days are celebrated with great pomp and magnificence; yet our duty is to make ourselves worthy of arriving at the eternal Festivals. You endeavour to be present at these feast-days, which pass and disappear; try, then, your utmost to be one day present, all together, at the never-ending celebration in heaven. What would it profit you to assist at our festivals now, were you never to be admitted to the festivities of the angels in heaven? Our present feast-days are only the shadow of those we are expecting, and, though year after year we are celebrating them, we are longing for those never-ending days in the kingdom of God. Renew in your hearts the desire of the eternal festivities by the celebration of the annual earthly festivals. Let the happiness granted to us in the present time penetrate us in such a way that we continue sighing for the eternal happiness prepared for us in heaven, and ardently desired by us on earth. Prepare yourselves for that eternal rest by amending your lives and practising virtue and holiness. Never forget that He Who in His Resurrection was meekness itself, will be terrible when coming to judge the world. On this awful day He will appear surrounded by Angels, Archangels, Thrones, Principalities and Powers. On that day heaven and earth and all the elements, being the ministers of His wrath, will be in a general conflagration. May this terrible Judge be ever present to the eyes of your mind, that, penetrated by a salutary fear of His severe judgment, that is to be held, you may confidently expect His coming. Let us fear now, that we may be without fear then, and this fear will help us to avoid sin and work out our salvation. For I tell you that the more we are now afraid to rouse the anger of our Judge against us, the greater will be our confidence when we appear before Him at the end of the world.

31. SECOND SUNDAY AFTER EASTER

GOSPEL: John 10: 11-16. *At that time*: Jesus said to the Pharisees: I am the Good Shepherd. The Good Shepherd giveth his life for the sheep. But the hireling, and he that is not the shepherd, whose own the sheep are not, seeth the wolf coming, and leaveth the sheep, and flieth; and the wolf catcheth and scattereth the sheep, and the hireling flieth, because he is a hireling, and he hath no care for the sheep. I am the Good Shepherd: and I know Mine and Mine know Me. As the Father knoweth Me, and I know the Father; and I lay down My life for My sheep. And other sheep I have, that are not of this fold: them also I must bring, and they shall hear My voice, and there shall be one fold, and one Shepherd.

HOMILY BY POPE ST. GREGORY, PREACHED IN THE CHURCH OF ST. PETER ON THE SECOND SUNDAY AFTER EASTER
Fourteenth Homily on the Gospel

I. THIS GOSPEL WHICH YOU HAVE HEARD, BELOVED brethren, is to you, both an instruction and a warning against danger. For our Lord, Who is infinitely good, not by an accidental gift of nature, but by the very essence of His being, says to us: *I am the Good Shepherd*. Then He tells us what is the character of His goodness, even of that goodness which we must endeavour to imitate. *The Good Shepherd giveth His life for His sheep.* This truth was proved by our Redeemer's own example; for both the instruction and the command were literally fulfilled in His life. The Good Shepherd gave His life for the sheep, and made His own Body and Blood to be the sacramental Food of the sheep He had redeemed. In this Divine Model we perceive the way we are to go, and the manner of imitating Him. For we see in Him the duty freely and tenderly to spend our temporal goods for His sheep, and, if necessary, to give our life for them. Again, the soul being more precious than all outward things that we possess, how shall we be ready to give our life for our brethren, seeing that we refuse to them even our worldly substance? However, there are many, loving the things of this world better than the sheep entrusted to them, who deserve no longer to be called shepherds. Of them it is said by our Redeemer: *The hireling, and he that is not the shepherd, whose own the sheep are not, seeth the wolf coming, and leaveth the sheep, and flieth.*

11. He is called a hireling, and is deprived of all the rights of a good shepherd, because he does not in reality love the sheep entrusted to him that is, their souls but wishes thereby to gain earthly wealth. He that takes a shepherd's place, and seeks not the salvation of souls, is only a hireling. He is seeking his happiness in the honours rendered to his dignity, and endeavours to procure to himself the commodities of life. And does not the reward of the hireling consist in the temporal profit he acquires by the care he takes of his flock, whilst he will be deprived of the eternal inheritance prepared by God for His faithful servants? But it is not very easy to recognise the true shepherd, and to distinguish him from the hireling, unless he be discovered by special circumstances or by dangers threatening the flock. For very often, when men are kept in safety by peace and tranquillity, the hireling seems, like a true and faithful shepherd, to watch over his sheep. But when a wolf comes near the flock, then will be noticed by what spirit the selfish shepherd is animated. Under the image of the ravenous wolf attacking the flock we usually understand a violent and unjust man, who attacks souls, and tries to bring them under his power. In such circumstances he, who has only the appearance of a zealous shepherd, will leave his sheep and fly away, because he is afraid of dangers, and has not the courage to resist the unjust attempts of the enemy. But the hypocritical shepherd does not

31. SECOND SUNDAY AFTER EASTER 177

always leave his place or go away from his flock; still, he may be said to fly, because he gives not his flock the necessary assistance and the spiritual help he owes to them. He flies, since he keeps silent at the time when he ought to raise his voice against injustice; he flies when, hiding under the cloak of dissimulation, he tries to escape the strokes of the enemy. The Prophet justly complains against such faithless shepherds, saying: *You have not gone up to face the enemy, nor have you set up a wall for the house of Israel, to stand in battle in the day of the Lord* (Ezech. 13: 5). To face the enemy means to resist with true freedom and strength of mind every kind of power misusing its authority and doing injustice. We stand in battle, and set up a strong wall for the protection of the house of Israel, when with the weapons of justice we defend the innocence of the faithful attacked without cause. But under such critical circumstances the hireling, perceiving the wolf coming near the flock, flies instead of resisting.

III. However, there is yet another wolf against whose fury, far more terrible than the former, we are to protect ourselves; for his cruelty ravishes not bodies, but souls. This is the infernal spirit, who kills souls and carries them off as his prey. Of the devil it is said: *The wolf catcheth and scattereth the sheep, and the hireling flieth.* This happens when the devil, by his temptations, tears souls to pieces, and when he, who ought to perform the duties of a good shepherd, thinks of earthly advantages only, and lets the souls go to their ruin, without even attempting to help them. The infernal wolf catches and scatters the sheep, attracting some to lust and impure sins, and others to avarice; tempting some to pride or violent anger; awakening in some sinful envy, and instructing others in the art of deceiving. Through these different temptations death is brought by the devil to Christian souls; yet the zeal of the hireling is not awakened neither is he prompted by godliness to save his flock from ruin and destruction. For, since he seeks only the comforts and commodities of life, he is not moved by the spiritual sickness nor the eternal death of his flock. Hence our Lord adds these words: *The hireling flieth, because he is a hireling*, as if to say: It is not possible to one, who is a shepherd of My sheep, to remain firm amidst dangers surrounding them, if he does not give to the flock an unselfish love, but is seeking for the perishable goods of the world. For, desiring honours and trying to find happiness in the enjoyment of earthly things, he will be careful to avoid those dangers by which the things he loves so well would be lost. After unfolding before us the defects and faults of the hireling, our Lord shows us in His own Person the qualities of the one we are to imitate, and says: *I am the Good Shepherd, and I know Mine* — that is, I love them — and Mine know Me, namely, they are subject to Me, because they love Me. He that has no love for the truth announced by our Saviour, cannot boast of knowing Him.

IV. You have seen, beloved brethren, the dangers to which the office of a pastor or shepherd is exposed; now recognise also, according to our Lord's words, those dangers to which you are exposed. Consider first whether you are of the sheep belonging to the Divine Shepherd, and hear His voice. Ask yourselves whether you know what truth is. For it is not enough to recognise the truth by faith — it must be sincerely loved; and it is not enough to believe the truth — it must be put into practice. St. John, who wrote this Gospel, says: *He who saith that he knoweth God, and keepeth not His commandments, is a liar, and the truth is not in him* (1 John 2: 4). And our Lord added these words: *As the Father knoweth Me, and I know the Father; and I lay down My life for My sheep* — that is, I wish them to recognise the love I have for My Father by the love that moves Me to give My life for their salvation. And since our Saviour came to redeem not only the Jews but also the Gentiles, he continued: *And other sheep I have that are not of this fold; them also I must bring, and they shall hear My voice, and there shall be one fold and one Shepherd.* Our Lord, speaking of these other sheep, had in view our own salvation, for *At that time we were among the number of the Gentiles.* And this is fulfilled every day, as you can witness the fact; for you are aware of the mystery of reconciliation among the idolaters, by which the two nations, formerly separated, are united in the one and the same fold, and Jews and Gentiles form one spiritual nation. St. Paul speaks of this: *For Jesus Christ is our peace, Who hath made both one*

(Eph. 2: 14). Thus our Lord gives life everlasting to simple and artless souls, chosen among the one and the other nation, and brings them as His sheep into His own fold.

V. Of these sheep our Lord was speaking, when He said: *My sheep hear My voice, and I know them, and they follow Me. And I give them life everlasting. By Me if any man enter in, he shall be saved; and he shall go in and out, and shall find pasture* (John 10: 27-29). That is, he will go in by faith, and go out of this life to see Me face to face. Then he will see with his own eyes that which he believed when on earth, and finally he will find eternal nourishment in this happy dwelling. These are the pastures promised by our Lord and found by His sheep; for since with a simple and willing heart they followed Him, they will be nourished with heavenly love, that fruitful field and that inexhaustible source of blessings. Indeed, what is the food of these beloved sheep but the interior joy felt at the ever-new spectacle prepared for them in heaven? God Himself, ever present to the elect, will be their food; and since there is no deficiency in Him, their souls will be continually satiated with this Bread of Heaven. In these delicious pastures of eternity, which alone can satisfy our desires, was found real happiness by those who have already been victorious over the pleasures of this world. The heavenly court resounds with the eternal songs of its blessed inhabitants. Among the citizens of this holy city are seen those who safely arrived there after a sad and long pilgrimage in this foreign country, in which we are still living. There are seen the Prophets who announced future events; the Apostles on their thrones judging the nations; the glorious army of the Martyrs, the more praiseworthy the greater their sufferings had been; Confessors rewarded for their constancy; faithful and fearless men never overcome by the wickedness of the world; holy women who, in spite of the weakness of their sex, conquered the world; children, whose virtues were beyond the number of their years; and old men, whose infirmities never prevented them from advancing on the road to perfection.

VI. Ah, let us eagerly seek for that spiritual food! The happiness, which so many heavenly citizens wish to share with us, will be obtained, and the festivities to which we are invited will be our portion. Were a great market or fair to be held in a city, or the feast of the consecration of a church to be celebrated, we should all endeavour to be present. You would feel very sorry, were you not able to enjoy the festivities by which those present are filled with delight and happiness. And we are indifferent about the eternal blessings, and make no efforts to possess them; we are not even desirous of assisting at these eternal festivities, and, though deprived of them, we still rejoice. Let us encourage ourselves, beloved brethren; let our faith be awakened by these truths, so that our desires may be inflamed with love for the eternal goods; for to love them is the only way to reach them. Let us not be prevented by any adversity; for this place of happiness must be the aim of our efforts, notwithstanding all troubles and obstacles encountered in the way. We should be like a foolish traveller, were we to tarry on the road looking at the variety of flowers and the beauty of the fields, without caring to reach the end of our journey. All our desires ought to take us to the lands above, our real Fatherland. Let us not desire the goods of this world, which soon forsake us; but, wishing to be faithful sheep of our heavenly Shepherd, instead of loving the worthless enjoyments of this life, let us be longing after the eternal pastures by which we shall be made happy for ever. Amen.

32. THIRD SUNDAY AFTER EASTER

GOSPEL: John 16: 16-22. *At that time*: Jesus said to His disciples: A little while, and now you shall not see Me; and again a little while, and you shall see Me; because I go to the Father. Then some of His disciples said one to another: What is this that He saith to us: A little while, and ye shall not see Me; and again a little while, and you shall see Me, and because I go to the Father? They said therefore: What is this that He saith: A little while? We know not what He speaketh. And Jesus knew that they had a mind to ask Him, and He said to them: Of this do you inquire among yourselves, because I said: A little while, and you shall not see Me; and again a little while, and you shall see Me? Amen, amen, I say to you, that you shall lament and weep, but the world shall rejoice: and you shall be made sorrowful, but your sorrow shall be turned into joy. A woman, when she is in labour, hath sorrow, because her hour is come: but when she hath brought forth the child, she remembereth no more the anguish, for joy that a man is born into the world. So also you now indeed have sorrow, but I will see you again, and your heart shall rejoice; and your joy no man shall take from you.

HOMILY BY ST. AUGUSTINE
Tract 101 on St. John

I. THESE WORDS OF OUR LORD, WHERE HE SAYS: *A little while, and now you shall not see Me; and again a little while, and you shall see Me; because I go to the Father*, seemed to the disciples so obscure, before the fulfilment of what He said, that, whilst asking themselves what they meant, they confessed that they could not understand them. The Gospel makes this remark, for it goes on: *Then some of His disciples said one to another: What is this that*

He saith to us: A little while, and ye shall not see Me; and again a little while, and you shall see Me, and because I go to the Father? They said therefore: What is this that He saith: A little while? We know not what He speaketh. For this was the very difficulty that staggered them; He said: *A little while, and now you shall not see Me; and again a little while, and you shall see Me.* Yet, when, without speaking of the short time, the meaning of which they could not understand, He had before that said to them: I go to the Father; and you shall see Me no longer, He seemed to have spoken openly, and they were not astonished, neither did they question among themselves about the words. Now, what to them *At that time,* before its fulfilment, was a mystery, and was shown to them only later on, is quite clear and intelligible to us. For after a little while He suffered, and they saw Him not; again after a little while He rose again, and they saw Him. And when before these words He said that He was going to His Father, and that they should see Him no longer, He wished them to understand that they would see Him no longer in His mortality.

II. *And Jesus knew,* as the Evangelist continues to say: *That they had a mind to ask Him, and He said to them: Of this do you inquire among yourselves, because I said: A little while, and you shall not see Me; and again a little while, and you shall see Me. Amen, amen, I say to yon, that you shall lament and weep, but the world shall rejoice: and you shall be made sorrowful, but your sorrow shall be turned into joy.* And the disciples experienced all this; for they were made sorrowful by the death of our Lord, and again were made glad by His Resurrection. But the world — that is, the enemies by whom Christ was killed — rejoiced at Christ's being put to death, whilst the disciples were made sorrowful. By the world, of which our Lord speaks, is undoubtedly meant the wickedness of this world, namely, of those men who are the friends of the world. Of this wickedness St. James says: *Whosoever will be a friend of this world, becometh an enemy of God* (Jas. 4: 4). This enmity of the world against God was the cause of their washing their hands in the Blood of the Son of God.

III. And to be the better understood by His disciples our Lord makes use of a similitude, and says: *A woman, when she is in labour, hath sorrow, because her hour has come; but when she hath brought forth the child, she remembereth no more the anguish, for joy that a man is born into the world.* It is not difficult to understand this similitude, and the point of comparison is seen at once in the exposition given by Himself of its meaning. The labour is compared to sorrow, the birth to joy. And this joy will be the greater when it is not a girl, but a boy that is born. This is a figure of the eternal felicity in heaven, a fruit of the tribulations of the just on earth. However, Jesus added: *Your heart shall rejoice; and your joy no man shall take from you.* He thus teaches His disciples that He Himself will be their joy, that He will never be taken from them, signifying what the Apostle says: *Christ rising again from the dead, dieth now no more; death shall no more have dominion over Him* (Rom. 6: 9).

IV. I also think that the words: *I will see you again, and your heart shall rejoice; and your joy no man shall take from you,* are not to be referred to the time when He was risen from the dead, and when He showed them His flesh to be looked at and touched, but rather to that time of which He had already spoken, when He said: *He that loveth Me, shall be loved of My Father; and I will love him, and will manifest Myself to him* (John 14: 21). In fact, He had already risen, He had already shown Himself to them in the flesh, and He was already sitting at the right hand of His Father, when this same Apostle John, who wrote this Gospel, said in his Epistle: *Dearly beloved, we are now the sons of God; and it hath not yet appeared what we shall be. We know that, when He shall appear, we shall be like to Him: because we shall see Him as He is* (1 John 3: 2). This vision, therefore, is not for this life, but for the life to come; it is not temporal, but eternal. For He that is the Truth and the Life says: *This is eternal life; that they may know Thee, the only true God, and Jesus Christ, Whom Thou hast sent* (John 17: 3). Of this blessed seeing, and this perfect knowing the Apostle says: *We see now through a glass in a dark manner; but then face to face. Now I know in part: but then I shall know even as I am known* (1 Cor. 13: 12). At present the Church is, so to speak, in labour by her desires, but then she will rejoice seeing the fruits of her efforts. Now she labours in sorrow and amidst prayers; then she will manifest her joy, and eternally praise God Who delivered her. Then she will arrive at the long expected end, by which alone she can be satisfied; that end of which St. Philip, inspired by the Holy Ghost, spoke when he said to our Saviour: *Show us the Father, and it is enough for us.* In this showing of the Father, which is enjoyed by the Saints in heaven, the Son promised to manifest Himself, saying: *Do you not believe that I am in the Father, and the Father in Me?* (John 14: 8-10). And in the possession of this blessing, by which alone our desires can be perfectly satisfied, consists our happiness, which, as our Lord said, no man can take from us.

V. This *little while* of which until now we have been speaking, must also be referred to this present time, flying away with such rapidity that the Apostle says: *It is the last hour* (1 John 2: 18). That the short duration of time may be understood, our Lord compared Himself to a wanderer on earth, for He said: *I go to the Father.* These words have reference to the *little while* spoken of to His disciples, during which they would not see Him, and not to that other time when, as they were assured, they would see him again. For, from the time He went to His Father, as He said at the beginning, He ceased to show Himself to His disciples. Finally, by these words a *little while* we are given to understand the short space of the times in which we live; for our Lord did not say to His Apostles that He would die, and that they would be deprived of His presence, until the day of His Resurrection; but He said that He would go to His Father, as it was done on the day of His Ascension, after showing Himself to His disciples, and being with them during the forty days following His Resurrection. As to these words, *And again a little while, and you shall see Me,* they must be understood of the special assistance He promised to His Church, when on another occasion He said: *Behold I am with you all days, even to the consummation of the world* (Matt, 28: 20). For as St. Peter says: *The Lord delayeth not His promise* (2 Peter 3: 9); and after a little while we shall see Him again, when there shall be no need of making request, no need of putting questions, because there shall be nothing left to be desired, nothing hidden to be inquired into. This *little while* seems long to us, because it is yet going on in our life; but when it shall be ended, then we shall feel how short it was. Let not our joy, therefore, be such as the children of the world have, of whom our Lord says: *The world shall rejoice.* Yet let us not in our labouring with this desire be without joy; we may be sorrowful, but, as the Apostle says, *Rejoicing in hope; patient in tribulation* (Rom. 12: 12), because the very mother we are likened to is more rejoicing over the offspring she is about to have, than she is sorrowful for her present pains.

33. FOURTH SUNDAY AFTER EASTER

GOSPEL: John 16: 5-14. *At that time*: Jesus said to His disciples: I go to Him that sent Me; and none of you asketh Me, Whither goest Thou? But because I have spoken these things to you, sorrow hath filled your heart. But I tell you the truth; it is expedient to you that I go: for if I go not, the Paraclete will not come to you; but if I go, I will send Him to you. And when He is come, He will convince the world of sin, and of justice, and of judgment. Of sin; because they believed not in Me. And of justice; because I go to the Father; and you shall see Me no longer; and of judgment, because the prince of this world is already judged. I have yet many things to say to you, but you cannot bear them now. But when He, the Spirit of truth, is come, He will teach you all truth. For He shall not speak of Himself, but what things soever He shall hear, He shall speak; and the things that are to come He shall show you. He shall glorify Me, because He shall receive of Mine, and shall declare it to you.

HOMILY BY ST. AUGUSTINE
Tract 94 on St. John

I. THE LORD JESUS, AFTER FORETELLING HIS DISciples the persecutions they would have to suffer after His departure, went on to say: *But I told you not these things from the beginning, because I was with you. And now I go to Him that sent Me.* Let us first inquire whether He had before this moment foretold them their future sufferings. That He had done so before the night of the Last Supper is testified by the three first Evangelists; but it was at the end of that supper that, according to St. John, He spoke these words: *But I told you not these things from the beginning, because I was with you.* Are we, then, to try and find the solution of this difficulty by asserting that, according to those three Evangelists, it was on the eve of the Passion, though before the supper, that He had said these things to them? That, therefore, not from the beginning of His being with them, but when He was about to leave them, and to go to the Father, He said these things? And so, even according to those Evangelists, this also is true what He said by the other: *But I told you not these things from the beginning.* But then, what credit shall we attach to the Gospel according to St. Matthew, who tells us that our Lord spoke to His Apostles of these things concerning their sufferings, not only when He was on the point of eating the Paschal Supper with them, immediately before His Passion, but also at the very beginning, when the names of the twelve were for the first time mentioned, and they were sent forth to do the Divine works? (Matt. 10). It seems, then, that when He said, *But I told you not these things from the beginning, because I was with you,* He meant by 'these things' not the sufferings they were to bear for His sake, but His promise of the Holy Ghost, Who should come to them and bear witness while they suffered. And these things He did not say from the beginning, because He was with them.

11. This Comforter, then, or Advocate (for both terms render the Greek word *Paracletos*], would be necessary to them when they saw Christ no more; and this is the reason why He had not spoken of Him to them at the beginning of His public life, while He was with them, since His visible presence was then their sufficient comfort. But now that He was about to depart from them, it behoved Him to tell them of the coming of that Spirit, through Whom it would come to pass that, by the love infused into their hearts, they should preach the word of God with boldness. And while the Holy Ghost inwardly that is, within them bore testimony of Christ, they also should bear witness, and feel no cause of stumbling when their enemies, the Jews, should put them out of the synagogues and kill them, imagining that they were doing a service to God; for 'charity endureth all things' (1 Cor. 13: 7), and that charity of God was poured forth in their hearts by the Holy Ghost given to them (Rom. v. 5). This, then, is the whole meaning of His discourse, namely, that He would make them His

33. FOURTH SUNDAY AFTER EASTER

martyrs — that is, witnesses — through the Holy Ghost; so that by His working they should endure any amount of persecutions, and not grow cold in their preaching, being then inflamed by that Divine fire. *But these things,* He said, *I have told you that, when the hour shall come, you may remember that I told you of them.* These things, therefore, I have told you, not only that you suffer them, but also that, when the Paraclete is come, He shall bear testimony that you may not keep silence through fear, when you ought to speak, but you also shall bear testimony to Me.

III. And when our Lord said, *Now I go to Him that sent Me, and none of you asketh Me, Whither goest Thou?* He wished to intimate that He was about to go in their presence, and in such a manner, that it would be useless to ask to what place He was going. For previously to this they *had* asked Him whither He was going, and He had answered that He was going whither they *At that time* could not come. But now He declared that His going will be in such a manner, that none of them shall ask whither He goes. For when He ascended into heaven, a cloud received Him; and as He went, they asked not in words *whither,* but with their eyes they escorted Him *thither.*

IV. Jesus saw what effect these words about His going produced in the hearts of His disciples, and He said: *Because I have spoken these things to you, sorrow hath filled your heart.* Indeed, they had not yet the spiritual consolation which they were to receive through the Holy Ghost, who would fill them with His gifts. They feared, therefore, to lose the visible presence of their Master; and, because they could not doubt that He spoke the truth, their human affection was saddened, being convinced that their carnal sight of Him would be left desolate. However, He knew that was most expedient to them, because that inner sight, wherewith the Holy Spirit should console them, was assuredly superior. This Spirit would not present a human body before the bodies of men, that they should see Him, but He would infuse Himself into the hearts of men who believed. And Jesus goes on to say: *But I tell you the truth; it is expedient to you that I go; for if I go not, the Paraclete will not come to you; but if I go, I will send Him to you.* As though He said: It is expedient to you that this human form of a servant be taken from you. I am indeed the Word made flesh dwelling among you; but I do not wish you to love only My corporeal and carnal presence, and, content with this milk, desire to be always infants. If you suffer not the tender aliments, wherewith I have fed you, to be withdrawn from you, you will never be longing for solid meat. If in a carnal way you cleave only to the flesh you see in Me, you will never be worthy to receive the communications of the Holy Spirit. But what is the meaning of these words: *If I go not, the Paraclete will not come to you; but if I go, I will send Him to you?* Who would say that our Lord, whilst on earth with His disciples, had not the power to send them the Holy Ghost? For it must not be imagined that He had left the place where that Spirit was, and that He had been sent by His Father in such a way as not to abide with the Father any longer. Who will believe that Jesus Christ had not the power, even when still on earth, to send the Holy Ghost, Who, as we know, came upon Him at His baptism in the Jordan, and remained upon Him, and from Whom, indeed, we know that He was never separable? Then the meaning of, *If I go not, the Comforter will not come to you*, will be: You cannot receive the Spirit, as you persist in knowing Christ after the flesh and loving Him in the flesh. Whence St. Paul, who also had received the Spirit, says: *If we have known Christ according to the flesh, but now we know Him so no longer* (2 Cor. 5: 16). For, even now he did not know the flesh of Christ in a carnal way, until brought to a spiritual knowledge of the Word that has been made flesh. And surely our good Master wished to intimate this, when He said: *If I go not, the Comforter will not come to you; but if I go, I will send Him to you.*

V. Let us also believe that, when Christ bodily withdrew from the presence of His disciples, not only the Holy Ghost, but both the Father and the Son were present to them spiritually. For if Christ departed from them in such a manner that the Holy Ghost was in them, instead of Him and without Him, what becomes of His promise: *Behold, I am with you all days, even to the consummation of the world?* And how can we explain these other words of our Redeemer: *We will come to him,* I and the Father, *and will make Our abode with him*, seeing that He had promised to send the Holy Ghost in such a way as to be Himself with them to the end of the world? In this way it was, on the other hand, that seeing they were out of their carnal or animal condition to become spiritual, they were also, with undoubted certainty, to have both the Father and the Son, with the Holy Ghost, in a more comprehensive way. But we are not to believe that the Father is present in any man without the Son and the Holy Ghost, or the Father and the Son without the Holy Ghost, or the Son without the Father and the Holy Ghost, or the Holy Ghost without the Father and the Son, or the Father and the Holy Ghost without the Son. But wherever any one of them is, there also is the Trinity, one God. Here, however, the notion of the Trinity had to be suggested in such a manner that, though there was no diversity of substance, yet, by the several mentioning of each Person, we should be informed of the distinction of the Persons, of Whom, to them that rightly understand, there can never be a separation of Natures.

VI. Our Lord, when promising that He would send the Holy Ghost, said: *When He is come, He will convince the world of sin, and of justice, and of judgment.* What does this mean? Did not the Lord Jesus convince the world of sin when He said: *If I had not come and spoken to them, they would not have sin; but now they have no excuse for their sins* (John 15: 22). And, that no one may take it into his head to say that this applied properly to the Jews, and not to the world in general, He said in another place: *If you had been of the world, the world would love its own* (15: 22). Did He not convince the world of justice, saying: *O just Father, the world hath not known Thee?* (17: 23). Again, did He not convince the world of judgment, when He declared that He would say to those on the left hand: *Depart from Me, you cursed, into everlasting fire, which was prepared for the devil and Us angels?* (Matt. 25: 41). And many other passages are found in the holy Gospel, where Christ convinced the world of these things. How is it, then, that He attributes this to the Holy Ghost, as if it properly belonged to Him? Is it, perhaps, that, because Christ spoke only among the nation of the Jews, He does not appear to have reproved the world, so that he only be understood to be reproved, who actually hears the reprover? Yet the Holy Ghost, Who was in His disciples when scattered through the world, is understood as having reproved not one nation, but the whole world. For, notice what He said to them when about to ascend into heaven: *It is not for you to know the times or moments, which the Father hath put in His own power; but you shall receive the power of the Holy Ghost coming upon you, and you shall be witnesses unto Me in Jerusalem, and in all Judaea and Samaria, and even to the uttermost part of the earth* (Acts 1: 7, 8). Surely this is to reprove or convince the whole world. But who would venture to say that through the disciples of Christ the Holy Ghost reproves the world, and that Christ Himself does not, when the Apostle exclaims: *Do you seek a proof of Christ that speaketh in me?* (2 Cor. 13: 3). When, therefore, the Holy Ghost reproves, assuredly Christ also reproves. But, in my opinion, because there was to be *poured forth in their heart that charity* (Rom. 5: 5), *which casteth out fear* (1 John 4: 1, 8), by which fear they might have been hindered from daring to reprove the world, roaring at them with persecutions, He said: *He shall convince (reprove) the world.* Being then strengthened by the Holy Ghost, they reproved the world without fearing either torture or death. We have often mentioned that the operations of the Trinity are not separable, yet there was need to set forth the Persons one by one, that, without separating Them nor confounding Them together, we may have a clear understanding of Their Unity and Trinity.

34. FIFTH SUNDAY AFTER EASTER

GOSPEL: John 16: 23-30. *At that time:* Jesus said to His disciples: Amen, amen, I say to you; if you ask the Father anything in My name, He will give it you. Hitherto you have not asked anything in My name. Ask, and you shall receive; that your joy may be full. These things I have spoken to you in proverbs. The hour cometh when I will no more speak to you in proverbs, but will show you plainly of the Father. In that day you shall ask in My name, and I say not to you, that I will ask the Father for you. For the Father Himself loveth you, because you have loved Me, and have believed that I came out from God. I came forth from the Father, and am come into the world; again I leave the world, and I go to the Father. His disciples say to Him: Behold, now Thou speakest plainly, and speakest no proverbs. Now we know that Thou knowest all things, and Thou needest not that any man should ask Thee. By this we believe that Thou comest forth from God.

HOMILY BY ST. AUGUSTINE
Tract 102 on St. John

I. THE WORDS OF OUR LORD, WHICH YOU ARE NOW to consider, are these: *Amen, amen, I say to you: if you ask the Father anything in My name, He will give it you.* It has already been said in the earlier part of this discourse of the Lord, with regard to those who ask some things of the Father in Christ's name, and receive them not, that whatsoever is asked and tends not to salvation, is not asked in the name of the Redeemer. For, not the sounds of letters and syllables, but what the sound signifies, and what by that sound is honestly and truly understood, that He is regarded to declare, when saying: *In My name.* Hence, he that has such ideas of

Christ as ought not to be entertained of the only Son of God, is not asking in His name, though he may not abstain from mentioning the name of Christ in so many letters and syllables; because by that sound he means not the real Christ, but a fancied being, who has no existence but in the speaker's imagination. But, on the other hand, whosoever thinks of Christ as he ought to, this one is asking in Christ's name, and will receive, provided he ask for nothing against his own salvation; and if it be good for him to receive, he will receive. Some things are not given at once, but are deferred, that they may be given at a more suitable time. This is the true interpretation of the words: *He will give it you*—that is, those benefits or blessings will be given which are good to them that ask. All the saints are heard, when asking for themselves, but not necessarily when asking for others, whether friends or enemies; because it is not said in a general way, *He will give*, but *He will give it you*.

II. *Hitherto*, says the Lord, *you have not asked anything in My name. Ask, and you shall receive, that your joy may be full*. This joy of theirs, which He calls *full*, is not to be understood as meaning a carnal joy, but a spiritual one. When that joy is so great, that it cannot be increased any more, then it will undoubtedly be full. Whatsoever, then, is asked for the fulfilment of this joy—viz., grace and everlasting life—is a thing that is just and meet to ask in the name of Christ. Should we ask anything else, and not this, we ask nothing, though we actually ask some thing; because in comparison with this all other things we covet are nothing. If we say that man is something, we hear the Apostle, saying: *If any man think himself to be something, whereas he is nothing, he deceiveth himself* (Gal. 6: 3). But the fact is, that in comparison with the spiritual man, who knows that by the grace of God only he is what he is, the one who entertains vain presumptions is nothing. In this way, therefore, may those words be rightly understood: *Amen, amen, I say to you: if you ask the Father anything in My name, He will give it you*; so that by the word *anything* should not be understood any thing that we please, but any thing that is not considered nothing in connection with a blessed life. And the following words: *Hitherto you have not asked anything in My name*, may be understood in two ways: either, that you have not asked in My name, because you have not known this name, as it ought to be known; or you have not asked anything, because, in comparison with the things you ought to have asked, what you have asked is to be accounted as nothing. And that they may ask in His name, not that which is nothing, but a full joy — since if they ask anything else, that *anything* is nothing, — He addressed to them this exhortation: *Ask, and you shall receive; that your joy may be full* — that is, ask this in My name, that your joy may be full, and you shall receive. For His saints, who persevere in asking such a good thing will, by the mercy of God, never be defrauded.

III. *These things*, He said, *I have spoken to you in proverbs. The hour cometh when I will no more speak to you in proverbs, but will show you plainly of the Father.* The hour of which He speaks might be supposed to mean the world to come, when we shall see openly as St. Paul says, *face to face;* and that what He says, *These things I have spoken to you in proverbs*, should be understood by the words of the same Apostle: *We see now through a glass in a dark manner* (1 Cor. 13: 12). But *I will show you*, because the Father shall be seen through the instrumentality of the Son, according to what is said elsewhere: *Neither doth anyone know the Father, but the Son, and he to whom it shall please the Son to reveal Him* (Matt. 11: 27). But this sense seems to be interfered with by what follows: *In that day you shall ask in My name.* For in the future world, when we have reached the kingdom, where *we shall be like to Him, because we shall see Him as He is* (1 John 3: 2), what shall we then have to ask, when our desires shall be *satisfied with good things?* (Ps. 102: 5). In another Psalm it is also said: *I shall be satisfied when Thy glory shall appear* (Ps. 16: 15). The asking for anything implies need, which cannot have any place there, where this fulness of satisfaction shall be attained and reign.

IV. It remains, therefore, for us, as far as I can conceive the matter, to understand Jesus as having promised His disciples that, of carnal or animal, they should through Him become spiritual, though not yet such as we shall be, when a spiritual body shall also be ours, but such as he was who said: *We speak wisdom among the perfect* (1 Cor. 2: 6), and *I could not speak to you as unto spiritual, but as unto carnal* (1 Cor. 3: 1); and: *We have received not the spirit of this world, but the Spirit that is of God, that we may know the things that are given us from God. Which things we also speak, not in the words of human wisdom, but in the doctrine of the Spirit, comparing spiritual things with spiritual. But the sensual man perceiveth not those things that are of the Spirit of God* (1 Cor. 2: 12-14). And thus the sensual man hears in such a way whatsoever is told him of the nature of God, that he can conceive of nothing else but some bodily form, however spacious or immense, however bright and splendid, yet still a body. They are, therefore, proverbs to him, whatsoever is said of the incorporeal and immutable substance of wisdom. Not that he accounts them as proverbs or riddles, but because his thoughts follow the same direction as those who usually listen to proverbs without understanding them. But the *spiritual* man, who judges all things and is judged by no one, perceives, though in this life it still be 'through a glass,' and 'in part.' He perceives, not by any bodily sense, and not by any imaginative conception, which takes in or fancies the likenesses of all sorts of bodies, but by the clearest understanding of the mind, that God is not a body, but a Spirit. In such a way does the Son of God openly show us of the Father, that He Who thus reveals, is also Himself of the same substance as the Father. Thus we see how it is that those who are asking, ask in His name, because they know that to ask in this name, is to ask in the name of God. They do not, in vanity or weakness of mind, fancy to themselves the Father being in one place and the Son in another; the Son humbly standing before the Father and making request in our behalf; both, in the material substance occupying each its own place, and the Word pleading verbally for us with Him Whose Word He is, whilst a definite space exists between the speaker's mouth and the hearer's ears. Such absurdities are fabricated for themselves in their own hearts by those who are natural and also carnal. But such things, suggested by the experience of bodily habits, if occurring to spiritual men when thinking of God, are at once denied, rejected, and driven away, like troublesome flies, from the eyes of their mind. They rest in the sincerity of that light, by whose testimony and judgment they prove how utterly false are these bodily images that haunt their inward vision. They are able, to a certain extent, to think of our Lord Jesus Christ as Man addressing the Father on our behalf; but as God hearing our prayers with the Father. And this, I suppose, He wished to indicate, when He said: *I say not to you that I will ask the Father for you.* But the perception of this, that the Son asks not the Father, but that Father and Son together hear those who ask, this height of conception can be reached only by the spiritual eye of the mind.

V. *For the Father Himself loveth you, because you have loved Me.* Does He love because we love — or, rather, do we love because He loves? Let the same Evangelist answer out of his own epistle: *We love God,* he says, *because God first hath loved us* (1 John 4: 19). This, therefore, is the cause of our love, namely, that we were loved; for to love God is the gift of God. He, while still unloved, gave us the grace to love Him. We were loved, even when displeasing Him, that there might be in us that whereby we should be pleasing in His sight; for we could not love the Son unless we also loved the Father. The Father loves us, because we love the Son, since we have received of the Father and the Son the power to love both the Father and the Son. For love is poured forth into our hearts by the Spirit of both; by which Spirit we love both the Father and the Son, and Him Whom we love together with the Son and the Father. God, therefore, it was, Who made that religious love of ours, whereby we worship Him, and He saw that it was good. Therefore He loved what He made; but He would not have made in us anything He could love, were it not that He loved us before He made us.

VI. And Jesus added: *You have believed that I came out from God. I came forth from the Father, and am come into the world; again I leave the world, and I go to the Father.* Yes, we have believed. Surely it ought not to be thought a thing incredible, only because that, in coming into the world, He came in such a manner out of the Father, as not to quit the Father, and, in leaving the world, He went to the Father in such a manner, as not to forsake the world. For He came forth from the Father, because He is of the Father, and He came into the world showing His bodily form, which He took to Himself of the Virgin Mary. He left the world by a bodily withdrawal; He went to the Father by His Ascension as Man, yet He quitted not the world in the ruling activity of His presence.

VII. Everywhere throughout the Gospels, the inward state of Christ's disciples is declared by many testimonies, when before His Passion He talketh with them, as with children, of great things. But He spoke in such a way, as was meet that great things should be spoken of to children. Not having yet received the Holy Ghost, as they did after His Resurrection, either by His breathing upon them, or by the descent from above, they had a mental capacity for the things of men rather than the things of God. This is also declared by what they said in the lesson before us. For, says the Evangelist: *His disciples say to Him: Behold, now Thou speakest plainly, and speakest no proverbs. Now we know that Thou knowest all things, and Thou needest not that any man should ask Thee. By this we believe that Thou comest forth from God.* The Lord Himself had said just before: *These things I have spoken to you in proverbs. The hour cometh when I will no more speak to you in proverbs.* How is it, then, that they say: *Behold, now Thou speakest plainly, and speakest no proverbs?* Was the hour now come, when He had promised He would no more speak to them in proverbs? No; that such an hour was not yet come is shown by the continuation of His words, which are as follows: *These things I have spoken to you in proverbs. The hour cometh when I will no more speak to you in proverbs, but will show you plainly of the Father. In that day you shall ask in My name, and I say not to you that I will ask the Father for you. For the Father Himself loveth you, because you have loved Me, and have believed that I came out from God. I came forth from the Father, and am come into the world; again I leave the world, and I go to the Father.* Since throughout all these words He is still promising that hour, when He shall no more speak in proverbs, but shall show them openly the Father, why do they say: *Behold, now Thou speakest plainly, and speakest no proverbs*, except because the things He knows to be proverbs to those that have no understanding, they are still so far from understanding, that they do not even know that they do not understand them? For they were babes, and had no spiritual discernment of what they heard regarding things which pertained not to the body, but to the spirit.

35. ASCENSION DAY

GOSPEL: Mark 16: 14-20. *At that time*: Jesus appeared to the eleven as they were at table; and He upbraided them with their incredulity and hardness of heart, because they did not believe them who had seen Him after He was risen again. And He said to them: Go ye into the whole world and preach the Gospel to every creature. He that believeth and is baptized shall be saved; but he that believeth not shall be condemned. And these signs shall follow them that believe: in My name they shall cast out devils; they shall speak with new tongues; they shall take up serpents; and if they shall drink any deadly thing, it shall not hurt them; they shall lay hands upon the sick, and they shall recover. And the Lord Jesus, after He had spoken to them, was taken up to heaven, and sitteth on the right hand of God. But they, going, preached everywhere, the Lord working withal, and confirming the word with signs that followed.

HOMILY BY POPE ST. GREGORY, PREACHED IN THE CHURCH OF ST. PETER ON THE FEAST OF THE ASCENSION OF OUR LORD
Twenty-Ninth Homily on the Gospels

I. THE SLOWNESS OF THE DISCIPLES TO BELIEVE that the Lord had indeed risen from the dead was not so much, if I may be allowed to say so, a sign of their weakness, as the motive of Divine Providence to strengthen us in our faith. Indeed, the consequence of their doubts was the demonstration of the Resurrection by many infallible proofs. And we read and acknowledge these proofs, and our faith is assured by the disciples' doubt. For my part, I do not put so much trust in Mary Magdalen, who believed at once, as in Thomas, who doubted so long; for by his doubting he came actually to touch the Lord's wounds, and thereby closed up any wound of doubt in our own hearts. However, to confirm to our minds the truth of the Resurrection of our Lord, we do well to take notice of one of the statements of St. Luke: *Eating together with them, He commanded them that they should not depart from Jerusalem* (Acts 1: 4); and a little afterwards: *While they looked on, He was raised up, and a cloud received Him out of their sight* (ver. 9). He ate, and ascended; so that the fact of His eating might show the reality of His body in which He went up. But St. Mark tells us that before the Lord ascended into heaven, He upbraided His disciples with their incredulity and hardness of heart. I know not what we should gather from this, unless that the Lord then reproached His disciples, from whom He was about to be parted in the body, to this end, that the words He spoke to them, as He left them, might be the deeper imprinted on their hearts.

II. And when He had rebuked the hardness of their heart, what command did He give them? Listen: *Go ye into the whole world, and preach the Gospel to every creature.* Was, then, the holy Gospel to be preached to things insensate, or to brute animals, that the Lord said to His disciples: *Preach the Gospel to every creature?* No; but by the words *every creature* we must understand man, who possesses qualities pertaining to all creatures. He has being in common with stones, life in common with trees, feeling in common with beasts, and understanding in common with angels. If, then, man has something in common with every creature, man is to some extent every creature. And if the Gospel is preached to man only, it is preached to every creature, because man has dominion over all things created by God on earth, and because everything created has in itself something like to man. However, we may also suppose that the intention of Jesus, commanding His Apostles to preach the Gospel to every creature, was to give them to understand that His Gospel was to be preached to all the nations in the world. On a former occasion He had told them not to go to the Gentiles, but now He commanded them to preach to all men. When, therefore, the Jews despised the preaching of the Apostles announcing Jesus Christ, the preachers turned to the Gentiles and were listened to. For, instead of imitating the pernicious pride and obstinacy of the Jews, the Gentiles humbly submitted to the yoke of the Gospel. When the Apostles were sent by the Eternal Truth to preach to the world, a most precious seed was sown, which seems very small, but which, through faith, will soon bring forth a rich harvest. How could the number of the faithful have increased in the world in such marvellous manner, had not the hand of the Almighty spread abroad among the different nations the small number of Apostles chosen for the purpose of extending His kingdom on earth?

III. *He that believeth and is baptized shall be saved; but he that believeth not shall be condemned.* Relying on the truth of these words every one among us will perhaps say: I shall be saved, for I believe. This will undoubtedly be the case if our actions agree with the faith we profess. For we shall be saved by that faith by which our life is in conformity with the principles it teaches. St. Paul confirms this when, speaking of bad Christians, he says: *They profess that they know God, but in their works they deny Him* (Titus 1: 16). The same is said by St. John: *He who saith that he knoweth God and keepeth not His commandments, is a liar, and the truth is not in him* (1 John 2: 4). If this be so, then our life must absolutely give testimony to the faith which we profess; and if our conduct be not against the rules prescribed by our holy religion, then we may trust to belong to the number of the faithful. Indeed, we do not forget the solemn promises made at our baptism — namely, to renounce Satan, all his works and all his pomps. Let each of us earnestly examine himself, and should he be able to testify to the fact that he has fulfilled all those duties taken upon himself in the Sacrament of Baptism, he may congratulate himself on the happiness of being a good Christian. But should he be forced to confess that he has been faithless to his promises, that he has been a member of that company which he had formerly renounced, and that his actions reproach him with having lost his innocence, then let him ask himself whether he feels deep contrition for his sins, and endeavours to wash them out with tears of repentance. Our Judge is a God of mercies, who will no longer recognise as faithless the servant who, after leaving Him, now feels contrite, and sincerely returns to Him; for our penance will make Him forget the sins that had rendered us guilty in His eyes.

IV. Then our Lord added these words: *And these signs shall follow them that believe; in My Name they shall cast out devils; they shall speak with new tongues; they shall take up serpents; and if they shall drink any deadly thing, it shall not hurt them; they shall lay hands upon the sick, and they shall recover.* Now, do not think because such miracles are not wrought by you, that you have not the true faith. These miracles were necessary at the beginning of the Church, that the faith should be accepted, and the number of the faithful increased by the signs of the Almighty power. For the beginning of the Church may be compared to the planting of a young tree, which is to be tended and watered until it has taken deep root in the ground. Therefore St. Paul says: *Tongues are for a sign not to believers, but to unbelievers* (1 Cor. 14: 22). But there is also an important lesson contained in these miracles and gifts of the Holy Ghost, provided we understand their meaning. For these miracles, which in former times were wrought by the Apostles in a corporal and visible manner, now take place in the Church of God in a spiritual and invisible manner. When we, priests and ministers of the Church, lay our hands upon the faithful, and see how by the power of exorcisms the evil spirit is prevented from entering souls, is it not as if we were casting out devils? When Christians, formerly addicted to bad conversations, so common in the world, now renounce such sins, are edifying in their words, conversing about the doctrine of salvation, and everywhere praising their Creator and Redeemer, are they not like those Christians who spoke *with new tongues*? Again, those who, by their zealous admonitions, withdraw others from a shameful and vicious life *take up serpents*, and are not poisoned by them. If anyone, hearing corrupting language, is not affected by it or led to evil, does he not seem to *drink a deadly thing, and is not hurt*? Lastly, all those who, seeing their brethren, not yet strong in virtue — on the point of yielding to sin, run to their help, in order to prevent their spiritual shipwreck; all others who by their good example strengthen their neighbour in virtue — all of them

35. ASCENSION DAY

lay hands upon the sick, and they recover. All these miracles are the more astonishing, since they are worked on souls, the resurrection of which to the spiritual life of grace is more wonderful than the rising of bodies. Well, beloved brethren, you can do these in visible wonders with the help of God, if only you are willing. As to the visible signs, proving the holiness of those who work them, they cannot of themselves sanctify, not even those by whom they are witnessed; whereas the spiritual gifts, spoken of just now, when imparted to souls, though not proving the virtue of the receivers, nevertheless give them the life of grace. Both the good and the wicked may be favoured by exterior gifts; yet the spiritual gifts are possessed by the just only. Therefore it was said by the Eternal Truth, speaking of those who boast of having done miracles in His Name: *Many will say to me in that day: Lord, Lord, have not we, prophesied in Thy Name, and cast out devils in Thy name, and done many miracles in Thy Name? And then will I profess unto them, I never knew yon; depart from Me, you that work iniquity* (Matt. 7: 22, 23). Beloved brethren, do not desire these exterior signs which are sometimes granted by God to His enemies and to the reprobate; but earnestly wish for those wonders of love and examples of true piety, I have spoken of to you. Their merits are the surer the more they are hidden — merits that will be the more generously rewarded by God, the less they are shining before the eyes of men.

V. *And the Lord Jesus, after He had spoken to them, was taken up to heaven, and sitteth on the right hand of God.* When we read in Holy Scripture (4 Kings 2) that Elias also was taken up to heaven, we easily understand the difference. The prophet was taken up in the air, whereas our Saviour ascended by His own power into heaven. As the birds, flying up in the air and again coming down, are called the *birds of the heaven,* so Elias is said to have passed through the space of the air or atmosphere, that he might be taken to an unknown land, there to spend painless and happy days, until the end of the world, when he will again appear and pay the debt of nature. Death is a punishment that was not remitted to him; it was only postponed. But our Redeemer, suffering death without delay, conquered it and destroyed its dominion by His

Resurrection, the glory of which was revealed in the triumph of His Ascension. Again, observe that the prophet Elias was taken up to heaven in a fiery chariot, showing that, as a human being, he had need of exterior help. Angels carried him into the atmosphere, wherein the great weakness of his human nature could not have supported him. But our Saviour ascended into heaven by His own power, without the assistance of angels or the help of creatures; and He saw the earth under His feet, since by His Almighty power He was elevated above all things. He ascended without any effort to the eternal dwellings, for He had never left His glory; and if as man He ascended into heaven, as God He had always been present in heaven and on earth.

VI. As Joseph, sold by his brethren, was a symbol of Jesus sold by Judas, so were also Henoch, translated by God to paradise, and Elias taken up to heaven, two types of His Ascension. Our Lord wished this great mystery to be announced by these two witnesses, the one living before the Law, the other under the Law. However, there are different degrees of glory in these translations, according to the different conditions of the persons. Holy Scripture says of Henoch: *He was seen no more, because God took him* (Gen. 5: 24); of Elias, that he was taken up in a fiery chariot. But our Saviour penetrated heaven without the help of another. He was not taken up nor carried up, but went up into the dwelling of glory by His own power. In His Ascension, and also in the translation of Henoch and Elias, are shown the different degrees of the virtue of chastity, of which He is our exemplar, and which He wished to be perpetuated in His Church. When first we consider Henoch in the bonds of matrimony, then see Elias without wife and children, we notice the progress of this holy virtue manifested in these two men, as compared with Jesus in His Ascension. We know that Henoch, being begotten like other men, in his turn begot children; that Elias, coming later, though born like others, never begot; and that Jesus Christ, not only in His miraculous birth, but in His whole life, was Purity itself.

VII. St. Mark says of our Lord: *And sitteth on the right hand of God.* Yet St. Stephen (Acts 7: 55) exclaimed: *Behold, I see the heavens opened, and the Son of Man standing on the right hand of God.* This does not seem to agree, namely, sitting on the right hand, and standing on the right hand. Yet, beloved brethren, you will not be astonished by this seemingly disagreeing testimony of Holy Scripture. You will take into consideration that it appertains to a judge to be sitting, whereas one fighting or helping is thought to be standing. Now, the Redeemer of the world, after ascending into heaven, is the Judge of all things, and will come at the end to judge the whole world; and in this capacity of highest judge He is represented by St. Mark as sitting on the right hand of God. But when Stephen, still in the throes of the battle, saw Him standing in the midst of His glory, we are to understand that Jesus in the highest heavens was fighting with this glorious martyr, giving him His help to overcome the fury of his persecutors.

VIII. *But they, going, preached everywhere; the Lord working withal, and confirming the word with signs that followed.* What are we to notice in this, and what are we to remember, but that obedience followed the commandment, and that great miracles followed their obedience? But now, since by the will of God we have lightly run over our reading from the Gospel, it remains that we should give you some considerations or reflections on this great festival.

IX. And first, let us ask why the angels, appearing at the birth of our Lord, were not in white garments; whereas, when the Lord ascended into heaven, it is written that they were clad in white. It is written: *While they looked on, He was raised up: and a cloud received Him out of their sight. And while they were beholding Him going up to heaven, behold two men stood by them in white garments* (Acts 1: 9, 10). White garments are an outward sign of an inward joy. But how is it that these heavenly spirits, announcing the blessed birth of our Saviour, were not seen in white garments? Because at the Ascension the angels, beholding the Man-God going up in triumph to heaven, were manifesting their joy, since His humanity received the glory due to Him; whereas in His Nativity the Divinity seemed to be humbled, taking the form of a servant, and the angels showed no special exterior joy. Their appearance in white garments at the Ascension was a sign of glory; at the Nativity a sign of the humiliation of the Son of God.

X. However, beloved brethren, what deserves our greatest consideration on this festival is the fact, that on this day Christ was *blotting out the handwriting of the decree that was against us* (Col. 2: 14), and that the sentence of corruption was reversed. For our human nature, of which it was said, *Thou art dust, and unto dust thou shalt return* (Gen. 3: 19), was taken up to heaven on this day. Foreseeing this elevation of our flesh, the holy man Job compared our Lord with a bird. And seeing that the Jews would not recognise this mystery, he reproached them with their incredulity, and said: *The bird hath not known the path* (Job 28: 7). The name of a bird is well given to the Lord, Who in His human body soared up into heaven. And those who do not believe in His Ascension, do not know the path of the Bird. It is of this glorious occasion that the Psalmist says: *Thy magnificence, O Lord, is elevated above the heavens* (Ps. 8: 2); again: *God is ascended with jubilee, and the Lord with the sound of trumpet* (Ps. 46: 6). And again he says: *Thou hast ascended on high, Thou hast led captivity captive; Thou hast received gifts in men* (Ps. 67: 19). Ascending to heaven, He led captivity captive, for by His Resurrection we were delivered from corruption; and He gave gifts to men when sending His Spirit: *To one, indeed, by the Spirit is given the word of wisdom to another the word of knowledge; to another the grace of healing; to another the working of miracles; to another divers kinds of tongues; to another interpretation of speeches* (i Cor. xii. 8-10). The prophet Habacuc spoke of the glory of Christ's Ascension in the words: *The Sun and the Moon stood still in their habitation* (Hab. 3: 11). Who is here signified by the Sun if not the Saviour? or by the Moon, if not the Church? This Church was, until the Lord's Ascension, exposed to violent storms, and lived in fear of her enemies. But when our Saviour had ascended into heaven, the Church was strengthened, took heart, and began to preach openly the faith which she had been holding secretly. Like the sun rising towards the south, the Lord rose, and gave strength and increase to His Church by the powerful command to preach His Gospel. And to confirm the truth, the

Church, taking the words of Solomon, exclaims: *The voice of my beloved; behold he cometh leaping upon the mountains, skipping over the hills* (Cant. 2: 8). For the Church contemplates the sufferings of our Saviour, Who, from the first moment of His coming into this world, *leaped* with giant's steps on painful roads. And would you know, beloved brethren, these steps taken by the Redeemer? Consider that from heaven He stepped into the womb of a Virgin, from the womb into the manger, from the manger on to the cross, from the cross into the sepulchre, and from the sepulchre up to heaven. Thus the truth manifested in the flesh took such steps for our sakes, that He might draw us to run after Him; and for this end *He hath rejoiced as a giant to run His way* (Ps. 18: 6), that we might passionately say: *Draw us; we will run after Thee to the odour of Thy sweetness* (Cant. 1: 3).

XI. Therefore, beloved brethren, we must follow in heart and mind Him Who on this day ascended into heaven. Let our hearts be separated from all earthly desires, so that we may henceforth taste no other happiness than the remembrance of Him Who is our Father in heaven. Let us remember, and often meditate on this truth, that, though He ascended as a peaceful King, He will one day come as a terrible Judge, and require of us with justice an account of our keeping those commandments given to us by Him in mercy. Let no man neglect the time, given to us for doing penance; let everyone work for the salvation of his soul whilst there is yet an opportunity. Our Redeemer will be all the sterner, when He comes in judgment, the more wondrously long-suffering He was before. Carefully consider my words, and dispose your life according to this important lesson. And should your soul be tossed about by the storms of this life, let it be fastened by the anchor of hope to the eternal dwellings, our true fatherland, and let your eyes steadfastly gaze on that heavenly light. After considering the Ascension of our Lord, let our faith meditate on this mystery, and, though we are still fastened to this earth by the bonds of our body, let us at least follow Jesus on the wings of our love, and ask Him, Who granted us these heavenly desires, not to forsake us, until they be perfectly fulfilled. Amen.

36. SIXTH SUNDAY AFTER EASTER

GOSPEL: John 15: 26 to 16: 4. *At that time*: Jesus said to His disciples: When the Paraclete cometh, Whom I will send you from the Father, the Spirit of Truth, Who proceedeth from the Father, He shall give testimony of Me: and you shall give testimony, because you are with Me from the beginning. These things have I spoken to you, that you may not be scandalized. They will put you out of the synagogues; yea, the hour cometh, that whosoever killeth you, will think that he doeth a service to God. And these things will they do to you, because they have not known the Father, nor Me. But these things I have told you, that when the hour shall come, you may remember that I told you.

HOMILY BY ST. AUGUSTINE
Tracts 92 and 93 on St. John

I. WHEN OUR LORD HAD TOLD HIS APOSTLES THAT the world, His enemies, hated both the Son and the Father without a cause—that is, both Him that was sent and Him by Whom He was sent—He added these words: *But when the Paraclete cometh, Whom I will send you from the Father, the Spirit of Truth, Who proceedeth from the Father, He shall give testimony of Me: and you shall give testimony, because you are with Me from the beginning.* But what connection has this with what He had just said: *Now they have both seen, and hated both Me and My Father; but that the word may be fulfilled which is written in their law: They have hated Me without cause* (John 15: 25). Is it that, when the Paraclete, the Spirit of Truth, is come, He will convict by a still clearer testimony those who have both seen and hated both God the Son and God the Father? Yea, indeed, some there were who had seen and still hated, whom the testimony of the Paraclete converted to the *faith which worketh by charity* (Gal. 5: 6). To make this view of the passage intelligible, we recall to your mind that so it actually came to pass. For on the day of Pentecost the Holy Spirit came down upon an assembly of 120 men, among whom were all the Apostles; and when these, filled with the Spirit, spoke in the tongues of all the nations, a great number of those who had hated, were amazed by so great a miracle, specially when they saw in Peter's speech, how great and how Divine a testimony was borne to the fact that the Christ, Whom they had murdered, and Whom they reckoned among the dead, had risen again, and was alive. And many of the bystanders *had compunction in their hearts* (Acts 2: 37), and were converted. They received pardon from that precious Blood, which had been so sacrilegiously and cruelly shed by them, and they themselves became redeemed by the very Blood they had shed; for the Blood of Christ was shed so efficaciously for the remission of all sins, that it had power to blot out the very sin by which it was shed. Towards this the Lord looked, when He said: *They hated Me without cause; but when the Paraclete cometh, He shall give testimony of Me.* This was as though He had said: 'They hated Me and killed Me when I stood visibly before their eyes; but the Paraclete shall bear such testimony concerning Me, that He will compel them to believe in Me, when I am no longer visible to their sight.'

II. *And you,* He says, *shall give testimony, because you aye with Me from the beginning.* The Holy Ghost shall give testimony, and so also shall you. Because you have been with me from the beginning, you can preach what you know; but you cannot do this just now, because the fulness of that Spirit is not yet within you. *He, then, shall give testimony of Me; and you shall give testimony; for the charity of God is poured forth in your hearts by the Holy Ghost Who is given to you* (Rom. 5: 5), and will give you the needful confidence for such witness-bearing. This certainly was still wanting to Peter's heart, who, terrified by a maid-servant's question, could give no true testimony, but, breaking his promise, was driven by fear thrice to deny Him. Now, *fear is not in charity; but perfect charity casteth out fear* (1 John 4: 18). In fact, before the Lord's Passion, his slavish fear was questioned by a serving-woman, but after the Resurrection his free love was asked by the very Prince of freedom. And so on one occasion he was troubled, on the other he was at peace; there he denied the One he loved, here he loved the One he had denied. But still even then this very love was weak and narrow, until strengthened and expanded by the Holy Ghost. And that spirit, pervading him with the fulness of richer grace, set on fire his once cold heart, to give testimony to Christ, and unlocked those trembling lips which had suppressed the truth. Therefore, while all on whom the Holy Ghost had descended were speaking with tongues of all the nations to crowds of the Jews that stood around, Peter alone, more promptly than the rest, broke forth to bear witness of Christ, and, giving an account of His Resurrection, confounded His murderers. And if anyone would like to look at such a sweetly holy spectacle, let him read the Acts of the Apostles (Acts 2: 5), there to be amazed at the preaching of blessed Peter, over whose denial of his Master he had just been mourning; there to behold that tongue translated from cowardice to boldness, from servitude to liberty, converting to the confession of Christ so many tongues of His enemies, not one of which he had had strength enough to bear, when lapsing himself into denial. What shall I say more? In him there shone forth such brightness of grace, such fulness of the Holy Ghost, such weight of most precious truth, proceeding from the mouth of the preacher, that of the vast multitude of Jews, who were the murderers of Christ, he transformed them into men who were ready to die for His Name, even those by whom he once dreaded to be put to death with Him. All this was done by the Holy Ghost, then sent, previously only promised. These were His own great and marvellous gifts, foreseen by the Lord, when He said: *They have both seen and hated both Me and My Father; but that the word may be fulfilled which is written in their law: They have hated Me without cause. But when the Paraclete cometh, Whom I will send you from the Father, the Spirit of Truth, Who proceedeth from the Father, He shall give testimony of Me*; and you shall give testimony. For He, giving testimony, and inspiring such witnesses with invincible courage, rid Christ's friends of their fear, and turned into love the hatred of His enemies.

III. In the words preceding this portion of the Gospel, the Lord strengthened His disciples to bear the hatred of their enemies, and prepared them also by His example to become more courageous by imitating Him. He then added the promise that the Holy Ghost would come and give testimony of Him, and also that they themselves should be made His witnesses through the powerful working of His Spirit in their hearts. This is the meaning of His words: *He shall give testimony of Me, and you shall give testimony* — that is, because He shall give testimony, you shall also give testimony, He in your hearts and you in your voices; He by inspiration, you by expression, that thus the words might be fulfilled: *Their sound hath gone forth into all the earth* (Ps. 18: 5). For it would not have been enough to cheer them on by His example, had He not also filled them with His Spirit. Thus we see that the Apostle Peter, after hearing His word, *The servant is not greater than his Master; if they have persecuted Me, they will also persecute you* (John 15: 20); and having seen that already fulfilled in his Lord, wherein he ought to have imitated His patient suffering, had example been sufficient, succumbed and fell into denial, because he was unable to bear what he saw Him enduring. But when he received the Holy Ghost, he preached Him Whom he had denied; and Whom he had been afraid to confess, he had no fear now openly to profess. He had already been taught by example to know what was meet to be done; but he was not yet inspired by the power to do what he knew; he was instructed that he might stand, but he was not strengthened that he might not fall. But when this was given by the Holy Ghost, he preached Christ even to the death, Whom, for fear of death, he had previously denied. Therefore the Lord, in the following chapter, of which we are now to speak to you, says: *These things have I spoken to you that you may not be scandalized.* Thus we sing in the psalm: *Much peace have they that love Thy law; and to them there is no stumbling-block* (Ps. 118: 165). Fittingly enough, then, after promising the Holy Ghost, by Whose operation in their hearts they should be made His witnesses, He goes on to say: *These things have I spoken to you, that you may not be scandalized. For when the charity of God is poured forth into our hearts* by the Holy Ghost, Who is given to us (Rom. 5: 5), those who love God's law have great peace, so that nothing may scandalize them.

IV. Then He expressly declares what they were to suffer: *They will put you out of the synagogues.* But what harm was it to the Apostles to be expelled from the Jewish synagogues? Were they not about to separate themselves therefrom, though none should expel them? Doubtless He meant to announce that the Jews would refuse to receive Christ, from Whom the Apostles as certainly would refuse to withdraw. And so it would come to pass that they, who could not be without Him, would also be cast out with Him by those who refused to be in Him. Certainly, as there was no other people of God than that seed of Abraham, had they only acknowledged and received Christ, they would have remained as the natural branches of the olive-tree; nor would the Churches of Christ have differed from the synagogues of the Jews, but would have been one and the same, had they also desired to abide in Him. But having refused, what remained but that, continuing to be out of Christ, they put out of the synagogues those who would not forsake Christ? For, having received the Holy Ghost, and so become His witnesses, they would certainly not belong to those of whom it was said: *Many of the chief men also believed in Him, but because of the Pharisees they did not confess Him, that they might not be cast out of the synagogues; for they loved the glory of men more than the glory of God* (John 12: 42, 43). And so they believed in Him, but not in the way He wished them to believe, when He said: *How can you believe, who receive glory one from another; and the glory which is from God alone, you do not seek?* (John 5: 44). It is, therefore, with those disciples who believe in Him that, being filled with the Holy Ghost or, in other words, with the gift of Divine grace they no longer belong to those who, *not knowing the justice of God, and seeking to establish their own, have not submitted themselves to the justice of God* (Rom. 10: 3); nor to those of whom it is said, *they loved the glory of men more than the glory of God,* that this prophecy harmonizes, which is fulfilled in their own persons: *They shall walk, Lord, in the light of Thy countenance, and in Thy Name they shall rejoice all the day, and in Thy justice they shall be exalted, for Thou art the glory of their strength* (Ps. 88: 16-18). Rightly enough it is said to them: *They will put you out of the synagogues* — that is, they, *who have a zeal of God, but not according to knowledge,* because, *not knowing the justice of God, and seeking to establish their own,* they expel those who are exalted, not in their own justice, but in God's, and the expelled have no cause to be ashamed at being expelled by men, because He is *the glory of their strength*. Finally, He added these words: *Yea, the hour cometh, that whosoever killeth you, will think that he doeth a service to God; and these things will they do to you, because they have not known the Father nor Me.* That is to say, they have not known the Father nor His Son, to Whom they think they will be doing a service in slaying you. Words which the Lord added in the way of consolation to His own, who would be driven out of the Jewish synagogues.

37. WHIT-SUNDAY, THE FEAST OF PENTECOST

GOSPEL: John 14: 23-31. *At that time:* Jesus said to His disciples: If anyone love Me, he will keep My word, and My Father will love him, and We will come to him, and will make Our abode with him; he that loveth Me not, keepeth not My words. And the word which you have heard is not Mine; but the Father's Who sent Me. These things have I spoken to you, abiding with you. But the Paraclete, the Holy Ghost, Whom the Father will send in My name, He will teach you all things, and bring all things to your mind, whatsoever I shall have said to you. Peace I leave with you; My peace I give to you; not as the world giveth do I give unto you. Let not your heart be troubled, nor let it be afraid. You have heard that I said to you: I go away, and I come again to you. If you loved Me, you would indeed be glad, because I go to the Father; for the Father is greater than I. And now I have told you before it come to pass: that when it shall come to pass, you may believe. I will not now speak many things with you; for the Prince of this world cometh, and in Me he hath not anything. But that the world may know that I love the Father; and as the Father hath given Me commandment, so do I.

HOMILY BY POPE ST. GREGORY, PREACHED IN THE CHURCH OF ST. PETER, APOSTLE, ON THE FEAST OF PENTECOST
Thirtieth Homily on the Gospel

I. IT WILL BE BEST, BELOVED BRETHREN, BRIEFLY to run through the words of the Gospel, read out to you, and afterwards dwell for a longer time upon the subject of this solemn festival. This is the day whereon *suddenly there came a sound from heaven*, and the Holy Ghost descended upon the Apostles, and changed their fleshly minds into minds filled with the love of God. And whilst without *there appeared parted tongues, as it were of fire, and it sat upon every one of them*, within their hearts were inflamed. They received the visible presence of God in the form of fire, and their hearts were filled with the flames of His love. The Holy Ghost Himself is love; hence St. John says: *God is charity [love]* (1 John 4: 8). Whosoever, therefore, desires God with all his soul, has already obtained Him Whom he loves; for no one is able to love God, if he has not gained Him Whom he loves. Now behold, if one of you were asked whether he love God, he would with boldness and quietness of spirit answer: 'I do love God.' Yet at the very beginning of this day's Gospel we heard the Divine Truth say: *If anyone love Me, he will keep My word*. The test of love, then, is whether it is shown by works. Hence the same John says in his Epistle: *If any man say, I love God, and keep not His commandments, he is a liar* (1 John 4: 20: 3). We do indeed love God and keep His commandments, when we deny ourselves the gratification of our appetites. Whosoever goes after unlawful desires, does not love God, for he is acting against the will of God.

II. *And My Father will love him, and We will come to him, and will make Our abode with him*. O, beloved brethren, consider what a dignity it is to have God abiding as a guest in our heart! Surely, if some rich man, or some powerful friend were to come into our house, we would hasten to have the whole house cleaned, lest perhaps the eye of the entering friend should be offended by something. So let him, who wishes to make his heart a dwelling of God, cleanse it from all filth of sinful works. For what says the Truth? *We will come to him, and will make Our abode with him*. There are some hearts into which God comes, but makes not His abode therein. With a certain contrition they feel His presence, but in the time of temptation they forget that which made them sorry; and so they turn again to commit sin, as though they had never repented. Whosoever truly loves God, and keeps all His commandments, will receive the Redeemer into his heart, and be the abode of God, because Divine love will enchain him so strongly that, in the time of temptation, he will not be separated from that love. The true love of God is made manifest by our firmness amidst temptations, and our courage in overcoming them; for it is certain that we are the further from the love of supernal things, the more pleasure we find in the sinful enjoyments of this life. Therefore our Saviour added: *He that loveth Me not, keepeth not My words.* Examine, then, yourselves, beloved brethren, whether you really love God; and do not believe what your mind answers if you have not the testimony of your good works. The heart, the tongue, and the whole life must give testimony; for real love cannot remain idle. Love works great things, and as soon as it ceases to work, it ceases to exist. *And the word which you have heard is not Mine, but the Fathers Who sent Me.* You know, beloved brethren, that the only-begotten Son Who speaks is the Word of the Father, and that the word He announced is not the Son's, but the Father's word, because the Son is the Word of the Father. But how do these words of Jesus — *These things have I spoken unto you, abiding with you* — agree with His other words promising His disciples to be with them *all days, even to the consummation of the world?* This will be easily understood, when we remember that the Word made flesh will after a certain time secede from the world corporally, yet remain with us by virtue of His all-powerful and invisible Divinity.

III. And our Lord added: *But the Paraclete, the Holy Ghost, Whom the Father will send in My Name, He will teach you all things, and bring all things to your mind, whatsoever I shall have said to you.* You know, beloved brethren, that the Greek word *Paraclete* means in our tongue *intercessor* or *advocate*, because the Holy Ghost defends, so to speak, the poor sinner before the tribunal of the Father's justice. Therefore, when it is said that the Holy Ghost, though one and the same with the Father and the Son, is interceding for sinners, it means that by His inspirations He moves our hearts to pray to God, as St. Paul says: *We know not what we should pray for as we ought, but the Spirit Himself asketh for us with unspeakable groanings* (Rom. 8: 26). Should you ask how it is that the Holy Ghost, not being inferior to, but as infinitely great and powerful as the Father, nevertheless intercedes for us, you will understand this to mean that He fills our hearts and inflames our desires to send our petitions to heaven and lay our necessities before the throne of the Almighty. He is also called the *Comforter*, because He takes away the sorrowfulness caused by the remembrance of our sins, and inspires us with the hope of being pardoned by God. Our Lord also says that the Holy Spirit will teach us all things, because the words of the most eloquent preacher would be useless, did not the Holy Ghost speak to the hearts of the hearers. Therefore, do not attribute to the art and eloquence of the teacher whatsoever you understand about the Divine doctrine, but to the Spirit of Truth speaking in your soul; for does it not every day happen that the voice of the preacher reaches the ears of his hearers, yet the meaning of his words is not understood by all in the same manner? The voice is the same, but the understanding is not the same, because the divine Spirit, this invisible Teacher, opens the mind of some, and they comprehend the doctrine, whilst others remain unmoved by the same sound of the words. St. John teaches this truth, when he says: *His unction teacheth you all things* (1 John 2: 27); and we understand that, were not the unction of the Holy Ghost poured forth into our hearts, the words of the preacher could not teach us. But why should we insist on this fact that human eloquence is not able to convince us of the truths of salvation, since God Himself would in vain speak for our instruction, did not the unction of the Spirit move our hearts at the same time? We are aware that God, knowing Cain's sinful intention to kill his brother, spoke to him, and said: *Thou hast sinned; now stop* (Gen. 4, iuxta 70.). Yet, though he heard the voice of God warning him not to stain his hands with the innocent blood of his brother, he remained deaf to that voice, because the unction of the Holy Spirit had not entered his heart, nor moved him to give ear to that voice. However, there is another difficulty. Our Saviour, speaking of the Holy Ghost, said to His disciples: *And He will bring all things to your mind, whatsoever I shall have said to you.* This seems to imply that the Son of God is superior to the Holy Ghost. But when we consider the words *bring all things to your mind*, we understand that the Holy Ghost does not lower Himself by such suggestions, as if drawing these things out of the innermost of the souls, but by His supernatural light makes known the truths which before were hidden to them. *Peace I leave with you, My peace I give you.* These words of our Lord mean that He leaves His peace with those who endeavour to walk on the road to salvation, and that He will give His peace for ever to those who enter the kingdom prepared for them.

IV. After briefly explaining the words of this day's Gospel, let us now give our attention to the mystery of this solemn festival. You heard, beloved brethren, that on this day the Holy Ghost came down upon the Apostles in parted tongues, as it were, of fire, and that they began to speak with divers tongues, according as the Holy Ghost gave them to speak. By this great wonder we understand that the holy Church, filled with the same spirit as the Apostles, and preaching to the nations of the world, will be heard by all of them. Indeed, when God, to confound the arrogance of the people building the Tower of Babel, also confounded their tongue, He in the same way united all languages in those who humbly feared Him, so that humility found its power there, where pride and arrogance felt their weakness and received their punishment.

V. Now let us examine why the Holy Ghost, one and co-eternal with the Father and the Son, appeared under the element of fire; why He appeared in fire and tongues; why He at one time appeared as a dove, and at another as fire; why He showed Himself as a dove when coming down upon the Son of God, and as tongues of fire upon the Apostles (Acts 2: 2); so that the dove was not visible when the Holy Ghost came upon the Apostles, neither the fire when He appeared upon the Person of the Son of God. These questions will be answered, when we first say that the Holy Ghost, co-eternal with the Father and the Son, showed Himself as fire, because God Himself is a spiritual and invisible fire, according to the words of St. Paul: *For our God is a consuming fire* (Heb. 12: 29). He is indeed a fire, for He consumes the rust of our sins; and this has been confirmed by the words of the Eternal Truth: *I am come to cast fire on the earth; and what will I but that it be kindled* (Luke 12: 49). The earth of which He speaks are the worldly hearts of men, which, being filled with earthly thoughts, are, so to speak, trodden upon by the infernal spirits. But when, through the breathing of the Holy Ghost, the Almighty sends His Divine fire, the carnal hearts of men are at once inflamed by His love; the earth is enkindled by this heavenly fire, and the worldly and cold hearts forsake the sinful desires, by which they are bound to this world, and they endeavour to belong only to God, now the sole object of their love. The Holy Ghost comes in fire, because by Him our cold hearts are warmed and filled with desires of eternity. And, being co-eternal with the Son, the same Spirit appeared in the shape of tongues of fire, and thus showed the intimate relationship between the tongue and the Word. For the Son is the Word of the Father, and since the Holy Ghost and the Son have the same Divine Nature, it was fit that this Spirit should appear in the form of a tongue, this being the organ of words. The Holy Ghost was seen in tongues, for he that receives this Spirit will confess the Word of God, the only-begotten Son; and he cannot deny the Word, since he already possesses the tongue of the Spirit. Again He appeared in the shape of tongues *of fire*, because all those filled with the gifts of the Holy Ghost are by Him inflamed with love and endowed with eloquence. The true teachers of the doctrine of Jesus Christ have, so to speak, *fiery tongues*, because they preach the love of God, and inflame the hearts of the hearers; for the most learned sermons are unprofitable, unless sparks of that holy fire are brought by them into the hearts of men. The heat of this fire was felt by the two disciples going to Emmaus, and, being taught by the Eternal Truth, they said: *Was not our heart burning within us, whilst He spoke in the way, and opened to us the Scriptures?* (Luke 24: 32). These are the effects produced in a soul listening to zealous preaching: the heart is inflamed, the ice of torpidness is melted, holy desires are aroused, and the longings for earthly things are removed. Real love, filling the soul, awakens in it sighs and tears; but by these pains, suffered under the yoke of Divine love, the real love is nourished and strengthened. Such a soul finds its delight in hearing the word of God and the Divine commandments, and these commandments are as many torches enlightening and guiding the soul on the road to salvation, whereupon it had been walking carelessly and inactively, but now zealously, because strengthened by the word of God. Thus Moses says: *In His right hand a fiery law* (Deut. 33: 2); for by the left hand are indicated the damned, one day to be placed at the left hand of the Judge; whereas the right hand shows the elect, who could not behold the fiery law in the right hand of the Almighty without being inflamed with fiery love to fulfil that law. As soon as the words of the law are heard, these souls find no other rest but in the sweetness of this fire consuming them. But as the Holy Spirit showed Himself under the form of fires, and on another occasion appeared under the form of a dove, this twofold symbol meant the effects produced by Him in the hearts of those who receive Him — that is, simplicity and ardour of love. By Him we are made artless through purity, and ardent through Divine zeal. For simplicity without zeal cannot please God, just as zeal without an artless heart cannot be accepted by Him. We hear, therefore, the Truth say to His Apostles: *Be ye, therefore, wise as serpents, and simple as doves* (Matt, 10: 16); meaning that wise zeal must animate simplicity, whilst simplicity is to temperate our zeal. This is corroborated by the great Apostle admonishing us in these words: *Brethren, do not become children in sense, but in malice be children, and in sense be perfect* (1 Cor. 14: 20). And Holy Scripture, speaking of Job as a simple man, says: *And this man was simple, and upright, and fearing God*. By which we are taught that there can be no uprightness without simplicity, nor simplicity agreeable to God without uprightness. And since the Holy Ghost came to teach us both these virtues, He appeared as a dove and as fire, in order to teach us meekness and peacefulness under the form of a dove, and ardent love for justice under the form of fire — virtues imparted to those that receive Him.

VI. The motive why the same Holy Spirit came upon the Redeemer as a dove, and upon the Apostles in tongues of fire, is apparent when we consider that the wrath of the justice of the Son of God could not have been borne by us, had He appeared in fire to judge and punish, before attracting us through the sweetness of His blessings. The Son of God became man to redeem all men, and He showed Himself full of meekness that we might find His yoke light and amiable; also because He wished to convert and to be merciful to all in this life, since in His justice He must condemn some of them on the day of His wrath. This is the reason why the Holy Ghost showed Himself first as a dove upon Him who had come to forgive the sins of men, and not to punish. But if on this day He appeared in consuming fire, it means that the Apostles, being mere men, and consequently sinners, were to be purified in the fire of Divine love, cleansed by their own penance from their faults, though God in His infinite mercy is always ready to forgive sins; for let us not imagine that the Apostles, entrusted with that heavenly ministry, were without sin. St. John writes: *If we say that we have no sin, we deceive ourselves, and the truth is not in us* (1 John 1: 8). The Holy Ghost came in fire upon men, and as a dove upon our Lord; for Christ has borne our sins patiently and mercifully; whereas we are carefully to examine our sins and burn them in the fire of penance and ardent love of God.

38. WHIT-MONDAY

GOSPEL: John 3: 16-21. *At that time*: Jesus said to Nicodemus: God so loved the world as to give His only-begotten Son; that whosoever believeth in Him, may not perish, but may have life everlasting. For God sent not His Son into the world, to judge the world, but that the world may be saved by Him. He that believeth in Him is not judged. But he that doth not believe is already judged: because he believeth not in the Name of the only-begotten Son of God. And this is the judgment: because the light is come into the world, and men loved darkness rather than the light: for their works were evil. For every one that doth evil hateth the light, and cometh not to the light, that his works may not be reproved. But he that doth truth, cometh to the light, that his works may be made manifest, because they are done in God.

HOMILY BY ST. AUGUSTINE
Tract 12 on St. John

I. JESUS CHRIST, THE DIVINE PHYSICIAN, IS COME into the world to heal the sick, as far as it lies in the Physician. For that man, who will not observe the orders of that Physician, is his own destroyer. He is come a Saviour to the world. And why is He called the Saviour of the world, but because He is come not to judge the world, *but that the world may be saved by Him*. Thou dost not choose to be saved by Him; of thy own self thou shalt be judged. And why do I say *shalt be judged*? See what He says: *He that believeth in Him, is not judged*; but he that doth not believe. What dost thou expect He is going to say, but *is judged*? He says, *is already judged*. The judgment has not yet appeared, yet it has already taken place; for the Lord knows them that are His; knows who shall persevere for the crown, persevere for the flame. He knows the wheat on His threshing-floor, and knows the chaff;

knows the good corn, and knows the tares. *He that believeth not is already judged.* Why judged? *Because he believeth not in the Name of the only-begotten Son of God.*

11. *And this is the judgment: because the light is come into the world, and men loved darkness rather than the light; for their works were evil.* But, my brethren, whose works will the Lord find to be good? The works of none. He finds the works of all evil. In what sense, then, is it said that some have done truth, and are come to the light? For this is what follows: *But he that doth truth, cometh to the light, that his works may be made manifest, because they are done in God.* In what sense have some done a good work to come to the light — that is, to Christ? And how have some loved darkness? For if He finds all men sinners, and heals all of sin, and that serpent, in which the death of the Lord was figured, healed them that were bitten, and on account of the serpent's bite the serpent was erected, that is, the death of the Lord, because of mortal men whom He found sinful; how are we to understand that *this is the judgment; because the light is come into the world, and men loved darkness rather than the light; for their works were evil?* What is this? Whose works were good? Hast Thou not come to justify the godless? But He says: *They loved darkness rather than the light.* Here He makes the great point; for many loved their sins, many confessed their sins. Now, he that confesses his sins and accuses his sins, henceforth works with God. God accuses thy sins, and if thou also accusest, thou art united with God. There are, as it were, two things: man and sinner. That thou art called man, is God's doing; that thou art called sinner, is man's own doing. Blot out what was thy doing, that God may save what was His doing. It behoves thee to hate thine own work in thee, and to love the work of God in thee. Now, when thy own works begin to be displeasing to thee, from that time thy good works begin, because thou accusest thy evil works. The confession of evil works is the beginning of good works. Thou dost truth, and comest to the light. *What means thou dost truth?* If thou dost not fondle thyself, nor soothe, nor flatter thy self, and dost not say, *I am just,* whilst thou art a sinner, thus thou beginnest to do the truth. Thou comest to the light, that thy works may be manifest

38. WHIT-MONDAY

that they are done in God. For thy sins, the very thing that gave thee displeasure, would not have displeased thee, had not God shone in thee, and His truth showed them to thee. But the man who, being admonished, loves his sins, hates the light admonishing him, and flees from it, that his works, which he loves, may not be proved as evil. Whereas he that does truth, accuses his evil works in himself, spares not himself, forgives not himself, that God may forgive him; for he himself acknowledges that which he desires to be forgiven by God, and he comes to the light, to which he is thankful for showing him what he should hate in himself. He says to God: *Turn away Thy face from my sins*; and with what assurance says it, unless he adds: *For I know my iniquity, and my sin is always before me* (Ps. 50: 3). Let that be before thee which thou desirest not to be before God. But if thou wilt put thy sin behind thee, God will force it back before thy eyes; and this He will do at a time when there will be no more fruit of repentance.

III. My brethren, run, that the darkness come not upon you. Awake to your salvation; awake while there is time. Let none be kept back from the temple of God, none kept back from the work of the Lord, none called away from continual prayer, none be defrauded of the customary devotion. Awake, then, while it is day; the day shines, Christ is the day. He is ready to forgive sins to them that acknowledge their sins; ready to punish those who defend themselves, and who boast that they are just, and think themselves to be something, when they are nothing. But he that walks in His love and mercy, and being free from these great and deadly sins, such crimes as murder, theft, adultery, but is also sorry for those which seem to be small, sins of thought or of tongue, or of want of moderation in things permitted, he does the truth of confession and comes to the light in good works, seeing that many small sins, if they be neglected, are fatal. Small are the drops which swell the river, small the grains of sand, but if such sand be heaped up, it presses and crushes. The bilge-water allowed to accumulate in the ships hold, does the same thing as a rushing wave. By little and little it leaks in through the hold; and by long leaking in and no pumping out it sinks the vessel. Now, what is this pumping out, but that by good works, by sighing, fasting, giving, forgiving, we take care that sins overwhelm us not? Truly the path of this life is troublesome, full of temptations; in prosperity let it not lift us up; in adversity let it not crush us. He who gave the happiness of this world, gave it for your comfort, not for your ruin. Again, He who scourges you in this world, does it for your improvement, not for your condemnation. You must bear Him as a Father Who corrects you for your training, lest you feel Him as a Judge Who will punish you. These things we tell you every day, and they must be said often, because they are good and wholesome.

39. TRINITY SUNDAY

GOSPEL: Matt. 28: 18-20. *At that time*: Jesus said to His disciples: All power is given to Me in heaven and in earth. Going, therefore, teach ye all nations; baptizing them in the Name of the Father, and of the Son, and of the Holy Ghost. Teaching them to observe all things whatsoever I have commanded you; and behold I am with you all days, even to the consummation of the world.

HOMILY BY ST. GREGORY OF NAZIANZUS
Treatise on the Faith

I. IS THERE A CATHOLIC IN THE WORLD WHO DOES not know that the Father is a very Father, the Son a very Son, and the Holy Ghost a very Holy Ghost? The Lord Himself said to His Apostles: *All power is given to Me in heaven and in earth. Going, therefore, teach ye all nations; baptizing them in the name of the Father, and of the Son, and of the Holy Ghost.* This is that perfect TRINITY, consisting in UNITY, of Whom we testify that His substance is ONE; for we make no division in God as divisions are made in bodies; but we testify that, according to the power of the Divine Nature, which exists not in matter, the Persons have a real existence, and that God is ONE. We also believe that these three names and the Persons meant by them, are all of one Substance, one Majesty, and one Power; and we do not say, as some have dreamt, that the begetting of the Son of God is an extension from one part to another part, neither do we say that He is the Word in the sense of a mere sound uttered by a voice, and not a reality.

II. We testify, therefore, that God is ONE, because this ONENESS of His Majesty forbids the use of the plural form of speech saying *Gods*. It is Catholic language to say *Father and Son*; but we cannot and must not say that the Father and the Son are two Gods. And that, not because the Son of God is not by Himself God — for He is true God of true God — but because we know that the Son of God is not from elsewhere, but from the One Father, therefore we say that God is ONE. This is the doctrine which the Prophets and the Apostles have transmitted to us; and it is the doctrine which our Lord Himself taught, when He said: *I and the Father are one* (John 10: 30). *One* refers to the one Divinity, as I said; whereas *are* means the Persons. Thus the Apostle says: *To us there is but one God, the Father, of Whom are all things, and we unto Him; and our Lord Jesus Christ, by Whom are all things, and we by Him. But there is not knowledge in everyone* (1 Cor. 8: 6, 7). Concerning this truth, and having explained these words which were a stumbling-block, not to me who know what I am saying, but to others, I believe to have removed every occasion of a false interpretation. The profession of faith is manifest: for PERSON agrees with the words used, while the Divinity is ONE. Should anything else in these words seem ambiguous to the reader, let him refer to the real meaning of the words. Though this meaning of the words is clear, the obstinacy of a biased intellect is often shown; and since our exposition agrees with the truth, the words also ought to be clear to a sincere mind.

40. FIRST SUNDAY AFTER PENTECOST

GOSPEL: Luke 6: 36-42. *At that time*: Jesus said to His disciples: Be ye merciful, as your Father also is merciful. Judge not, and you shall not be judged. Condemn not, and you shall not be condemned. Forgive, and you shall be forgiven. Give, and it shall be given to you; good measure, and pressed down, and shaken together, and running over, shall be given into your bosom. For with the same measure that you shall mete withal, it shall be measured to you again. And He spoke also to them a similitude: Can the blind lead the blind? Do they not both fall into the ditch? The disciple is not above his master; but every one shall be perfect, if he be as his master. And why seest thou the mote in thy brother's eye; but the beam that is in thy own eye thou considerest not? Or how canst thou say to thy brother: Brother, let me pull the mote out of thy eye, when thou thyself seest not the beam in thy own eye? Hypocrite, cast first the beam out of thy own eye, and then thou shalt see clearly to take out the mote from thy brother's eye.

HOMILY BY ST. AUGUSTINE
Fifteenth Sermon on St. Matthew, Words of Our Lord

I. THERE ARE TWO WORKS OF MERCY WHICH deliver us, and which are briefly laid down by our Lord in the Gospel: *Forgive, and you shall be forgiven. Give, and it shall be given to you.* The words *forgive, and you shall be forgiven* are a promise of pardon; *give, and it shall be given to you* relate to doing kindnesses. As to what He says of pardoning, thou hast sins which thou wishest to be pardoned thee, and thou hast another, who trespassed against thee, whom thou canst forgive. Again, as to doing kindnesses, there are beggars that ask of thee, and thou art God's beggar. For when we pray, we are all God's beggars. We stand before the door of the Great Householder; we even fall down on our knees; we groan in supplications, wishing to receive something, and this something is God Himself. What does a beggar ask of thee? Bread. And what dost thou ask of God but Christ, Who says: *I am the living bread, which came down from heaven* (John 6: 51). Would you be forgiven? Forgive. *Forgive, and ye shall be forgiven.* Would you receive? *Give, and it shall be given to you.*

11. But now, why should there be a difficulty in such a plain precept? In this question of forgiveness, when pardon is asked and is due from him who should grant it, there may be a difficulty to us, as it occurred to St. Peter: *How often shall my brother offend against me, and I forgive him? till seven times? Jesus saith to him: I say not to thee, till seven times; but till seventy times seven times* (Matt, 18: 21, 22). Now reckon up how often thy brother hath sinned against thee. If thou canst reach the seventy-eighth fault, so as to go beyond the seventy times seven, thou mayst take revenge. Is this, then, what He really means? and is it in reality so, that if he shall sin *seventy times seven,* thou shouldst forgive him; but if he shall sin seventy times and eight, it will be lawful for thee not to forgive? No; for I dare say and venture to assert, that should he even sin seventy-eight times, thou must forgive. Yea, if he should sin, as I have said, seventy-eight times, forgive. And if he sin a hundred times, forgive. Why need I say this, and so often? Because, as often as he shall sin, forgive him. Have I, then, taken upon me to overstep the measure of my Lord? He fixed the limit of forgiving in the number seventy-seven; shall I presume to go beyond this limit? This is not so; I have not presumed to go beyond. I have heard our Lord Himself speaking through His Apostle, where no measure nor number is fixed. For He says: *Forgiving one another, if any have a complaint against another. Even as God hath forgiven you in Christ* (Col. 3: 13, Eph. 4: 32). You hear the rule. If Christ has forgiven thy sins *seventy-seven times* only, and has pardoned thee to this point only, and refused to pardon beyond it, then do thou also fix this limit, and be loath to go beyond. But if Christ has found thousands of sins upon sins, and has yet forgiven them all,

do not withdraw thy mercy, but ask the forgiveness of that large number. It was not without a special motive that the Lord said seventy-seven times, because there is no trespass whatever which thou oughtest not to forgive. See the servant in the parable, who, being a debtor, and himself having a debtor, owed ten thousand talents. And I suppose that ten thousand talents are at least ten thousand sins, for I will not say that but one talent includes all sins. And how much did the fellow-servant owe him? He owed a hundred denarii. Now, is not this more than *seventy and seven*? And yet the Lord was angry, because he did not forgive. For not only is a hundred more than seventy-seven, but a hundred denarii are perhaps a thousand *pence*. And what is this to ten thousand talents of gold or silver?

III. Let us, therefore, be ready to forgive all the trespasses which are committed against us, if we wish to be forgiven. For if we consider our sins, and reckon up what we do in deed, what by the eye, what by the ear, what by thought, and what by numberless motions, I know not whether we be able to say that our sleep is free from sin. Therefore, we daily beg, we daily entreat God in prayer, and say to Him: *Forgive us our trespasses, as we forgive them that trespass against us* (Matt 6: 12). And what trespasses? All, or a certain part? Thou wilt answer: All. So, then, must we do with our debtors. This is the rule thou layest down, this the condition thou speakest of, this the agreement thou dost mention when saying: *Forgive us our trespasses, as we forgive*.

IV. What, then, is the meaning of *seventy-seven*? Listen, for it is a great mystery — a wonderful sacrament. Justice, as you know, consists in the observance of the Law of God; this is true. And the Law is set forth in ten precepts. This is the reason why the servant in the parable is said to owe *ten thousand* talents. This is the memorable decalogue written by the finger of God, and delivered to His servant Moses. He owed *ten thousand talents*; and this signifies all sins, with respect to the number of the Law. And the other servant owed *a hundred denarii*, equally derived from the same number, since a hundred times hundred make ten thousand, and ten times ten make a hundred. There was no departure from the number of the Law. Both are debtors, and both implore and beg for pardon; but the wicked, ungrateful servant would not repay what *he* had received, and would not grant to his fellow-servant the mercy which had been undeservedly accorded to him. Now consider what sin is. The law is denoted by *ten*, and sin by *eleven*. Why by eleven? Because to get to eleven there is the transgression of ten; when you have passed beyond the ten, you come to eleven. This high mystery was figured out when the tabernacle was ordered to be built. There are many things mentioned there in numbers, which are a great mystery. Among others, curtains of goats' hair were ordered to be made to cover the top of the tabernacle, not *ten*, but *eleven*, because by goats' hair (haircloth) is signified the confession of sins. Do you require anything more? Would you know why all sins are contained in this number *seventy-seven*? Seven is usually put for a whole, because in seven days the revolution of time is completed, and when the seventh is ended, it returns to the first again, that the same revolution may be continued. Therefore, He spoke of all sins when He said *seventy times seven*; for multiply that *eleven* seven times, and it makes seventy-seven. Therefore, He would have all sins forgiven by marking them out by the number seventy-seven. Let no one, then, refuse to forgive, lest it be refused to him when he prays. God says: *Forgive, and you shall be forgiven*; I have forgiven thee first; do at least forgive after that. If thou wilt not forgive, I will call thee back, and again put upon thee all that I had remitted to thee. The Truth does not speak falsely. Christ neither deceives nor is deceived; and He said at the end of the parable: *So also shall My heavenly Father do to you.* You find a Father, imitate your Father; for if you will not imitate Him, you renounce your inheritance of sons of God. *So also shall My heavenly Father do to you, if you forgive not everyone his brother from your heart.* Do not say with the tongue, I forgive, and put off forgiving in the heart; for by His threat of vengeance God shows the punishment. Man can hear your voice; God looks into the heart and conscience. If you say, *I forgive*, forgive. Better it is that you should be violent in words, and forgive in the heart, than to be gentle in words and relentless in your heart.

V. Unruly boys will beg and take it hard when we are about to chastise them, and they say: *I have sinned, but forgive.* Well, I have forgiven, and he sins again. *Forgive me,* he cries, and I have forgiven him. He sins a third time, and is forgiven; a fourth time. Let him be chastised, and he will say: *What! have I tired you out to seventy-seven times?* Now, if by such exceptions the severity of discipline were to sleep, I am sure that wickedness would rage with impunity upon the suppression of discipline. What is to be done? Let us reprove with words, and, if necessary, with scourges; but let us forgive the sin, and cast away the memory of it from our heart. Therefore, the Lord added, *from your heart*; so that, though through affection discipline must be exercised, gentleness may not depart from the heart. What is so kind and gentle as the surgeon with his knife? He that is to be cut cries out, yet cut he is; he that is to be cauterized cries, but he is cauterized. There is no cruelty in this. The surgeon is cruel against the wounded part, that the patient may be cured; for should the wound be too softly dealt with, the man would be lost. Thus, then, my brethren, my advice is that we love our brethren, though they may have sinned against us; that we do not let affection for them depart from our hearts, and that, when necessary, we exercise discipline towards them, lest wickedness increase by the relaxation of discipline, and we should be accused on God's behalf, since it is said to us: *Them that sin reprove before all; that the rest also may have fear* (1 Tim. 5: 20). If the sin be secret, rebuke it in secret; if the sin be public and open, rebuke it publicly, that the sinner may be reformed and *that the rest also may have fear.*

41. FEAST OF CORPUS CHRISTI

GOSPEL: John 6: 56-59. *At that time*: Jesus said to the multitude of the Jews: My Flesh is meat indeed, and My Blood is drink indeed. He that eateth My Flesh and drinketh My Blood, abideth in Me and I in him. As the living Father hath sent Me, and I live by the Father, so he that eateth Me, the same also shall live by Me. This is the Bread that came down from heaven; not as your fathers did eat manna and are dead. He that eateth this Bread shall live for ever.

HOMILY BY ST. AUGUSTINE
Tract 26 on St. John

I. BY THE USE OF MEAT AND DRINK MEN SEEK TO attain to this, that they should neither hunger nor thirst any more. Yet, there is but one Meat and one Drink which renders those who feed thereon incorruptible and immortal—that is, the very communion with that general assembly and Church of God's holy children, where there shall be peace and unity full and perfect. Therefore it is, as men of God before our times understood, that our Lord Jesus Christ set before us His Body and His Blood in the likeness of things, which from being many, are reduced into one. In one loaf there are many grains, and in one cup of wine, the juice of many grapes. And now He explains how that which He spoke of comes to pass, and what it is to eat His Body and drink His Blood. *He that eateth My Flesh, and drinketh My Blood, abideth in Me, and I in him.* To abide in Christ, therefore, and to have Him dwelling in us, is for a man to eat that meat and to drink that cup. And he that dwells not in Christ, and in whom Christ abides not, undoubtedly does not spiritually eat His Flesh nor drink His Blood, though he carnally and visibly press the Sacrament with his teeth. But rather *he eateth and drinketh judgment to himself*, because, being unclean, he dares to come to that secret and holy thing of Christ, whereunto no one draws nigh worthily, unless he be pure; for of such it is said: *Blessed are the clean of heart, for they shall see God* (Matt. 5: 8).

11. *As the living Father hath sent Me, and I live by the Father; so he that eateth Me, the same also shall live by Me.* Notice that our Lord does not say, As I eat the Father, and live by the Father; so he that eats Me, the same shall live by Me. For the Son, Who was begotten equal to the Father, does not become better by the participation of the Father, just as we are made better by the participation of the Son through the unity of His Body and Blood, signified by the eating and drinking. We live by Him, eating Him — that is, by receiving Him as the eternal life, which we had not from ourselves. He lives by the Father, being sent by Him, because *He humbled Himself, becoming obedient unto death, even to the death of the cross* (Phil. 2: 8). *I live by the Father as One that is greater than I* (John 14: 28). Just as we also live by Him, Who is greater than we are; and this results from His being sent. The sending is, in fact, the humbling Himself, *taking the form of a servant*; and this is rightly understood, while also the Son's equality with the Father is entirely preserved. For the Father is greater than the Son, considered as man only; but He has the Son equal to Himself as God; whilst the same is both God and man — Son of God and Son of man, the one Christ Jesus. If these words are rightly understood, then we know why He said: *As the living Father hath sent Me, and I live by the Father; so he that eateth Me, the same also shall live by Me.* Just as if He had said: My humbling Myself — in that He sent Me — effected that I should live by the Father that is, that I should refer My earthly life to Him as the greater. But that anyone should live by Me is effected by that communion in which he eats Me. Therefore, being humbled, *I live by the Father*, and man, being raised up, lives by Me. But if it was said, I live by the Father, so as to mean that He is of the Father, not the Father of Him, it was said without any detriment of equality. And yet, when saying, *He that eateth Me, the same shall live by Me*, He did not mean to say that His own

equality was the same as our equality, but He thereby showed the grace of the Mediator.

III. *This is the Bread that came down from heaven,* that by eating it we may live for ever, since we cannot have eternal life from ourselves. *Not,* He says, *as your fathers did eat manna and are dead. He that eateth this Bread shall live for ever.* That those fathers are dead, He wished us to understand as meaning that they do not live for ever. For even those who eat Christ shall without doubt die temporally; but they live for ever, because Christ is life everlasting.

42. SECOND SUNDAY AFTER PENTECOST

GOSPEL: Luke 14: 16-24. *At that time*: Jesus spoke this parable to the Pharisees: A certain man made a great supper, and invited many. And he sent his servant at the hour of supper to say to them that were invited, that they should come, for now all things are ready. And they began all at once to make excuse. The first: said to him: I have bought a farm, and must needs go out and see it; I pray thee, hold me excused. And another said: I have bought five yoke of oxen, and I go to try them: I pray thee, hold me excused. And another said: I have married a wife, and therefore I cannot come. And the servant returning, told these things to his lord. Then the master of the house, being angry, said to his servant: Go out quickly into the streets and lanes of the city, and bring in hither the poor, and the feeble, and the blind, and the lame. And the servant said: Lord, it is done as thou hast commanded, and yet there is room. And the lord said to the servant: Go out into the high ways and hedges, and compel them to come in, that my house may be filled. But I say unto you, that none of those men that were invited, shall taste of my supper.

HOMILY BY POPE ST. GREGORY, PREACHED IN THE CHURCH OF SS. PHILIP AND JAMES, ON THE SECOND SUNDAY AFTER PENTECOST
Thirty-Sixth Homily on the Gospels

I. BETWEEN THE PLEASURES OF THE BODY, beloved brethren, and the pleasures of the mind, there is that difference, that the pleasures of the body, when we miss them, raise up a great longing after them, and when we greedily taste them, our fulness soon produces dislike and aversion. Whereas the pleasures of the mind seem disagreeable as long as we lack them, but when we fill ourselves with them we feel hungry after them, and the more we feed on them, the more hungry we get after them. Bodily or corporal pleasures are full of sweetness when taken, but soon excite nausea; whereas in the spiritual feeding, which at first seems bitter, real pleasure is found at the end. What is sensual stirs up our appetite, yet we cannot take it for a time without feeling a strong aversion against it. But what is spiritual excites the appetite in the very act of eating. We see, therefore, that souls tasting spiritual dainties, feel greater hunger and thirst for Divine things through the sweetness they taste. If we taste them not, we cannot love them, for we know not how sweet they are. And who can love that thing whereof he knows nothing? We are, therefore, invited by the Psalmist, saying: *O taste, and see that the Lord is sweet* (Ps. 33: 9); that is, as it were, if you taste not, you shall not know His goodness, but let your heart once taste the food of life, then, indeed, having tasted and proved its sweetness, you will be able to love Him. These are the dainties which were lost to man, when he sinned in the earthly paradise; and he lost Paradise when he shut his own mouth against the sweet bread, whereof if any man eat he shall live for ever. And as we are born of the first man under the afflictions of this pilgrimage, and came into this world smitten with aversion, we know not what to desire. And the disease of this aversion grows worse, the more our soul is estranged from this bread of sweetness. We are no longer hungering after interior dainties, since we have lost the use of eating them. And so in this aversion we starve, and the sickness of long fasting destroys our health. We would not eat of the interior sweetness made ready for us, and we love outward things, even our starvation; yet the infinite Goodness does not forsake those by whom It is forsaken.

11. This goodness of God recalls to our mind these holy dainties, so often despised, and by trying to shake off our sluggishness, invites us to overcome the aversion we feel against this spiritual food. Listen to the words of our Redeemer: *A certain man made a great supper, and invited many.* This man is the same of whom

the prophet said: *It is a Man, and who hath known Him?* (Jer. 17: 9). He prepared a great supper, for He wished to give us the fill of interior sweetness. Many were invited, but a few came; for it often happens that some of those who receive the light of faith, keep away from the eternal banquet through a bad life that is opposed to their calling. This man *sends out his servant at the hour of the supper to say to them that were invited, that they should come.* And what is the meaning of these words, *the hour of the supper?* The end of the world, as St. Paul explains, saying: *All these things happened to them in figure, and they are written for our correction, upon whom the ends of the world are come* (1 Cor. 10: 11). And since we know that the Lord calls us *now*, because the hour of the supper, to which we are invited, has come, we cannot find any excuse not to appear at it, especially because, on account of the offered and yet neglected grace, we must fear that the favourable hour will never return. Then, this banquet prepared by God, is called in the Gospel a supper, to give us to understand that, supper being the last meal of the day, the banquet spoken of means the eternal supper prepared by God at the end of the world. And who is the servant sent out to call *them that were invited*, if not the preachers bidden by God to announce His truths? As one of these servants, God has sent us, though unworthy of this high office, being bowed down under the burden of our own sins. God has sent us to you on this day; and whilst I speak to you that you may be edified and instructed, I obey the commands of the Divine Householder. Exhorting you to despise the world, I am like the servant of the Gospel, and I invite you to the supper prepared for you by God. Do not consider my person, but only my office; for if you see in me a servant unworthy to invite you, your esteem ought, at all events, to be given to the pleasures of the spiritual banquet to which you are invited. You know, beloved brethren, that a master, being of a high rank, often has a servant who, seeming low, is despised. But when this servant brings a message to his master's friends, it is gladly accepted in consideration of the master, no attention being paid to the faults or shortcomings of the servant. Do likewise, beloved brethren, and be not disturbed by my unworthiness, but highly esteem the call of the Lord. Obey, and promptly, the invitation of the Divine Householder to His Banquet. Prepare your hearts, and expel from them the mortal indifference which keeps you away from His sanctifying Banquet. And should your minds be still carnal, desiring only corporeal food, consider that the Flesh of your God is offered to you for the nourishment of your souls. The sinless Lamb of God, killed for you, is prepared for you on God's altar.

III. How shall we be made worthy of this invitation? *And they began all at once to make excuse*, says the Gospel. God in His infinite love offers, without being asked for, an actual favour, which we could not expect, not even by our most ardent desires; yet this favour is despised. He promises food for our eternal happiness; yet everyone makes excuse not to accept it. Let us take an ordinary example to understand higher things. A mighty Prince invites a poor man to his banquet. You will easily imagine that this poor man will be overwhelmed with joy, that he will express his gratitude with modest and humble words, and, taking off his tattered garments, will endeavour to appear one of the first in the banquet-hall, not to be before-handed by another. This poor man would certainly behave in this manner. And we are invited by God Himself to His Banquet, and we make excuse, and do not appear. Yet it seems to me, your answer in your heart will be that you do not excuse yourselves, and that you will be only too glad to partake of this supper prepared for you.

IV. Your testimony seems plausible enough, were it not for your own conscience telling you that you are inclined to love the world more than heaven, and corporeal and perishable things more than spiritual and invisible goods. Consider the motives alleged by the invited guests for not appearing at the supper. *The first said: I have bought a farm, and must needs go out and see it; I pray thee hold me excused.* This farm he speaks of, what does it mean but the earthly and perishable goods? He goes out to see it, for he is only busy with and fettered by exterior and temporal possessions. *And another said: I have bought five yoke of oxen, and I go to try them; I pray thee hold me excused.* Cannot the five corporal senses of man be understood under the number of these yoke of oxen? And is it not with a special reason that animals are put before us under the yoke, or in couples, as both sexes are subject to the exterior sense? By these senses we are not elevated to the knowledge of *supernatural* things, but we remain with the *corporeal* ones. Through these man forsakes the knowledge of the things within him, and clings to those without. And this is the cause of our inquisitiveness concerning the life of our neighbour, whilst we overlook our own life. The human mind is, indeed, of this disposition, trying to know things which are of no concern, and overlooking those which ought to be the first and paramount care. Not without a special reason is it said about the five yoke of oxen: *I go to try them; I pray thee hold me excused.* Such excuse clearly shows the curiosity of the man. This vice mastered him entirely, and led him to go and try *exterior* and not spiritual things. Now, consider how those who wished to be excused by the householder for not coming to his banquet—the one on account of the farm and the other on account of the five yoke of oxen—at first made use of very humble language, *I pray thee hold me excused.* Yet this humility is in their words only, while the contempt for the householder resides in their doings. And such is the conduct of many Christians towards the ministers of God, when punished by them for their misdeeds. Being admonished in such words as: 'Do be converted; return to God; avoid the world and its sins;' their answer to the zealous servant of God, inviting them to the Lord's banquet, will be: 'We are not worthy of the grace offered to us; we are sinners; we cannot obey you; but do not forget to pray the Lord for us.' Are they not like the invited guests, who asked the servant to excuse them? Saying that they are sinners, they seem to humble themselves, but adding that they cannot be converted, their pride is only too obvious. Their false humility is shown by their words, and by their acts, their real pride.

V. *And another said: I have married a wife, and therefore I cannot come.* The real reason of his refusal is found in the vice of voluptuousness. Indeed, though marriage is in itself good and lawful, being instituted by Divine Providence for the propagation of the human race, yet it is often desired, not for that legitimate purpose, but for the satisfaction of vicious desires; so that under the words of an action, just in itself, unlawful intentions are often hidden. The Divine Master of the house invites you to His heavenly Banquet; yet you refuse, since the love of earthly goods, inquisitiveness, and sinful lust keep you away. You act in the same manner as those who, on account of their excuses, were rejected by the householder of the Gospel. They alleged the same reasons you make use of, and showed the same aversion against the heavenly food offered to men.

VI. *And the servant, returning, told these things to his lord. Then the master of the house, being angry, said to his servant: Go out quickly into the streets and lanes of the city, and bring in hither the poor, and the feeble, and the blind, and the lame.* The Lord, therefore, shuts out of His Banquet those who are only and solely clinging to the goods of this earth, those addicted to useless curiosity, and those given up to sinful lust. The proud also are rejected, and the poor are chosen. How is this? Listen to St. Paul saying: *The foolish things of the world hath God chosen, that He may confound the wise; and the weak things of the world hath God chosen, that He may confound the strong* (1 Cor. 1: 27). Now, notice that those brought to the banquet are called *poor* and *feeble*, to point out that they were not relying on their own strength, but recognised their weakness. For he that, in the midst of his poverty, has a high opinion of himself, is proud in spite of his needs. Again, the blind may be said to be those deprived of the interior light; the lame, those who do not go straight in the path of justice. Now, these exterior deformities seem to be the marks of interior defects; it follows, then, that they are sinners, like the first who refused to come to the Banquet. But because they are humble they are preferred and received, on account of their humble sentiments.

VII. The despised by the world are therefore chosen by God; for it often happens that the little esteem in which they are held makes them reflect on themselves, and urges them to follow the prodigal son of the Gospel, who, having wasted his substance living riotously, and being in want, returned to himself, and said:

42. SECOND SUNDAY AFTER PENTECOST

How many hired servants in my father's house abound with bread? (Luke 15: 17). As long as he was living in sinful abundance, he knew not himself, but went, so to speak, away from himself, not to see the sad condition in which he was plunged. He would not have returned to himself, had not the corporal hunger he suffered shown him the terrible spiritual distress of his soul. The poor and the feeble, the blind and the lame, are called by God, and they come, because they are infirm and despicable in the eyes of the world. They are the more willing and prompt to listen to the voice of God, the less attention and comfort they receive from the world.

VIII. However, the sentence pronounced by our Lord against all those who refused to accept the invitation, is exceedingly terrible. I entreat you, therefore, you, beloved brethren, and you, my teachers, you who are sinners and you who are just—I entreat you to give your serious attention to His words, that He may be the less feared on the day of the judgment, the more He is feared by you now, when attentively listening to my words. He adds: *I say unto you, That none of those men that were invited, shall taste of My supper.* At sundry times and in divers manners you have been called by God: through His Angels, sent to guide us; through the Prophets and Fathers, gone before us; through the Apostles and pastors; and, lastly, through our ministry; do not despise His invitation. Should the voice of God be heard by you in miracles or punishments, in blessings or adversities, do not refuse to listen to it. For, were you unwilling to accept the invitation now, the time might come when the entrance to the banquet will be refused to you, just when you are most desirous to obtain that favour. Remember what Wisdom tells us through Solomon: *Then they shall call upon me, and I will not hear; they shall rise in the morning, and shall not find me* (Prov. 1: 28). And the foolish virgins, coming late, exclaim: *Lord, Lord, open to us. But the Bridegroom, answering, said: Amen I say to you, I know you not* (Matt. 25: 11, 12). And now need I tell you, beloved brethren, to forsake all things, to renounce the cares and concerns of this world, and to think only of eternity? Such a blessing is given to a few only; and I do not flatter myself that you will be induced, in consequence of my admonitions, to forsake all the things you possess. But if you cannot do so, at least keep your earthly goods in such a way as not to be possessed by them; keep them in your possession, so that your heart may not be enslaved by them; make use of the goods of this world, and desire the eternal gifts. Temporal goods help us on the journey of this life, but eternal goods alone are deserving of our continual desires and efforts to possess them. Whatsoever happens in this world ought to be looked upon with indifference, whilst the eyes of our soul are to be continually directed towards the desired eternal felicity. Let us entirely root out the vices of our heart, so that we may be ready not only to avoid every sinful act, but even to banish the least sinful thought. Then neither the lust of the flesh, nor over-curiosity or desire for honours will keep us away from the Banquet of the Lord. When applying ourselves to honest and necessary occupations, let not our mind be so intent on them, as to give them our whole heart. You see, therefore, beloved brethren, that you are not asked to forsake all things, but that, though keeping what you possess, you may in spirit deprive yourselves of all things that is to say, you will make use of earthly things, so as to found all your hopes and desires upon eternal goods. Follow this advice of St. Paul: *The time is short; it remaineth, that they that weep, be as though they wept not; and they that rejoice, as if they rejoiced not; and they that buy, as though they possessed not; and they that use this world, as if they used it not; for the fashion of this world passeth away* (1 Cor. 7: 29 and following).

43. THIRD SUNDAY AFTER PENTECOST

GOSPEL: Luke 15: 1-10. *At that time*: The publicans and sinners drew near unto Jesus to hear Him. And the Pharisees and Scribes murmured, saying: This man receiveth sinners, and eateth with them. And He spoke to them this parable, saying: What man of you that hath an hundred sheep, and if he shall lose one of them, doth he not leave the ninety-nine in the desert, and go after that which was lost until he find it? And when he hath found it, lay it upon his shoulders rejoicing; and, coming home, call together his friends and neighbours, saying to them: Rejoice with me, because I have found my sheep that was lost. I say to you, that even so there shall be joy in heaven upon one sinner that doth penance, more than upon ninety-nine just who need not penance. Or what woman, having ten groats, if she lose one groat, doth not light a candle, and sweep the house, and seek diligently until she find it? And when she hath found it, call together her friends and neighbours, saying: Rejoice with me, because I have found the groat which I had lost. So I say to you, there shall be joy before the angels of God upon one sinner doing penance.

HOMILY BY POPE ST. GREGORY, PREACHED IN THE CHURCH OF SS. JOHN AND PAUL ON THE THIRD SUNDAY AFTER PENTECOST
Thirty-Fourth Homily on the Gospels

I. YOU HAVE HEARD, BELOVED BRETHREN, FROM the Gospel just read out to you, that the publicans and sinners drew near our Lord, and were received by Him, not only to speak, but also to eat with Him; and the Pharisees and Scribes, seeing this, murmured. Learn from this that true justice is merciful, whereas false justice is full of contempt, though even the just sometimes feel moved with indignation against sinners. However, we distinguish between a feeling of indignation through pride, and another such feeling through love for the law. He that has a true zeal feels indignant against sin, but he despises not the sinner; he feels a holy impatience, but he loses not hope; he will fight against sinners so as yet loving them; and though he will exteriorly punish them with strong words, he will always preserve in his heart the sweetness of love. The just man prefers to himself in his heart those whom he is correcting, and thinks those he judges, better than himself. And, so doing, he preserves discipline in those who are subject to him, and in himself, real humility. Whereas those possessing a false justice, by which they are rendered prouder, have only contempt for others; they spare them not; they are unmerciful to their misery, and thus are the more sinful, because they perceive not that they themselves are sinners. Such were the Pharisees who judged our Lord because He received sinners. Their hearts were mortally dry, whilst they rebuked the very fountain of mercy.

II. Their sickness was so desperate that they recognised not even they were sick. But the heavenly Physician, that they might know of their sickness, applied to them soft ointments by means of a gracious parable, and lanced the abscess of their proud heart. He said: *What man of you that hath an hundred sheep, and if he shall lose one of them, doth he not leave the ninety-nine in the desert, and go after that which was lost until he find it?* We cannot sufficiently admire the infinite wisdom and goodness of our Redeemer, who in this parable compels man to recognise himself, whilst his Creator's image is placed before him. Consider that one hundred is a perfect number representing angels and men, created by God and being His sheep. You will easily recognise that man is the lost sheep, since through sin he left the life-giving pastures allotted to him by God; and that this lost sheep might be found, the ninety-nine were left in the desert. For our Redeemer left the choirs of the angels in heaven, and came into this world to His human creatures. Why is heaven compared to a desert? Because man, by his sins, deserted that place created for him. And the angels, prefigured by the other sheep, inhabited that desert, whilst the lost sheep on earth were sought after by the Divine Shepherd. This desert had its beginning, when the number of angels and men, created for the contemplation of the Almighty, was diminished by the transgression of man. The lost sheep on earth were gone after, that the full number of His sheep in heaven might be restored. Thus we see that another Evangelist (Matt. 18: 12) uses the expression *mountains* instead of desert, clearly indicating that the angels, dwelling in the highest, are those sheep which remained in the heavenly pastures prepared by their Creator. *And when he hath found it, lay it upon his shoulders rejoicing.* Do we not recognise in this image our Saviour Himself, who, taking our human nature, burdened Himself with our sins? *And, coming home, call together his friends and neighbours, saying to them: Rejoice with me, because I have found my sheep that was lost.* After finding the lost sheep He came home; for after redeeming the human nature, that lost sheep, Jesus Christ returned to His home, the eternal kingdom. There He found His friends and neighbours that is, the choirs of the angels. They are His friends, for they have continually and faithfully done His will. They are His neighbours, for, walking in His presence, they are enlightened by the rays of His glory. The Divine Shepherd does not say: Rejoice with My sheep, but *Rejoice with Me*; for His joy is to give us life, and His desire and joy will be complete when we enter His kingdom.

III. This is explained by our Lord Himself: *I say to you, that even so there shall be joy in heaven upon one sinner that doth penance, more than upon ninety-nine just who need not penance.* Why does our Lord say that heaven will rejoice upon sinners doing penance, more than upon the just who persevere in their justice? It is because, according to our daily experience, the just, not forsaking the ways of justice, are not over anxious to win heaven, since they do not feel themselves burdened with sins, and are free from all unlawful doings. They abstain the less from lawful things, the more convinced they are of their renouncing forbidden things; thus they do not endeavour to attain to higher things, being conscious of their never committing any grievous fault. Whereas sinners, remembering their former vicious life, and penetrated by deep and sincere contrition, return to God with an ardent love. They begin to practise the most heroic virtues, and fight hard for a glorious victory over themselves. They are no longer moved by the pleasures of the world, nor by honours or dignities, but they rejoice in bearing with injustice and iniquities. Their only longing is after heaven, their only desire, to obtain the eternal felicity; and thus they make amends for their former sins by the rich treasure of their merits. Do not wonder, therefore, that there is joy in heaven upon one sinner doing penance, more than upon the just persevering in justice. A soldier who at the first shock of the battle lost heart and ran away, but at once returned with great courage to strike and overwhelm the enemy, will receive from the commander more praise than another who, though not turning his back to the enemy, never showed any act of real courage. Thus also a field, formerly covered with thistles and thorns, but now yielding a rich harvest, will be preferred by the farmer to a soil which, though never covered with thistles, has not been as fertile as the other.

IV. However, we must confess that among the just there are to be found many, who rejoice in heaven more than converted sinners do by their most sincere penance. For there are a great many who, leading a perfectly innocent life, nevertheless punish themselves with great severity, as if they had committed grievous sins. Such Christians renounce all the commodities of life; with heroic contempt they rise above the world; what is lawful seems to them sinful; justly acquired goods are rejected, whilst all visible things are despised in order to ascend to invisible riches. Tears and sighs are their comfort, and humiliations their happiness. And when others are weeping on account of their really sinful actions, they are sorry for the least sinful thought. We conclude, therefore, that such Christians, being really good and innocent, yet reap the merits of severe penance, because they continually practise the most sublime virtues. We may, therefore, recognise how much God rejoices upon the just suffering and humbling themselves for sins they never committed, since He rejoices upon a sinner deeply sorry for his past sins.

V. But, though our Lord said: *There shall be joy in heaven upon one sinner that doth penance*, the same Lord announces through His prophet: *If the just, trusting in his justice, commit iniquity, all his justices shall be forgotten* (Ezech. 33: 13). Consider the mystery of God's wisdom and goodness, threatening the just with His wrath, should they forsake the road of justice, and at the same time inspiring sinners with hope of forgiveness, provided they forsake and rise from their sins, and do penance. What a mystery! God inspiring the just with fear, lest their justice and good works make them presumptuous, and giving hope and courage to sinners, to prevent them from despairing on account of their sins! Learn, therefore, you good Christians, to fear the justice of God, Who may suffer you to fall, and you, sinners, hope in the mercy of God helping you to rise from your sins. Though oppressed by the burden of their wickedness, the sinners are awaited by Him, Who created them in justice, to rise again. The arms of His mercy are stretched out to receive them as soon as they return to Him. Yet, only a sincere penance can reconcile us to God, and this penance, the qualities of which must be acknowledged, consists in the deep sorrow for sins committed, and the firm purpose of avoiding them in the future. However, he that is repentant for past sins, and is again committing new ones, knows nothing about real penance, or is acting as if he knew nothing. What does it profit you to be sorry for sins against chastity, if at the same time you are given up to avarice? What advantage will be derived from tears shed about anger, if the fire of envy is not extinguished in your heart?

VI. Our penance will be perfect if, besides true contrition for past sins and sincere purpose not to commit them again, we also abstain from lawful things, in order to satisfy Divine Justice for unlawful actions. It is meet and just to renounce some pleasure, when the great commandments were transgressed. Let me illustrate this by an example taken from Holy Scripture. It was forbidden to covet the neighbour's wife (Exod. 20: 17), but the King was not forbidden to impose very difficult tasks on his soldiers, neither to ask for water by the fetching of which they would be exposed to great dangers. But all of you know how King David, yielding to his passions, took away the wife of one of his subjects; how his sin was severely punished, and how he made amends for it by severe penance and bitter tears. A long time afterwards the same King, fighting against his enemies, and suffering terrible thirst, was longing for the living waters of the cisterns at Bethlehem. Some fearless soldiers at once went, in spite of extreme dangers, through the ranks of the enemy, and brought him the longed-for fresh water. But David, reflecting on the great danger to which these soldiers exposed themselves, only to satisfy his desire, was sorry, and at once poured out the water upon the ground before the Lord, to bring Him a sacrifice, and thus to expiate by this generous self-denial the burning desire he had to get water. You see how this repentant and converted sinner deprived himself of the water so ardently desired, whilst he did not mind before that to take the wife of another man, to satisfy his lust. David, therefore, denied to himself the use of a thing allowed by the law, because he remembered the sin he had committed against the law by a forbidden act. Our penance must be of the same kind, if we wish to atone for our sinful actions. Consider also the infinite mercies of God, Who, though seeing us commit sin, bears with us in incomprehensible patience.

VII. It is true, when God had created man, He prohibited sin, yet since man's misfortune of committing sin, God's mercy has never tired in offering him forgiveness. He still calls us, though we give no ear to His voice; we forsake God, and He does not forsake us. This is expressed by Isaias the Prophet, saying: *Thy eyes shall see the teacher, and thy ears shall hear the word of one admonishing thee behind thy back* (Isa. 30: 20, 21). Man was created in justice and instructed by his Creator, at Whose countenance he gazed as long as he remained in the state of innocence and accepted His commands. But when he had transgressed these commands, he turned, so to speak, his countenance from His Creator. Yet, this despised and forsaken good God did not cease running after him, following him, and continually beseeching him to return. And this is God's conduct towards us; for when He was despised by us, He nevertheless continued to call us. We offend Him, not listening to His exhortations, and considering His commandments, too severe to be obeyed; nevertheless, He invites us to return to Him. His Divine commandments call us, whilst His invincible patience is awaiting us. Beloved brethren, consider a slave who, in his pride, will not listen to your words, who, instead of obeying, will turn his back on you; shall not his impudence be most severely punished? We easily recognise ourselves in this comparison, since by our repeated sins we have turned against God, our Creator, Who, in spite of them, still continues to preserve our life. We have proudly resisted Him, yet, in spite of our contempt, He meekly calls us, and is not only satisfied with remitting us the punishment deserved by our sins, but offers us, as a reward for our return, an eternal happiness in heaven. The most hardened heart ought to be moved by such infinite mercy. Let us also learn, by God's infinite patience after our heinous sins, to be ashamed of our ingratitude, which in justice deserves the most severe punishment.

44. FOURTH SUNDAY AFTER PENTECOST

GOSPEL: Luke 5: 1-11. *At that time*: When the multitude pressed upon Jesus to hear the Word of God, He stood by the Lake of Genesareth. And He saw two ships standing by the Lake; but the fishermen were gone out of them, and were washing their nets. And, going up into one of the ships that was Simon's, He desired him to draw back a little from the land. And, sitting, He taught the multitudes out of the ship. Now, when He had ceased to speak, He said to Simon: Launch out into the deep, and let down your nets for a draught. And Simon, answering, said to Him: Master, we have laboured all the night, and have taken nothing; but at Thy word I will let down the net.

And when they had done this, they enclosed a very great multitude of fishes, and their net broke. And they beckoned to their partners that were in the other ship, that they should come and help them. And they came and filled both the ships, so that they were almost sinking. Which when Simon Peter saw, he fell down at Jesus's knees, saying: Depart from me, for I am a sinful man, O Lord. For he was wholly astonished, and all that were with him, at the draught of fishes which they had taken. And so were also James and John, the sons of Zebedee, who were Simon's partners. And Jesus saith to Simon: Fear not; from henceforth thou shalt catch men. And having brought their ships to land, leaving all things, they followed Him.

HOMILY BY ST. AMBROSE
Bk. IV, Chapter 5, On St. Luke

I. SINCE THE LORD WROUGHT SO MANY WORKS of healing, we are not astonished to see that neither time nor place could restrain the multitude from seeking relief and health. Evening had come, and still they followed Him; He went down to the lake, and still they pressed upon Him, and therefore He entered

Peter's ship. This is the ship which, according to the expression of St. Matthew, is spiritually buffeted by tempests even up to this time, but which is still, according to St. Luke, filled with fishes, signifying that for a while *to labour* is the present state of the Church, whilst hereafter it shall be *to rejoice*; for the fishes represent those who swim in the troublesome waters of this human life. When Jesus Christ seems to sleep in this ship, and afterwards commands the winds and the sea, He teaches us that He is sleeping for the lukewarm, and watching for the perfect. However, our Lord's sleep must be considered according to the meaning attached to it in Holy Scripture: *I sleep, but My heart watcheth* (Cant. 5: 2). Therefore St. Matthew, in his Gospel, did not omit to mention the visible signs given by our Lord Himself to prove His power when calming the tempestuous sea. This was not the action of human power, as the Jews imagined when they exclaimed: *What manner of man is this, for the winds and the sea obey Him?* (Matt. 8: 27). It was the proof of the Divinity of Jesus Christ, revealing to men the mysteries of His grace, whilst commanding the waves of the sea, calming the elements, and forcing unfeeling creatures to obey His word. Indeed, when we see that at His word the sea is calmed, that the devil is forced to leave those he possessed, both these miracles prove the Almighty Power of the Man-God, Who commands material elements, and makes known His power over the supernatural order of things. There is a specially mysterious coincidence in the fact that St. Matthew relates the calming of the tempest, while St. Luke describes St. Peter's miraculous draught of fishes. Take notice that Peter's ship was not driven to and fro, like the one in which was Judas; for though this one contained also some good disciples of our Lord, yet, on account of the faithlessness of Judas, she could not safely progress in her course. Peter's own merits could not prevent the uneasiness he felt on account of one of the disciples; and thus we are warned to remove, as far as possible, the faithless ones from our society, lest we expose the multitude to perish through one whom we have not the courage to expel. No fear for the ship where Wisdom is steering, where no false teaching is known, and faith is swelling the sails. How could she be in trouble under the steering of the Lord Himself, the Church's sure foundation? It is where faith is weak that there is fear; but there is safety where perfect love abides.

II. To the other disciples it was commanded to loose their nets; but to Peter alone it was said: *Launch out into the deep* — that is, into the depths of the doctrine of faith, What, indeed, is there so deep, so incomprehensible, as to gaze upon the depth of Divine Wisdom revealed to this Apostle to recognise the Son of God, and to take up the profession of His Divine generation? This is a thing which the human mind is not able to grasp, but which is embraced by a hearty faith; for though it is not known to me how He was born of the Father, yet that born He was, I cannot be ignorant. What the order of His Divine generation was, I know not, but I acknowledge God, the source of His generation. No one beheld the begetting of the Son of God by the Father, but the Church stood by to hear the Father testify that this is His beloved Son (Luke 3: 22). Whom shall we believe, if we believe not God? For whatsoever we believe comes either by sight or by hearing; but our eyes oftentimes deceive us, while *faith cometh by hearing* (Rom. 10: 17). Shall we scrutinize the authority of him that speaks to us in order to believe his testimony? When we are made sure of a thing by honest people, we believe their words. And we are assured by God Himself of this mystery which we are to believe, and which is confirmed by the Son of God Himself. The sun was darkened at His death; the earth was quaking and shaking in its foundations; they all proclaim the same truth. In the depth of this mysterious sea the Son of God is seen by the Church under the guidance of Peter. He rises full of glory, and the Holy Ghost is pouring out all His gifts into the hearts of the faithful.

III. As to the nets, which by order of our Lord were let down by the disciples into the deep sea, we understand them to be the words of truth, forming, so to speak, the tissue of the evangelical sermons. These sermons, like the material nets, have some depths and corners, by which men caught in the spiritual nets are prevented from slipping out and being lost again in the deep. It is not without a special reason that the instruments used by the evangelical labourers are compared to *nets*; for they do not bring death to the fishes, but spiritual and everlasting life. Souls are taken out of the spiritual darkness, and receive light; they are delivered from the deep abyss, and guided up to heaven. Another manner of fishing is spoken of in the Gospel, when our Lord asked Peter to cast a hook, and to take the fish which first came up (Matt. 17: 23-26). This event suggests an important lesson; for by this miracle Christians are admonished to be subject to their temporal rulers, and also obedient to them. The Son of God Himself teaches this truth by His own act; He possessed nothing, yet He paid tribute to Caesar. It was to teach those endowed with earthly riches the obligation to recognise the rights of the Sovereign, and to teach others, the slaves of the perishable things of this world, not to think themselves above the princes of the earth. Our Lord paid this tribute, the same as was imposed in the old law, for the sum was twopence, to signify the great value of the redemption of man, who has both a spiritual and a corporeal nature. There is also another mystery in the fact that the money for the tribute was found in the mouth of the fish; for the mouth gives testimony to our justice and confesses our faith, the source of our salvation. The Apostle says: *With the mouth confession is made unto salvation* (Rom. 10: 10). This first fish caught by St. Peter may also represent St. Stephen, the first martyr, who had in his mouth the tribute paid by the Redeemer. Jesus Christ, giving Himself up for our redemption, is our tribute; we may therefore say that St. Stephen, confessing Jesus amidst his torments, bore, so to speak, the treasure of our redemption on his lips.

IV. Now consider the deep humility of St. Peter, saying to his Divine Teacher: *Master, we have laboured all the night, and have taken nothing; but at Thy word I will let down the net.* The Apostle seems to say: 'O Lord, I recognise that my labours would be useless, since I worked all the night in the darkness, hadst Thou not come to dispel my darkness and help me. I do not see anybody yet coming into my boat, in which there is truth. Thou hast manifested Thyself to the Gentiles, and the wise men came from the East; yet I have not caught any one in my net. I have uselessly laboured all the day, and am waiting for Thy command, that at Thy word I let down my net not uselessly.' Oh, how vain and useless is presumption and self-confidence, and how powerful and fruitful the humility of those who at the simple word of the Redeemer filled their nets with fishes after their previous useless work! By this we are given to understand that the miraculous draught of human creatures made by the evangelical labourers, was not the result of human eloquence, but the work of their divine vocation. Nations were converted through the faith being preached to them, and not through being convinced by the logical arguments of human wisdom. And what is the meaning of the other ships manned by Peter's companions and asked to give help, but the land of Judea, the country of James and John? The Prophet, in his songs, tells us that *Judea was made His sanctuary* (Ps. 113: 2). We learn thereby that these two disciples, leaving their own ship to enter that of Peter, left the Synagogue and joined the Church, and that Jews and Gentiles, figured by the two ships filled with fishes, will recognise Jesus as their Saviour, in Whose Name all knees shall bow in heaven and on earth.

V. Yet, considering this enormous quantity of fishes, I am seized with fear, lest the ships be submerged. But my fear disappears, when I remember the words of the Apostle: *There must be also heresies; that they, who are reproved, may be made manifest among you* (1 Cor. 11: 19). We may also see in the ship coming near to that of St. Peter a figure of those Churches which received their beginning from the first. Should the astonishment of St. Peter at the multitude of fishes caught in his net seem to indicate his uneasiness about the preservation of the great number of the faithful entrusted to his care, we have no motive to fear that he will lack the means of preserving them, as long as they remain in his ship, since he received the gift of drawing into it even those who were without. Nevertheless, the Apostle is far from attributing to his own efforts the success of taking souls into his net; for he gives this credit to his Saviour, Whose power he acknowledges, falling down at His knees and saying: *Depart from me, for I am a sinful man, Lord*. St. Peter is seized with astonishment at the favours he received; for the more worthy he was, the more unworthy he considered himself. Follow his example, and say: *Depart from me, for I am a sinful man, O Lord*, and the same answer will be given to you. Fear not to confess your sins before the merciful God, Who is ready to pardon you. For our sake He deprived Himself of everything; let us for His love generously give to Him what is our own. God, immensely rich and generous, cannot deprive us of nor envy us our possessions, especially when considering that, in the excess of His goodness, He granted to men the power of reconciling us to Him.

45. FIFTH SUNDAY AFTER PENTECOST

GOSPEL: Matt. 5: 20-24. *At that time*: Jesus said to His disciples: Unless your justice exceed that of the Scribes and Pharisees, you shall not enter into the kingdom of heaven. You have heard that it was said to them of old: Thou shalt not kill. And whosoever shall kill shall be in danger of the judgment. But I say to you, that whosoever is angry with his brother, shall be in danger of the judgment. And whosoever shall say to his brother, Raca, shall be in danger of the council. And whosoever shall say, Thou fool, shall be in danger of hell fire. Therefore, if thou bring thy gift to the altar, and there shalt remember that thy brother hath anything against thee, leave there thy gift before the altar, and go first to be reconciled to thy brother, and then come and offer thy gift.

HOMILY BY ST. AUGUSTINE
On the Lord's Sermon on the Mount, Bk. I, Chapter 9

I. THE JUSTICE OF THE PHARISEES WAS *NOT TO kill*, whereas the justice of those who shall enter the kingdom of heaven consists in *not to be angry with his brother*. The least, therefore, is, *Thou shalt not kill*, and whosoever shall break this commandment *shall be called the least in the kingdom of heaven*; but whosoever shall fulfil it, and *not kill*, is not yet great and worthy of the kingdom of heaven, though he has risen a step. But he will have advanced farther, if he be not angry with his brother without a cause, and, doing this, he will be farther off from manslaughter. Wherefore, He Who teaches us not to be angry without a cause, does not destroy the law, *Thou shalt not kill*, but rather fulfils and increases it, making us not only to be free of the sin of outward killing, but also innocent of anger within.

II. There are divers degrees or steps in the sins referred to. And first, a man is angry, and keeps that feeling unexpressed in his heart. But now, if that angry motion calls forth an exclamation of anger, not having any definite meaning, yet giving evidence of the trouble of him who is provoked, this is certainly more than anger restrained by silence. Next, this outburst of indignation may contain open and direct reviling of him who had roused it. Who can doubt but that this is something more than an empty exclamation of anger? Hence, in the first there is one thing only, that is, anger; in the second, two things, both anger and a word expressing that anger; in the third, three things, both anger and words expressing it, and in these words a distinct censure and reviling. Now look at the three degrees of liability and guilt, open respectively to the judgment, to the council and to hell fire. In the judgment there is still place for the defence; in the council, however, though this also is in a sense a judgment, yet we may suppose distinct from the judgment proper, because the council pronounces sentence, not as the result of a trial whereat the accused is present, but as the result of a consultation among the judges, to find out to what punishment he is to be sentenced, being already found guilty. When we get to hell fire, there remains no longer any doubt about sentence, as in the council. In hell fire both the condemnation and the punishment of him that is condemned are alike certain. Thus are seen certain degrees in the sins and the liability to punishment. But who can tell in what manner they are invisibly shown in the punishment of souls? We may ask, what is the difference between the justice of the Pharisees and that greater justice procuring admittance into the kingdom of heaven? For it is a more serious crime to kill than to inflict reproach by means of words. In the one case killing exposes one to the judgment, and in the other anger, the least of these three sins, also exposes one to the judgment. The answer will be that in the former case the question of murder is discussed among men, whereas in the latter all sins and vices are disposed of by the Divine judgment, and the final fate of the sentenced sinners is hell fire. However, let us not lose sight of this fact that, if the angry brother is punished by God with hell fire, as well as the other who murdered his brother, there must be, and certainly there is, a difference in the inflicted punishment.

III. *Therefore*, added our Lord, *if thou bring thy gift to the altar, and there shalt remember that thy brother hath any thing against thee, leave there thy gift before the altar, and go first to be reconciled to thy brother, and then come and offer thy gift.* From this it is clear that anger against one's brother is forbidden by our Lord. For the following sentence is connected by such a conjunction, as to confirm the preceding one. Our Lord did not say: But if thou bring thy gift; He said: *Therefore,* if thou bring thy gift to the altar. For, if it is not lawful to be angry with one's brother without a cause, or to say *Raca,* or *Thou fool,* it is still less lawful to keep in one's mind indignant motions often turned into hatred. To this belongs what is said in another part of Holy Scripture: *Let not the sun go down upon your anger* (Eph. 4: 26). Therefore, when we are about to bring our gift to the altar, and remember that our brother has anything against us, we are commanded to leave our gift before the altar, and to go and be reconciled to our brother, then to come and offer the gift. If this is to be understood literally, we might suppose that such a thing ought to be done if the brother is present; for it cannot be delayed too long, since we are commanded to leave the gift before the altar. Should, therefore, such a thing come to your mind respecting one who is absent, or even, as it may happen, beyond the sea, it would be absurd to imagine that your gift is to be left before the altar, until you have journeyed over both lands and seas. Therefore, we must have recourse to an internal and spiritual interpretation, then what is said will be understood without difficulty.

IV. There ought also to be on our part purity of intention when we present our offering; for our heart is the altar, the inner temple of God, according to the words of St. Paul: *For the temple of God is holy, which (temple) you are* (1 Cor. 3: 17). Again: *That Christ may dwell by faith in your hearts* (Eph. 3: 17). If it occur to your mind that a brother has aught against you — that is, if you have injured him, for then he has something against you; (whereas you have something against him, if he has injured you, and in that case you will not ask pardon of one who has done you an injury, but merely forgive him as you hope to be forgiven by God what you have committed against Him). Now, if your brother has anything against you, at once proceed to reconciliation, not only with your bodily feet, but with the emotions of your mind, prostrating yourself with humble disposition before your brother, to whom you have hastened with affectionate thought. And should he be present when you offer, you will be able to soften him and to recall him to good will by asking pardon. And God, witnessing your good dispositions, will forgive you and accept your present on your return to Him. But who acts in this way, so that he is neither angry with his brother without a cause, nor says *Raca* without a cause, nor calls him a *fool* without a cause — all sins most proudly committed? Or has he perchance fallen into any of these sins, who adopts the only remedy and asks pardon with suppliant and contrite minds? Who, but the man who is not puffed up with the spirit of empty boasting. Therefore, *Blessed are the poor in spirit, for theirs is the kingdom of heaven* (Matt. 5: 3).

46. SIXTH SUNDAY AFTER PENTECOST

GOSPEL: Mark 8: 1-9. *At that time*: When there was a great multitude with Jesus, and they had nothing to eat, calling His disciples together, He said to them: I have compassion on the multitude, for behold they have now been with Me three days, and have nothing to eat; and if I send them away fasting to their own home, they will faint in the way, for some of them came from afar off. And His disciples answered Him: From whence can anyone fill them here with bread in the wilderness? And He asked them: How many loaves have ye? Who said: Seven. And He commanded the people to sit down on the ground; and taking the seven loaves, giving thanks, He broke, and gave to His disciples for to set before them, and they set them before the people. And they had a few little fishes; and He blessed them, and commanded them to be set before them. And they did eat and were filled; and they took up that which was left of the fragments, seven baskets. And they that had eaten were about four thousand; and He sent them away.

HOMILY BY ST. AMBROSE
On St. Luke, Bk. VI, Chapter 9

I. AFTER THAT WOMAN, WHO IS A TYPE OF Christ's Church, was healed of an issue of blood (Luke 8: 43); after our Lord had sent His disciples to preach the kingdom of God (9: 2), food was given to men by His heavenly tenderness. However, consider who they are to whom He gave that food. He gave it not to such as live at ease, not to men in cities nor in synagogues, not to those who sit in places of worldly dignities; but to men seeking Him in a desert place. Those who do not despise His word, but hunger after it, are received by Christ; He speaks to them not of earthly things, but of the kingdom of God. And if any bear the sores of carnal passion, He willingly heals them. Then it happened that, after healing those who were in need of healing, He fed their hunger with spiritual meat. Thus we are given to understand that no man takes Christ's food, unless he be first healed; and they that are invited to the supper, are first cured by that invitation. Should they be lame, they receive the power to walk, that they may be able to come. If blind, and not able to find the door of the house of the Lord, His light will be given to them. In the mysteries, or Sacraments, presented by our Lord, order is preserved. The sinful soul is first purified by the remission of sins, and afterwards filled at the table of the Lord. Yet, that multitude following Him, was of such as being unable to feed on those strong meats, or to pasture their starving spirits upon the Body and Blood of Christ, as is done by those of a stronger faith, according to St. Paul: *I gave you milk to drink, and not meat; for you were not able as yet, but neither indeed are you now able* (1 Cor. 3: 2). The five loaves are, so to speak, your milk; the stronger meat will be the Body of Christ; the more generous cup, the Blood of the Lord.

II. Jesus Christ does not at first give to those, who follow Him, His Body and Blood to appease their spiritual hunger and thirst. In order to prepare them by degrees for the adorable Sacrament, He first satiates them with five loaves, then by another miracle with the seven loaves which He multiplied, finally giving Himself to us as our food. By this we ought to be intimately united with our Saviour, since He measures the food according to our strength, so that the weak shall not be oppressed by a heavy nourishment, and the strong shall find in it preservation and support. *He that is weak, let him eat herbs* (Rom. 14: 2); whereas he that has already left this state of weakness will enjoy in the five loaves and the two fishes a stronger nourishment. But should he desire something more for his sustenance, and yet hesitate to ask for it, then, let him forsake everything fastening him to this earth, and come to listen with more attention to the word of God. As soon as he begins to hear and to understand it, he will feel real hunger for it. Thus the Apostles began to live on this word of life, for which

46. SIXTH SUNDAY AFTER PENTECOST

they felt an unsatiable hunger. And though this Divine word, stimulating their hunger, was not yet understood by them, our Lord knew of their desire. He also was aware of their not longing after corporeal nourishment, so eagerly desired by the children of the world, but after spiritual food, which He gave them to taste in His admirable teaching. Our Redeemer did not wish to send these people *away fasting to their own home*, lest they would *faint in the way*. Divine goodness acts with us in the same manner. Our care and zeal are required to seek and to know, whilst strength to find it is imparted to us. O dear Jesus! grant that none of us, neither I nor these present, should be deprived of these gifts and be sent away by Thee. Give us this food, by which we are strengthened and preserved from the weakness overcoming us, when we are without this Bread of life. I will not ask Thee, O my Saviour, why Thou dost not dismiss me without food, since I am told by Thee that for want of this heavenly nourishment I should faint in the way. Indeed, I should be starved in this mortal life, before I could come to Thee, my sole object and end. Without Thee I should never be able, during this earthly life, to understand that Thou art the Son of the Eternal Father, that Thou hast come from heaven, and art the same Redeemer Who ascended into the highest heaven. Thou givest strength to my weakness, which, without Thy supernatural light, would have seen in Thee only the Son born of a Virgin, without taking any notice of Thy Divine Person that assumed our humanity.

III. The Apostles did not understand that the bread which, by order of our Lord, they were to distribute among the multitude, was not the common bread sold among us. But the Lord, Who came to redeem us by His precious Blood, and from Whom we receive our daily bread, knew this well. For the disciples had not yet received the power to distribute the Divine food by which souls are sanctified. They could only give the material bread, then in their hands, and by which the bodies were strengthened. The Redeemer has compassion on our misery, and is justly anxious lest our strength should fail us in our earthly journey. And should we be overcome by our weakness, let us accuse ourselves and not Him,

Who can easily justify Himself before His accusers. Indeed, what will be our answer, when He reminds us of the powerful assistance and help placed at our disposal amidst the dangers and struggles of life? Is He not our Father giving us life and strength with His supernatural nourishment? Should we be deprived of this spiritual and strength-giving food, then not Heaven's assistance was failing us, but our own will to make use of it in our necessities. For God, Who lets the rain fall upon the just and the unjust, takes also care of the food given to the wicked and to the good.

We read in Holy Scripture how the prophet Elias, being in the desert, and quite exhausted, received food from an angel of the Lord, and how in the strength of that food he walked forty days and forty nights (3 Kings 19: 5-9). Now, what will be your strength and power after eating the spiritual food prepared for you by Jesus Christ Himself? I go even further, and, basing my words upon examples offered by the Scriptures, I say that, with the help of this food, you will walk forty years through the deserts of Egypt — that is, you will leave them to enter the promised Land, flowing with milk and honey, a land, with which that once promised by God to our forefathers cannot be compared. You should be longing after this blessed Land, which will be possessed by the meek. The barren land now under your feet ought not to be the object of your desires or ambitions. Strongly and steadfastly endeavour to possess that Land gladdened by the presence of Jesus — that Land, the happy dwelling of the saints, and the eternal kingdom of God's glory and majesty, Who will also be your own eternal happiness.

IV. Our Lord, *taking the seven loaves, giving thanks, broke, and gave to His disciples for to set before them.* He does not act otherwise in regard to all men; for He refuses His gifts to nobody; He grants them to all. Yet, should you not stretch out your hands to receive the bread distributed by His disciples, you will be weak and faint in the way, and have no reason to complain that the Lord had not compassion on you. Remark also that the gifts of our Redeemer were handed to those who had remained with Him in the desert, and persevered not only the first day, but also the second and the third. He said so Himself: *I have compassion* on the multitude, *for behold they have now been with Me three days, and have nothing to eat.* Admire, therefore, God's infinite goodness towards men. What condescension! He sees their weakness and finds means to provide for all their wants. Thinking of the great care God takes of us, we ought to feel ourselves obliged to follow His guidance and to offer to Him our submission, even when for our spiritual advantage He punishes us. And should He chastise you now, you will not find irksome the yoke by which you are burdened, lest, by shaking it off, you will feel weak and exhausted later on. What answer will you then give to the Almighty now so infinitely generous to you? What justifiable excuse will you allege by which to explain your carelessness, since you neglect the salutary nourishment given by God for strengthening you on the long journey of this life? You will not be able to reprove our Lord for taking from you the spiritual food that is offered by Him to all men. Neither will you be able to pretend that it was not His wish to make you good, and to guide you on the road to perfection. For He places before you both good and evil, so that if you prefer virtue to sin, your choice will be free without constraint. There is, indeed, a great difference between the one acting by necessity, and the other freely resolving to practise virtue and good works; for only freedom of action deserves either reward or punishment. Moreover, consider that all of us must one day appear before the judgment-seat of our Redeemer; and should, then, the building of our life be consumed by flames and changed into ashes, we shall not have cause to complain or to excuse ourselves. On that great day God will say to us what He announced to the Jews by His Prophet: *O My people, what have I done to thee, or in what have I molested thee? Answer thou Me* (Mich. vi. 3). Then our Saviour will say to the one that fainted in the way: Why wast thou weak and feeble on the road? Did I not break the bread so necessary to thee? Did I not bless it and command My disciples to give it to thee? Why didst thou refuse that bread? Yet, how many will there be among those here present, now hearing and understanding my words (though the words I now utter are also the words of the Redeemer, and are bread, since no one can pronounce the name of Jesus, without the help of the Holy Ghost) — how many, I ask, will there be found fainting on the way? How many will leave the right road, and walk in the paths of infidels? Ah, would to God that one only might suffer such misfortune, and that the greater part of Christians be not included in that number! But Jesus is not the cause of this perdition; for He gives the necessary and strengthening bread to all who follow Him, and is as generous to every single one, as to the five thousand and the seven thousand in the desert.

47. SEVENTH SUNDAY AFTER PENTECOST

GOSPEL: Matt. 7: 15-21. *At that time:* Jesus said to His disciples: Beware of false prophets, who come to you in the clothing of sheep, but inwardly they are ravening wolves. By their fruits you shall know them. Do men gather grapes of thorns, or figs of thistles? Even so every good tree bringeth forth good fruit, and the evil tree bringeth forth evil fruit. A good tree cannot bring forth evil fruit, neither can an evil tree bring forth good fruit. Every tree that bringeth not forth good fruit shall be cut down, and shall be cast into the fire. Wherefore by their fruits you shall know them. Not every one that saith to me, Lord, Lord, shall enter into the kingdom of heaven; but he that doth the will of My Father who is in heaven, he shall enter into the kingdom of heaven.

HOMILY BY ST. HILARY
Commentary on St. Matthew, Chapter 6

I. WE ARE HERE WARNED BY THE AUTHOR OF ALL truth to value the worth of soft words and seeming meekness by the fruits brought forth in their works by those who show such things. He teaches us, in order to find out what a man is, to look not at his professions, but at his deeds, since there are many in whom sheep's clothing is but a mask hiding their wolfish ravening. *Do men gather grapes of thorns, or figs of thistles? Even so every good tree bringeth forth good fruit, and the evil tree bringeth forth evil fruit.* Thus it is with men; evil men do not bring forth good fruits, and we are to know them hereby. Words alone do not win the kingdom of heaven; and those who say to Christ, *Lord, Lord,* cannot expect to enter into that kingdom. Indeed, what merit is there in these words, *Lord, Lord?* Would He not be Lord all the same, whether or not we call Him so? Do we imagine that we have already attained perfection and holiness by calling the name of the Lord, since the true way of entering into the kingdom of God is to do the will of our Father who is in heaven? *Many will say to Me in that day, Lord, Lord, have not we prophesied in Thy name, cast out devils in Thy name, and done many miracles in Thy name?* (7: 22). Yet the Lord rebukes the deceit of false prophets, and the feigning of hypocrites, who take glory to themselves on account of the power of their words, their prophesying in doctrine, their casting out of devils and similar mighty works.

II. Those hypocrites flatter themselves that they will enter into the kingdom of heaven, as though their preaching to nations, and the power of the holy office they are endowed with, were the work of their own, and not the almighty working of God helping them. Meanwhile it is an undoubted truth that the constant reading of Scripture gives to the ministers of Christ the true knowledge of doctrine, and that their power of driving out devils is derived from the Divine power of the Name of Jesus. Therefore, if we wish to win the blessed eternity in heaven, we must do something of our own; we must be willing to do right, to turn away from sin, to obey with our whole heart the commandments laid on us from heaven, and thus to become the friends of God. It should be our duty to do the will of God rather than to boast of God's power in us; for God forgets and thrusts away such as are already by their wicked works estranged from His friendship.

III. And our Lord adds these words: *Everyone therefore that heareth these My words, and doth them, shall be likened to a wise man that built his house upon a rock.* The meaning of these words is intimately connected with the preceding discourse. For, after showing us the conceited and useless merit of the false prophets and their cunning hypocrisy, He places before our eyes a man animated by a perfect and truthful belief in God, thus making known to us the difference between this one and the false prophets. The believing man, spoken of by Jesus, is placed upon an immovable foundation. It is in vain that the most violent storms rage against him, for the strong Rock, upon which the building of the wise man is founded, is no other but Jesus Christ Himself, Who by His invincible power preserves every building erected upon Him from the fury of the winds, from the violent showers of rain, and from the devastating inundations. By these torrents of rain, mentioned by our Lord, are meant the tempting attractions of lust, penetrating our soul by little and little, and rendering our faith weak and faint. After the first attack made against us by the love of lust, the raging storms of the passions take possession of our heart, and the violent winds storming from all sides — that is, the whole fury of the devils are ready to overthrow and even to destroy us. But the wise man, who built his house upon the strongest foundation, cannot be removed from his place; whereas the foolish man, who despised this precaution, and built his house upon the sand, cannot be sure of the solidity of his building; for the falling rain, and the floods, and the blowing winds will *beat upon that house, and it will fall, and great will be the fall thereof.*

IV. Our Redeemer, giving us the parable of the wise man building his house upon a rock, and of the foolish man building upon the sand, teaches us that true merits consist in the obeying His commandments, and in a strong and lively faith in all He has done and promised. And the Gospel adds these beautiful words: *And it came to pass when Jesus had fully ended these words, the people were in admiration at His doctrine; for He was teaching them as One having power, and not as their Scribes and Pharisees.*

48. EIGHTH SUNDAY AFTER PENTECOST

GOSPEL: Luke 16: 1-9. *At that time*: Jesus spoke to His disciples this parable: There was a certain rich man who had a steward; and the same was accused unto him that he had wasted his goods. And he called him, and said to him: How is it that I hear this of thee? Give an account of thy stewardship; for now thou canst be steward no longer. And the steward said within himself: What shall I do, because my lord taketh away from me the stewardship? To dig I am not able; to beg I am ashamed. I know what I will do, that when I shall be removed from the stewardship they may receive me into their houses. Therefore calling together every one of his lord's debtors, he said to the first: How much dost thou owe my lord? But he said: An hundred barrels of oil. And he said to him: Take thy bill and sit down quickly, and write fifty. Then he said to another: And how much dost thou owe? Who said: An hundred quarters of wheat. He said to him: Take thy bill, and write eighty. And the lord commended the unjust steward, forasmuch as he had done wisely; for the children of this world are wiser in their generation than the children of light. And I say to you: Make unto you friends of the mammon of iniquity, that when you shall fail, they may receive you into everlasting dwellings.

HOMILY BY ST. JEROME
Letter 151 to Algesia

I. THE UNJUST STEWARD, SPOKEN OF BY JESUS IN this parable, is commended by his lord, because he had done wisely though wickedly. And this lord, though himself defrauded, could not but praise the shrewdness of his dishonest servant, because he had cheated him with profit to himself. Now, how much more will our Master Jesus Christ, Who cannot be defrauded by us, and

Who is Himself ready to forgive, praise us His disciples, if we deal mercifully with those who are to believe in Him? And after the parable the Lord said: *Make unto you friends of the mammon of iniquity.* This word *mammon* is a Syriac, not a Hebrew word, signifying ill-gotten riches. If, then, even ill-gotten riches can be so used by such as possess them as to profit by them, how much more can they who, like the Apostles, are *dispensers of the mysteries of God* (1 Cor. 4: 1), the true and blameless riches how much more can they profit themselves, even to be received *into everlasting dwellings,* by the right use of them?

II. And that we may be brought to understand this lesson, our Lord added: *He that is faithful in that which is least* — that is to say, in temporal things — *is faithful also in that which is greater* — that is, in spiritual things. *And he that is unjust in that which is little* — that is, who is not giving to his needy brother help of those things which are needful for the body and which God has created for all men — such a one *is unjust also in that which is greater;* that is, he will deal out spiritual things unfairly: this to one, and that to another, and not according to their spiritual needs. *If then,* says our Lord, *you have not been faithful in the unjust mammon* — that is, in the use of worldly riches which pass away — *who will trust you with that which is the true,* the spiritual riches of the word of God?

III. The Son of God condemns the avaricious, and teaches us that those, who love money and the riches of this world, cannot at the same time love God; that His disciples, therefore, who wish to love Him truly and really, are to despise riches. The Scribes and Pharisees, being avaricious, had only contempt for the words of the Redeemer. They understood that the parable was meant for them, yet they were ashamed to acknowledge this fact. Since these carnal men delighted in the present and visible goods, their great and only hope, we are not astonished to see that they preferred them to the spiritual and future riches, considered by them as most uncertain.

IV. And why was this evangelical steward called an *unjust steward,* since the old Law, the steward of which he was, came from God and was holy? Because this man was faithless in the administration of the service of God. The Jew adored God the Father, and at the same time persecuted God the Son; he recognised an Almighty God, and denied the Holy Ghost. The Apostle Paul, forsaking the Law and serving Jesus, was wiser than the Jews, who at one time were the *children of light*. For, since in the course of time the Jews kept only the Law, they lost Jesus Christ, the eternal Light and the only Way to salvation.

V. And this will be the real profit gained from this parable: that we should endeavour to make unto ourselves friends by means of the riches, the instruments of iniquity. However, among the poor, to whom we distribute them, we must especially consider those who will be able to take us, after this life, to the eternal dwellings. There, instead of the perishable goods we gave to the poor, we shall receive riches of an infinite value. For the temporal things, we give now, we shall be made partakers of everlasting blessings and happiness. So let us sow in blessings, that we may reap in blessings, remembering the words of the Apostle: *He who soweth sparingly, shall also reap sparingly* (2 Cor. 9: 6).

49. NINTH SUNDAY AFTER PENTECOST

GOSPEL: Luke 19: 41-47. *At that time*: When Jesus drew near to Jerusalem, seeing the city, He wept over it, saying: If thou also hadst known, and that in this thy day, the things that are to thy peace; but now they are hidden from thy eyes. For the days shall come upon thee, and thy enemies shall cast a trench about thee, and compass thee round, and straiten thee on every side, and beat thee flat to the ground, and thy children who are in thee; and they shall not leave in thee a stone upon a stone, because thou hast not known the time of thy visitation. And entering into the temple, He began to cast out them that sold therein and them that bought, saying to them: It is written: My house is the house of prayer; but you have made it a den of thieves. And He was teaching daily in the temple.

HOMILY BY POPE ST. GREGORY, PREACHED IN THE BASILICA OF ST. JOHN, CALLED THE CONSTANTINE
Thirty-Ninth Homily on the Gospels

I. NO ONE, THAT HAS READ THE HISTORY OF THE destruction of Jerusalem by the Roman princes Vespasian and Titus, can be ignorant of the fact that the Lord spoke of this destruction, when He wept over the ruin of that city. These princes were pointed at when He said: *For the days shall come upon thee; and thy enemies shall cast a trench about thee, and compass thee round, and straiten thee on every side, and beat thee flat to the ground, and thy children who are in thee.* And the truth of what follows, *they shall not leave in thee a stone upon a stone,* is even now fulfilled by the change of site of the city, which has been rebuilt round about the place without the gates, where the Lord was crucified, whilst the ancient city, as I am told, has been destroyed down to the very foundations. And a little after the preceding words we find what the sin of Jerusalem was, which brought upon her the punishment of this destruction: *Because thou hast not known the time of thy visitation.* The Creator of all things was pleased to visit her through the mystery of the Incarnation, but she remembered not to fear or to love Him. Hence, also, the prophet Jeremias, rebuking man's hardness of heart, calls the birds of the air to testify against it, and says, *The kite in the air hath known her time, the turtle, and, the swallow, and the stork have observed the time of their coming; but My people have not known the judgment of the Lord* (Jer. 8: 7). The Saviour wept over the ruin of the faithless city, while she herself knew not that it was coming. *If thou also hadst known,* He said, *even thou;* and we may understand Him to have meant, 'Thou wouldst have wept, instead of making merry, as thou now dost, not knowing what is hanging over thee.' And he added, *at least in this thy day, the things that are to thy peace.* While she was giving herself up to carnal pleasures, and never looked forward to the coming sorrows, she had still for a day in her power the things which might have brought peace to her. *But now they are hidden from thy eyes,* says the Lord. For, had the misfortunes threatening her been known, she would not have founded her hope and happiness upon that prosperous state by which she was deceived. And for this reason were foretold to her by the Redeemer all the evils she had later on to bear from the Roman army.

II. And as we see Jerusalem destroyed, and the temple, once the abode of thieves before our Lord had cast them out, now a mass of ruins, do we not perceive in these ruins an image of the spiritual destruction of our own moral conduct, destruction which we have every reason to be afraid of? *Seeing the city, He wept over it.* Indeed, our Lord once wept over Jerusalem and foretold her ruin; and He does the same every day, since He and His ministers and elect behold how some souls forsake the road to holiness and give themselves up to corrupt ways. He laments the blindness of these people, who ignore His lamentations and confirm the words of Solomon: *Who are glad when they have done evil and rejoice in the most wicked things* (Prov. 2: 14). For should these wicked people recognise their impending damnation, they would shed tears with the good Christians, who bewail their destruction. In all truth we may apply to such souls running to their perdition these words of Jesus: *If thou also hadst known, and that in this thy day, the things that are to thy peace; but now they are hidden from thy eyes.* These perverse souls, thinking only of the present time, and looking at this time, which quickly passes away, as their happiest days, seem to find true peace in earthly pleasures. Amidst the perishable things of this world by which they are dazzled — honours, puffing them up, carnal lust by which they are carried away with delight — such souls are in peace, and will not be disturbed by anything or the peaceful and bright day that destroys in their memory the fear of the terrible punishments awaiting them. But another, a different day will throw such souls into the eternal damnation, when they will see themselves in great affliction, whilst the just will be overwhelmed with joy and comfort; for on that terrible day the sweetness tasted now will be changed into bitterness and wrath. Then the reprobate souls will turn their anger and fury against themselves; they will upbraid themselves for not being terrified by the terrible condemnation threatened by God, and for having shut their eyes so as not to foresee the punishments heaped up and reserved for their unhappy future. Therefore it is said: *But now they are hidden from thy eyes.* Giving themselves entirely up to earthly things and rushing after the pleasures of this life, these souls cannot see the misery following their footsteps. And should the consideration of the future inspire such souls with fear, amidst the worldly pleasures they dismiss such a terrible sight from their mind, and blindfoldly rush amid frivolous amusements towards the everlasting flames. The wise man was right when he said: *In the day of good things be not unmindful of evils; and in the day of evils be not unmindful of good things* (Ecclus. 11: 27). And St. Paul says: *And they that rejoice be as if they rejoiced not* (1 Cor. 7: 30). Though it be lawful to rejoice in this world, the fear of the coming judgment should not forsake us; then our soul, at the sight of the Lord's wrath, would be penetrated with terror, be moderate in the pleasures of life, and would courageously look forward to the beginning of the great day. *Blessed is the man,* says Solomon, *that is always fearful; but he that is hardened in mind shall fall into evil* (Prov. 28: 14). Meanwhile the wrath of God will be the more terrible on that fearful day, the less we now fear to irritate Him by our sins.

III. Our Lord continues the history of the evils befalling Jerusalem, saying: *For the days shall come upon thee, and thy enemies shall cast a trench about thee, and compass thee round, and straiten thee on every side.* Who are these enemies but the devils, our sworn foes, laying snares to our soul which, by their allurements, is kept up in the love of the pleasures of this life, but will be besieged by them at the moment when it has to leave the body? Indeed, we may say that at the moment of our death the devil will make to himself a trench of our sins, and compass us round, and thus drag our soul down into hell. In that unhappy moment the sinful soul will be straitened on every side by this cruel enemy, without any hope of escaping, since the time for doing penance or good works, neglected during life, will now be passed. Truly, it may be said of that poor soul, that it is attacked by the enemy on every side, for not only the wicked actions, but also the bad thoughts and desires, are brought up against it. *In that day all their thoughts shall perish* (Ps. 145: 4). And these thoughts may be compared to stones, for our Lord said: *And they shall not leave in thee a stone upon a stone.* The perverse mind and the wicked thoughts form, so to speak, stones upon stones, and the more so, since that poor soul made such bad use of its former freedom.

IV. And what was the cause of that great evil? Listen to our Lord, saying: *Because thou hast not known the time of thy visitation.* Almighty God visits the soul of the sinner in different ways: now He announces by His ministers the great and Divine truths; now He chastises that soul with the scourges of His justice; again He meets that soul in a wonderful manner with His richest blessings. Acting thus, and making use of different means, God endeavours to convince that soul of the eternal truths so long unknown to it. When the word of God is not powerful enough to convert that soul; when the severity of His punishments cannot humble it, nor conquer its hardness; when all these means have been useless, then the infinitely merciful God sometimes pours out His blessings with a generous hand, that the ingratitude of the sinful soul might perhaps put it to shame. But should this soul wilfully refuse to recognise the time of visitation, then God will give it over to its enemies, with whom it must suffer the pains of damnation. Let us, therefore, make good use of the advice given by our Lord: *When thou goest with thy adversary to the prince, whilst thou art in the way endeavour to be delivered from him; lest perhaps he draw thee to the judge, and the judge deliver thee to the exacter, and the exacter cast thee into prison* (Luke 12: 58). This adversary, spoken of here, is the word of God, by which our passions are continually opposed during life. If the sinner humbly submits to the commands of this adversary, and faithfully obeys them, he shall be delivered from his persecutions. Whereas if he does not endeavour to be delivered in this manner, he will be drawn to the judge, and by him delivered to the officer of justice. The word of God, now despised by the sinner, will witness against him before the judgment-seat of the Almighty. He will be delivered by his Judge to the officer of His wrath — that is, the devil — by whom the poor sinner will be tortured with so much greater fury, the easier he had yielded during life to all vicious temptations. When it is said that the sinful soul will be cast into prison by the officer of justice, this means that it will be kept in hell until the day of the last judgment, when the bodies of the damned united with their souls, will be cast into the everlasting flames, there to suffer with the infernal spirits.

V. Our Lord, after ending the description of the destruction of the unhappy city, which is applied to the perdition of a sinful soul, *entering into the temple, He began to cast out them that sold therein, and them that bought*. This temple is also an image of a Christian soul, for our conscience is the temple and house of God. Yet, when the human mind is filled with sinful thoughts against the neighbour, it becomes like a den of thieves and murderers; for such a soul is armed with murderous designs against simple and innocent Christians, and discharges its arrows for their destruction. Thus our soul, deprived of innocence and simplicity of justice, instead of being a house of prayer and meditation, becomes a den of thieves, as it is to others a cause of scandal and perdition. According to the Gospel, *He was teaching daily in the temple.* This certainly means that He is still continuing to teach — that is, that He is *teaching daily in the temple,* enlightening the souls of the faithful, and showing them how to avoid sin. However, we ought to know that we shall be powerfully instructed in the truth, only when the future evils we ought to be afraid of are continually placed before our eyes, and that we endeavour to avoid them, never losing sight of these words of wisdom: *In all thy works remember the last end, and thou shalt never sin* (Ecclus. 7: 40). So let us, then, every day consider these words Jesus addressed to us: *If thou hadst known, and that in this thy day, the things that are to thy peace; but now they are hidden from thy eyes.* And since that severe Judge still patiently bears with us, and does not stretch out His arm to strike us; since the day of His wrath seems to be far off, let us think of the great calamities following that day, and let us endeavour to avoid them by being sorry for our sins. Let us despise the pleasures of the present life, and let us never be dazzled by its sinful amusements; then we shall not be dragged into the deep abyss now hidden by them from our eyes.

50. TENTH SUNDAY AFTER PENTECOST

GOSPEL: Luke 18: 9-14. *At that time:* Jesus spoke this parable to some who trusted in themselves as just, and despised others. Two men went up into the temple to pray; the one was a Pharisee, and the other a Publican. The Pharisee, standing, prayed thus with himself: O God, I give Thee thanks that I am not as the rest of men, extortioners, unjust, adulterers, as also is this Publican. I fast twice in the week: I give tithes of all that I possess. And the Publican standing afar off would not so much as lift up his eyes towards heaven; but struck his breast, saying: O God, be merciful to me a sinner. I say to you, this man went down into his house justified rather than the other, because everyone that exalteth himself shall be humbled, and he that humbleth himself shall be exalted.

HOMILY BY ST. AUGUSTINE
One Hundred and Fifteenth Homily on the Words of the Lord

I. THE PROUD PHARISEE, BOASTING OF HIS VIRtues, might at least have said: 'I am not as many men are.' But what is the meaning of *the rest of men?* All other men, but himself. Indeed, to say 'I am just,' does it not mean that all others are sinners? *I am not as the rest of men, extortioners, unjust, adulterers.* And, lo, the presence of the Publican gives him an occasion of greater pride: *As also this Publican.* He was alone, according to his proud thoughts, and the Publican was of the rest of men. My own justice makes the difference between me and the wicked, such as he is. *I fast twice in the week; I give tithes of all that I possess.* Now it would be in vain to look in his prayer for anything he went to the temple to ask for; you will find nothing. He went up to pray; but his prayer was not a request for anything from God, it was a glorification of himself. It was but little not to pray to God; but what do you think of his praising himself, and even despising his neighbour who did pray? *And the Publican standing afar off* was yet praying near to God. Conscious of his own self he kept at a distance, while his piety drew him near to God. Though the Publican stood afar off, the Lord was at hand to hear him. *For the Lord is high and looketh on the low, and the high,* as was this Pharisee, *He knoweth afar off* (Ps. 137: 6). The proud, indeed, God knows afar off, but He does not pardon them. Consider still more the humility of the Publican. It was not only that he stood afar off, but *he would not so much as lift up his eyes to heaven.* He looked not, that he might be looked upon. He dared not to look, for self-knowledge kept him down, but hope raised him up. Consider again how he *struck his breast.* He punished himself; therefore God had compassion on his confession of guilt. *He struck his breast, saying: God be merciful to me a sinner.* Behold him that is praying. And what are you wondering at? The sinner remembers, and God forgets!

II. After seeing the difference between the Pharisee and the Publican, let us now examine how they are judged by God Himself. The first praises himself, thinking himself better than the rest of men; the other, in his humility, accuses himself of his sins. And what is the Judge's sentence? *Amen, I say to you: this man went down to his house justified rather than the other, the Pharisee.* O Lord, I ask Thee for the cause of this difference; why did the Publican and not the Pharisee go down to his house justified? Thy answer will be: *Because everyone that exalteth himself shall be humbled, and he that humbleth himself shall be exalted.* Have you heard the sentence? Then take care lest your pride be the cause of your condemnation.

III. Those who rely on their own power and make use of the language of infidels, let them consider that, when saying: God gave me my nature, but I made myself just, they are worse than this Pharisee. For, after all, this Pharisee, though praising himself, was grateful to God, since he added: *O God, I give Thee thanks that I am not as the rest of men.* He is blamed, not for giving thanks to God, but because by his words, boasting of not being *as the rest of men,* he expressed the pride of his heart. Indeed, he seemed to say in as many words, that nothing could be added to his merits, and that he was asking for nothing. *I am not as the rest of men, extortioners, unjust, adulterers.* Does he not seem to say that he alone was just, that he was in need of nothing from God, since in his conceit he was already overwhelmed with merits and virtues? Therefore, boasting in this way he imagines himself not to be in need of God's help, and gives the lie to the Truth, saying: *The life of man upon earth is a warfare* (Job 7: 1). O proud Pharisee, thou seemest to say to thyself that it would be useless to ask God to forgive thy sins, for thou thinkest thyself just! Now that this man is justly condemned for thanking God in a proud manner, what shall we think of those who wickedly attack the grace of God?

IV. After the justification of the Publican and the condemnation of the Pharisee, children are presented, and our Lord is asked to receive and even to touch them. Did it not become Jesus Christ, the great Physician, to touch them so as to cure them? Do not object and say that these children were not afflicted with any corporal disease; for my answer will be, that these children were in need of a Saviour, and that they were received by the Saviour who had said: *The Son of Man is come to seek and save that which was lost* (Luke 19: 10). But how were they lost, and in what consisted their sins, since they were innocent children? What was their sin? Listen to the Apostle saying: *By one man sin entered into this world, and by sin death, and so death passed upon all men, in whom all have sinned* (Rom. 5: 12). Let, then, the children come; let them come and hear the Lord: *Suffer children to come to Me.* Let them come to the heavenly Physician, that He may touch them; let them come to the Saviour and be saved by Him. They have not sinned; yet they are like the branches of a tree the roots of which are infected with disease. May the Lord bless the little ones and the big ones, and touch them both to cure them. We beseech you, who are grown up, to take care of the little ones; to speak for those who are still mute; to pray for those who have but tears. Consider that, at an age when work is your duty, you must be the protectors of the little ones, and defend their cause. We were lost like them, so let us be united with them in Jesus Christ. They are less guilty than we are, but the grace of Jesus is given to all. The children have but the sin of their origin — that is, the original sin; why then should those, who to this first sin have added many other sins, place obstacles to the salvation of the little ones? Is it not true that the more we advance in years the more we increase in wickedness? However, the grace of God blots out both the sin brought with us into this world and all sin added to it; for *where sin abounded, grace did more abound* (Rom. 5: 20).

51. ELEVENTH SUNDAY AFTER PENTECOST

GOSPEL: Mark 7: 31-37. *At that time:* Jesus, going out of the coast of Tyre, He came by Sidon to the Sea of Galilee, through the midst of the coast of Decapolis. And they bring to Him one deaf and dumb, and they besought Him that He would lay His hand upon him. And, taking him from the multitude apart, He put His fingers into his ears, and spitting, He touched his tongue; and looking up to heaven, He groaned, and said to him, Ephpheta — that is, Be thou opened. And immediately his ears were opened, and the string of his tongue was loosed, and he spoke right. And He charged them that they should tell no man; but the more He charged them, so much the more did they publish it. And so much the more did they wonder, saying: He hath done all things well; He hath made both the deaf to hear and the dumb to speak.

HOMILY BY POPE ST. GREGORY
On Ezechiel, Bk. I, Homily 10

I. WHAT IS THE MEANING OF THIS FACT THAT, when God, the Creator of all men, was about to heal a deaf and dumb man, *He put His fingers into his ears, and spitting, He touched his tongue*? Are not the gifts of the Holy Ghost figured by the fingers of the Redeemer? Hence it is mentioned in another place that, after casting out an evil spirit, He said: *If I by the finger of God cast out devils, doubtless the kingdom of God is come upon you* (Luke 11: 20). The same idea is expressed by another Evangelist in these words: *If I by the Spirit of God cast out devils, then is the kingdom of God come upon you* (Matt. 12: 28). And setting these two passages together, we see that the *finger of God* is called the *Spirit of God*; that our Lord, putting His fingers into the deaf man's ears, enlightened by the gift of the Holy Ghost his dark mind into obedience. And what is the meaning of *spitting, He touched his tongue?* Out of the Redeemer's mouth we receive spittle upon our tongues, when the wisdom of speaking God's truth is given to us. Spittle flows from the head into our mouth; and so that wisdom, which is Himself, the great Head of the Church, as soon as it has touched our tongue, at once takes the form of preaching. *And, looking up to heaven, He groaned.* Not that He had any need to sigh or to groan, He Who gave whatsoever He asked. But He wished to teach us to look up and sigh towards Him Whose throne is in heaven, and, confessing our needs, to obtain that our ears should be opened by the gifts of the Holy Ghost, and our tongue loosed by the saliva of our Saviour's mouth—that is, by the knowledge of His Divine word, before using it to preach to others. *And He said to him, Ephpheta— that is, Be thou opened. And immediately his ears were opened, and the string of his tongue was loosed.* Let us remark that the command Be thou opened was addressed to the deaf ears; yet the tongue also was loosed. Just so. When the ears of a man's heart are opened to learn the obedience of faith, the string of his tongue also is loosed, that he may exhort others to do the good things which he does. It is well added, *And he spoke right.* For he only does well preach obedience to others, who has first learnt to obey.

II. *And so much the more did they wonder, saying: He hath done all things well.* These words were spoken by the admiring multitude, uttered by them in a transport of wonder at the great miracle wrought by our Lord on the deaf and dumb man brought to Him. The condition of this man was truly deplorable, and rendered him an object of our Saviour's compassion. He is also a figure of the much more deplorable condition of wilful and habitual sinners, who are spiritually deaf and dumb; who do not, because they will not, hear those things that belong to their great and eternal interest; who, though having tongues, may be said to be dumb, because of their making a wrong use of their faculty of speech. It is to cure these unhappy sinners that Christ, by His ministers, offers His assistance, to put His fingers into their ears, and to touch their tongues. Yet, they must be willing to accept the remedies, and to be aware of the danger in which they are. Thus our first duty is to show wilful sinners that they are truly and spiritually deaf and dumb; then to make them willing to apply the proposed remedies.

III. The Royal Psalmist, speaking of the heathen idols, says: *They have ears, and hear not; they have a mouth, and speak not* (Ps. 113). The same may be said, in a spiritual sense, of sinners who, in spite of all exhortations, choose to proceed in their sinful ways. Holy Scripture calls them *deaf,* and pronounces them *dumb dogs;* for though they enjoy the senses of hearing and speaking, by the wrong use of them, they make their condition worse than if they had them not. To be corporally deaf, so as not to hear what is said, is a very great misfortune and deserves compassion, though there is nothing criminal in it. But a wilfully spiritual deafness, and an obstinate refusing to hearken to what is said, is more than a misfortune: it is a voluntary crime. Such are sinners, viz., those obstinately continuing in their criminal ways. They have ears, but will not hear; they are deaf, not by misfortune, but by choice. They are often called upon, and often spoken to; and what is told them is in the name of God, Who said: *He that heareth you, heareth Me; and he that despiseth you, despiseth Me* (Luke 10: 16). Nay, God Himself often speaks to them and calls upon them to leave the broad and dangerous road of sin, assuring them that it leads to destruction. To continue on this dangerous road, to persist in this fatal and broad way, what is it, but a proof that we do not and will not hear, and stop our ears against every admonition, and that, if we perish, it is our own fault.

IV. What has been said of sinners being spiritually and wilfully deaf, is equally true of the faculty of speaking, which they have lost in the same way. To be dumb is generally considered as a natural consequence of being deaf. For not being able to hear what is said, it is not easy to learn how to speak. In like manner, when sinners have contracted a spiritual deafness, and will not hear what is said to them about their duties, there is no wonder that they become likewise spiritually dumb, as to the right use of speech. A proof of spiritual dumbness is the too frequent omission of prayer, of devotion, and of other religious duties. In this respect many are dumb; for though they know how to speak, and do so very often, and with great eloquence, about the things of this world, yet, in regard to God and His honour and service, they know not how — that is, they will not open their mouths. And, while they often run on with great volubility of speech in speaking ill of their neighbours, they will not say one single word in his defence. Again there are many and horrible abuses of the tongue by cursing and swearing, by calumny, lying and detraction, vain and immodest conversations. It is quite clear that those, who employ their tongues in such discourses, are in a worse condition than the dumb man in the Gospel. In these, and many other cases, sinners show themselves to be deaf and dumb; and since they are in this unhappy condition, it will be a great work of charity to endeavour to cure them, greater even than to cure a man who cannot hear or speak. For such a cure to be effected, sinners spiritually deaf and dumb must be sensible of their sad state. Of this they are often told, and they are also reminded of the danger they are in of being lost for ever. Such sinners also must have recourse to Jesus, and by sincere sorrow and contrition, seek to obtain pardon. This sorrow must be accompanied by firm and sincere resolutions of amendment, and a careful avoiding of sin and occasions of sins. Thus disposed let them apply to the ministers of God in the holy Sacrament of penance. It is there Jesus will put His fingers into their ears, will touch their tongue and say these powerful words: *Ephpheta — that is, Be thou opened.* And their ears will be opened and their tongues loosed, and they will speak plain and right. Yet let them take care of not relapsing into former sins, but of being faithful to their good purposes.

52. TWELFTH SUNDAY AFTER PENTECOST

GOSPEL: Luke 10: 23-37. *At that time*: Jesus said to His disciples: Blessed are the eyes that see the things which you see. For I say to you, that many prophets and kings have desired to see the things that you see, and have not seen them; and to hear the things that you hear, and have not heard them. And behold a certain lawyer stood up, tempting Him, and saying: Master, what must I do to possess eternal life? But He said to him: What is written in the law? how readest thou? He answering said: Thou shalt love the Lord thy God with thy whole heart, and with thy whole soul, and with all thy strength, and with all thy mind; and thy neighbour as thyself. And He said to him: Thou hast answered rightly: this do and thou shalt live. But he, willing to justify himself, said to Jesus: And who is my neighbour? And Jesus answering, said: A certain man went down from Jerusalem to Jericho, and fell among robbers, who stripped him, and having wounded him, went away, leaving him half dead. And it chanced that a certain priest went down the same way, and seeing him, passed by. In like manner also a levite, when he was near the place and saw him, passed by. But a certain Samaritan, being on his journey, came near him, and seeing him, was moved with compassion. And going up to him, bound up his wounds, pouring in oil and wine; and setting him upon his own beast, brought him to an inn, and took care of him. And the next day he took out two pence and gave to the host, and said: Take care of him, and whatsoever thou shalt spend over and above, I at my return will repay thee. Which of these three, in thy opinion, was neighbour to him that fell among the robbers? But he said: He that showed mercy to him. And Jesus said to him: Go, and do thou in like manner.

HOMILY BY THE VENERABLE BEDE
On St. Luke 10, Bk. III, Chapter 43

I. *AND TURNING TO HIS DISCIPLES, HE SAID: BLESSED are the eyes that see the things which you see.* Blessed were the eyes— not of Scribes and Pharisees, which saw only the body of the Lord but of those who were able to see the things belonging to faith and salvation, and of whom it is written: *Thou hast hidden these things from the wise and prudent, and hast revealed them to little ones* (Luke 10: 21). Blessed, therefore, are the eyes of the humble and little ones, to whom the Son of God deigned to reveal Himself and the Father also. *I say to you that many prophets and kings have desired to see the things you see, and have not seen them.* Even patriarchs desired to see these things: *Abraham your father rejoiced that he might see My day*—the day of My Birth; *he saw it*—in his strong faith *and was glad* (John 8: 56). Isaias and Micheas and many other holy prophets saw in the darkness of future times the glory of the Lord, wherefore they are called SEERS in Holy Scripture. But they all beheld it afar off, seeing it *through a glass, in a dark manner* (1 Cor. 13: 12). But the Apostles, having the happiness of seeing our Lord face to face, of eating with Him, and learning from Him by their questions whatsoever they liked, had no need of being taught by angels or by different kinds of visions. They who by Luke are called *prophets and kings*, are named by Matthew *prophets and just men* (13: 17). Just men are mighty kings indeed, for they know how to govern their rebellious passions, instead of falling under them, and thus becoming their slaves.

II. *And behold a certain lawyer stood up, tempting Him, and saying: Master, what must I do to possess eternal life?* This lawyer, who stood up to ask the Lord a tempting question about eternal life, took the subject of his asking, as I think, from the words just uttered by our Lord: *Rejoice in this, that your names are written in heaven* (10: 20). But his attempt was certainly a proof of these other words

52. TWELFTH SUNDAY AFTER PENTECOST

immediately following: *I confess to Thee, Father, Lord of heaven and earth, because Thou hast hidden these things from the wise and prudent, and hast revealed them to little ones.*

III. However, our Lord answered the lawyer, and put this question to him: *What is written in the law? And the lawyer, answering, said: Thou shalt love the Lord thy God with thy whole heart, and with thy whole soul, and with all thy strength, and with all thy mind; and thy neighbour as thyself.* And the Lord praised that answer as very good, since by the love of God we attain perfection, and walk on the road to eternal life; and He said: *This do, and thou shalt live.* Again, when the lawyer, answering Jesus, said that the *neighbour* was he who showed mercy to the man fallen among robbers on the road to Jericho, Jesus said to him: *Go, and do thou in like manner.* And by these words our Redeemer seems to say: Remember that the charity and help thou owest to thy neighbour must be like that of the Samaritan — must consist, not in words only, but in deeds, if by thy charity thou wish to obtain eternal life.

IV. *But he, willing to justify himself, said to Jesus: And who is my neighbour?* Consider the foolishness of his vainglory! He wished to justify himself, and at the same time to obtain the favour and esteem of the people who were listening to him. Trying to show his presumptuous wisdom before the eyes of the world, he only disclosed his ignorance concerning the first commandment prescribed by the Law. Yet, though pronounced by Jesus as wise and prudent, this lawyer deserved to be deprived of the special knowledge of the mysteries of God, revealed to pure and innocent souls, because he refused to humble himself with the little ones so dear to Jesus, and wished to justify himself.

V. Let us finally consider that, by His answer to the lawyer concerning our neighbour, our Lord wished to convey this lesson, that the neighbour is he who does mercy and gives assistance to those in need. But besides this, we are taught by the parable that, under the word neighbour may be understood the Son of God Himself, Who approached us in a visible manner, when assuming our human nature. Yet, this meaning of Jesus Christ, being our neighbour, must not be taken in a figurative sense, as if dispensing us from the duty of rendering to our brethren all the works of love and charity commanded by the Law.

VI. Carefully considering the parable in this Gospel, we shall at once see that the Samaritan, giving a helping hand to the man found on the road and covered with wounds, is a figure of Jesus Christ, Who, in a more worthy and sublime sense and with a special love, became our neighbour by taking upon Himself our wounds to heal them. Let us, therefore, love Him, for He is our Lord and God; let us love Him as our neighbour, since, being our Head and we His members, He cannot be nearer to us. Let us also love those that follow Him, and show that we love our neighbour as ourselves by giving them all spiritual and temporal help in our power.

53. THIRTEENTH SUNDAY AFTER PENTECOST

GOSPEL: Luke 17: 11-19. *At that time:* As Jesus was going to Jerusalem, He passed through the midst of Samaria and Galilee. And as He entered into a certain town, there met Him ten men that were lepers, who stood afar off and lifted up their voice, saying: Jesus, Master, have mercy on us. Whom, when He saw, He said: Go, show yourselves to the priests. And it came to pass, as they went, they were made clean. And one of them, when he saw that he was made clean, went back, with a loud voice glorifying God. And he fell on his face before His feet, giving thanks; and this was a Samaritan. And Jesus, answering, said: Were not ten made clean, and where are the nine? There is no one found to return and give glory to God, but this stranger. And He said to him: Arise, go thy way; for thy faith hath made thee whole.

HOMILY BY ST. AUGUSTINE
On Gospel Questions, Bk. II, Chapter 40

I. THE TEN LEPERS MET BY JESUS WHEN GOING to Jerusalem *lifted up their voice, saying: Jesus, Master, have mercy on us. Whom, when He saw, He said: Go, show yourselves to the priests. And it came to pass, as they went, they were made clean.* Considering this fact, we ask: Why did the Lord send them to the priests, that they might be cleansed as they went? Lepers were the only class among those whose bodies were cured by Jesus, who were sent by Him to the priests. In another place it is written that our Lord said to a leper whom He had cleansed: *Go, show thyself to the priest, and offer for thy cleansing according as Moses commanded for a testimony to them* (Luke 5: 14). We ask, then, of what leprosy was a type, since those who were delivered were called, not *healed*, but *cleansed*. This disease first appears in the colour of the skin, but does not immediately destroy the health, nor the use of the feeling and the limbs. Lepers, we may not absurdly suppose, are the types of those who have not the knowledge of the true faith, but show forth various teachings of error. They do not hide their ignorance, but make use of all the wit they have to manifest and proclaim it in high-sounding words. There is no false doctrine, but has some truth mixed with it. A man's discourse with some truths in it mingled with errors, and all confounded in one mass, is like to the body of one stricken with leprosy, whereon various foul colours appear in different places along with the true colour of the skin.

II. It follows that such men are to be avoided by the faithful, to the end that, standing afar off, they may lift up their voices and cry to the Lord, just as the ten lepers, standing outside the village, *lifted up their voice, saying: Jesus, Master, have mercy on us.* Notice that they called Him Master; and I know not that any of those who were cured by Him, ever called Him by this title. I think by this it is sufficiently shown that leprosy signifies false doctrines, whereof we are cleansed by the Good Master.

III. As to the priests, to whom the ten lepers were sent, it is known to every good Christian that they were a figure or type of the kingly priesthood — that is, the Church, by whom the faithful, belonging to the body of Christ, are consecrated, He being the true High Priest. Now all the faithful are anointed, what among the Jews was the privilege only of kings and priests. St. Peter, therefore, in his first Epistle (1 Pet. 2: 9) calls them *a kingly priesthood,* because in some manner the dignity of king and priest belongs to them by reason of their unction. There is no doubt that the diseases of our soul and the defects of our mind and senses are cured and corrected in our conscience by Jesus Himself. However, when our ignorance is to be enlightened by words suitable to our needs; when we are to receive the Sacraments, then we must have recourse to the ministers appointed by our Lord. These ministers are to pronounce on the colour of the leprosy, so as not to confound it with the true and sincere doctrine manifested by the good works brought forth. St. Paul was thus instructed. He heard the voice: *Saul, Saul, why persecutest thou Me? Who said: Who art Thou, Lord? And He: I am Jesus Whom thou persecutest* (Acts 9: 4, 5). Yet, he was sent to Ananias, who, by virtue of the power of the priesthood, was to instruct him in the doctrine of faith, and afterwards to pronounce on the genuineness of his colour — that is, of his mission to the Gentiles.

IV. It does not follow from this that Jesus could not do all that by Himself, for who else does all these things in His Church? But if He wishes us to consult His ministers, and thus to be made sure of the doctrine and faith we profess, it is to unite all the members of His Church into one and the same society or fold, with the one and same doctrine, and thus to preserve the unity and soundness of colour — that is, of faith, the one sure mark of the Church. This is confirmed by the words of St. Paul to the Galatians: *Then after fourteen years I went up again to Jerusalem with Barnabas, taking Titus also with me. And I went up according to revelation, and conferred with them the Gospel which I preach among the Gentiles, but apart with them who seemed to be something; lest perhaps I should run or had run in vain* (Gal. 2: 1). And soon after he adds: *And when they had known the grace that was given to me, James and Cephas and John, who seemed to be pillars, gave to me and Barnabas the right hand of fellowship* (2: 9). This conference of St. Paul with the three Apostles clearly shows the necessity of knowing whether his doctrine agreed with the true doctrine of the Church of Christ. We hear him, therefore, beseeching the Corinthians to remain in the unity of doctrine: *I beseech you, brethren, by the name of our Lord Jesus Christ, that you all speak the same thing* (1 Cor. 1: 10).

V. Then the centurion Cornelius was told by an Angel of God that his prayers and almsgivings had *ascended for a memorial in the sight of God* (Acts 10: 4); yet he was ordered *to send men to Joppe, and call hither one Simon, who is surnamed Peter,* to receive from him the true doctrine and the unity of the Sacraments. Telling him and his whole house to send for Peter seems as if our Lord had said: *Go, show yourselves to the priests. And, as they went, they were made clean.* Peter had already come to them; but since they had not received the Sacrament of Baptism, they had not been spiritually presented to the priests, though their cleansing had been declared by the Holy Ghost coming into them, and by the gift of tongues imparted to them.

VI. There is no doubt about this; yet it may happen that we are delivered from leprosy — that is, from false doctrines after accepting the true faith and embracing the doctrine of the Church in all its points, so as to be able to distinguish between the things coming from the Creator and those proceeding from His creatures. But we still remain ungrateful towards God, by Whom we were cleansed from our spiritual leprosy. Our pride and our presumption, preventing us from humbly recognising the blessings of our Creator, are the cause of our ingratitude. We are like those spoken of by the Apostle: *When they knew God, they have not glorified Him as God, or given thanks* (Rom. 1: 21). Note these words of the Apostle. They mean that these people knew God, and were freed from the leprosy of error, yet were still afflicted with ingratitude towards their Creator Who had enlightened them. They must, therefore, be reckoned among the nine lepers of the Gospel. This number *nine* is imperfect, and must increase by one, and thus be made perfect, since nothing can be added to the number *ten*, perfect in itself. This tenth is the leper who came back, *with a loud voice glorifying God and giving thanks*. He represents the Church, in whom alone there is unity. He is praised by our Lord, whereas the nine others are rejected and condemned on account of their ingratitude. Consider also that these nine lepers were a type of the Jews, who, through their pride and ingratitude, lost the kingdom of heaven; whereas the one who came back giving thanks was a Samaritan, who, like a faithful keeper of entrusted goods, preserved this kingdom by his humility and thankfulness, and could say with the prophet: *I will keep my strength to Thee, for Thou art my Protector* (Ps. 58: 10).

54. FOURTEENTH SUNDAY AFTER PENTECOST

GOSPEL: Matt. 6: 24-33. *At that time*: Jesus said to His disciples: No man can serve two masters. For either he will hate the one, and love the other; or he will sustain the one, and despise the other. You cannot serve God and mammon. Therefore I say to you, Be not solicitous for your life, what you shall eat, nor for your body, what you shall put on. Is not the life more than the meat, and the body more than the raiment? Behold the birds of the air, for they neither sow, nor do they reap, nor gather into barns; and your Heavenly Father feedeth them. Are not you of much more value than they? And which of you, by taking thought, can add to his stature one cubit? And for raiment, why are you solicitous? Consider the lilies of the field how they grow; they labour not, neither do they spin. But I say to you, that not even Solomon in all his glory was arrayed as one of these. And if the grass of the field, which is today, and to-morrow is cast into the oven, God doth so clothe, how much more you, O ye of little faith? Be not solicitous, therefore, saying: What shall we eat, or what shall we drink, or wherewith shall we be clothed? For all these things do the heathens seek. For your Father knoweth that you have need of all these things. Seek ye, therefore, first the kingdom of God, and His justice, and all these things shall be added unto you.

HOMILY BY ST. AUGUSTINE
On the Lord's Sermon on the Mount, Bk. II, Chapter 14

I. THESE WORDS OF OUR LORD, *NO MAN CAN SERVE two masters*, are explained by the following: *For either he will hate the one, and love the other; or he will sustain the one, and despise the other.* We ought carefully to weigh these words, for our Lord shows who the two masters are, saying: *You cannot serve God and mammon.*

Mammon is a term which the Hebrews are said to use for *riches*. It is also a Carthaginian word, for the Punic word for *gain* is *mammon*. He that serves mammon—that is, loves riches—serves that evil one who has perversely chosen to be the lord of these earthly things, and is called by the Lord *the prince of this world* (John 14: 30). Of these two masters man will either hate the one, and love the other—that is, God—or he will sustain the one, and despise the other. He that serves mammon sustains a hard and pernicious master; for, led captive by his lust, he is a slave of the devil, though he love him not. Is there any one who loves the devil? Yet there are those who sustain him.

II. Our Lord does not say that a man serving two masters — that is, God and mammon will hate God; he will *despise* Him. For there is no one reproached by his conscience for hating God. Yet God is despised, because, His goodness being abused, He is not feared. We are warned by the Holy Ghost not to give ourselves up to such carelessness and pernicious security, for the prophet says: *My son, add not sin upon sin; and say not: The mercy of the Lord is great* (Ecclus. 5: 5, 6). These words are confirmed by the Apostle: *Knowest thou not that the benignity of God leadeth thee to penance?* (Rom. 2: 4). Indeed, what greater mercy can there be imagined than that of God forgiving sins, however great, to a converted and penitent sinner, and giving the fertility of a good olive-tree to a sterile oleaster? And has God not revealed the severity of His justice by not sparing the natural branches — that is, the Jews — but cutting them off, on account of their infidelity? If we wish to be pleasing to God, let us not think that we can serve two masters, and divide our heart; for God must be thought of in goodness and sought in the simplicity of our heart.

III. And our Lord said: *Therefore I say to you, Be not solicitous for your life, what ye shall eat, nor for your body, what you shall put on*, lest, perhaps, though such things are not superfluous, but necessary, our heart should be divided by the seeking of needful things, and that our intention should be corrupted when doing something, as it were, from compassion — that is, lest, when we seem to be seeking another's good, it should be a profit to ourselves rather than a benefit to him that we are seeking. Thus we do not seem to ourselves to sin, because we wish to obtain, not superfluities, but necessaries. And our Lord, by His teaching, admonishes us to understand that we may be guilty, if we are *too* solicitous in seeking needful things. He also reminds us that, when God created man, He gave him not only a body and a soul, but also life, more preferable than raiment and meat, so much coveted. *Is not the life more than the meat, and the body more than the raiment?* Why should He, Who gave us life, not also give us that which is necessary to sustain life? And since the body is more than the raiment, why should He, after creating our body, refuse to give us wherewithal to cover it?

IV. And should anyone ask, why the soul spoken of by our Lord, and being incorporeal, is in need of this corporeal food, I answer that the soul mentioned in this Gospel is meant for the life of man, and that the meat is to keep up that life, according to the words: *He that loveth his life shall lose it* (John 12: 25). Indeed, were not the soul taken here for the life which we are bound to lose for the kingdom of God, as the martyrs were able to do, then this command would be contradictory to the sentence in which it is said: *What doth it profit a man, if he gain the whole world, and suffer the loss of his own soul?* (Matt. 16: 26).

V. *Behold*, He said, *the birds of the air, for they neither sow, nor do they reap, nor gather into barns; and your Heavenly Father feedeth them. Are not you of much more value than they?* Indeed, the rational being — that is, man — possesses a higher rank in creation than irrational beings like birds, and is, moreover, destined to a supernatural end. *Which of you*, He added, *by taking thought, can add to his stature one cubit? And for raiment, why are you solicitous?* These words clearly tell us that, since our body, without the help and protection of God, cannot attain its present stature, we ought to leave to His power and providence the care to cover it with raiment.

VI. After speaking about the food for the body, our Lord also mentions the clothing: *And for raiment, why are you solicitous? Consider the lilies of the field how they grow; they labour not, neither do they spin. But I say to you, that not even Solomon in all his glory was arrayed as one of these. And if the grass of the field, which is today, and to-morrow is cast into the oven, God doth so clothe, how much more you, ye of little faith?* Let us not imagine that, under the figure of the birds of the air and the lilies of the field, our Lord wished to hide mysteries. He made use of these common and ordinary things to teach us more important truths. For on another occasion He made use of the parable of a certain judge *who feared not God, nor regarded man* (Luke 18: 2); yet, because the widow was troublesome, he avenged her, lest, continually coming, she weary him. We cannot say that, under the figure or allegory of this unjust judge, the person of God is meant; yet our Lord wished to convey the lesson that, when even an unjust man yields to the impetuous prayers of petitioners, God, this infinitely good and just Lord, will not refuse to be merciful to those who beseech Him.

VII. Then He says: *Be not solicitous, therefore, saying: What shall we eat, or what shall we drink, or wherewith shall we be clothed? For after all these things do the heathens seek. For your Father knoweth that you have need of all these things. Seek ye, therefore, first the kingdom of God, and His justice, and all these things shall be added unto you.* By these words we are admonished that those things we desire, as necessary to life, must not be considered as our aim, when we exert ourselves to attain virtues. For the difference between blessings, which are to be sought, and the necessaries, that are to be taken for our use, is made plain by this sentence, when He said: *Seek ye first the kingdom of God, and His justice, and all these things shall be added unto you.* The kingdom of God, therefore, and His justice are to be our principal aim and object, to which our efforts must be directed, since our eternal felicity will depend on them. This life is given to man to fight on earth as a soldier for the kingdom of heaven. But, since man cannot live without the necessary means, God promises to give them to him: *All these things shall be added unto you.* Yet He warns him to work first for the obtaining of the immortal glory prepared for him: *Seek ye first the kingdom of God.* The needful things for our corporal maintenance are to be considered as means only to obtain the everlasting goods, our final aim and object.

55. FIFTEENTH SUNDAY AFTER PENTECOST

GOSPEL: Luke 7: 11-16. *At that time*: Jesus went into a city called Naim, and there went with Him His disciples, and a great multitude. And when He came nigh to the gate of the city, behold a dead man was carried out, the only son of his mother, and she was a widow; and a great multitude of the city was with her. Whom when the Lord had seen, being moved with mercy toward her, He said to her: Weep not. And He came near, and touched the bier. And they that carried it stood still. And He said: Young man, I say to thee, arise. And he that was dead sat up, and began to speak. And He gave him to his mother. And there came a fear on them all; and they glorified God, saying: A great Prophet is risen up among us, and God hath visited His people.

HOMILY BY ST. AUGUSTINE
Forty-Fourth on the Words of the Lord

I. THE JOY OF THAT WIDOWED MOTHER, WHEN her son was again called to life, is a figure of the joy of our Mother the Church, when souls of men, spiritually dead through sin, are called to life every day. He was dead in body; they have been dead in soul. His death was exterior and visibly bewailed; whereas their inward death has neither been seen nor mourned for. But He, who had known them to be dead, sought them; and He alone knew them to be dead, Who was able to make them live. Had the Lord not come to raise the dead, the Apostle could not have said: *Rise thou that sleepest; and arise from the dead; and Christ shall enlighten thee* (Eph. 5: 14). You hear the words: *Rise thou that sleepest*, and you think they are said to an ordinary sleeper; but you understand them being said of one really dead, when you hear: *Arise from the dead*. Indeed, in Holy Scripture we see that the dead are often said to be asleep. And certainly they are all but sleeping in respect of Him Who can awaken them; but in respect of you a dead man is dead indeed, seeing he will not awake, though you call or prick or pull him to and fro. But the young man heard the word of the Lord: *Arise*, and immediately he arose, though he had been dead. No one can so easily awaken another asleep in bed, as Christ can the dead in the tomb.

II. In the Gospel we read that three dead persons were raised by our Lord visibly, thousands invisibly. But how many more were raised by Him visibly? Who knows? For all the things that He did are not written. St. John says: *There are also many other things which Jesus did; which if they were written every one, the world itself, I think, would not be able to contain the books that should be written* (John 21: 25). Doubtless there were many more raised to life; but it is not without a meaning that three only are expressly recorded. For our Lord wished that those things He did carnally, should also be understood spiritually. He did not merely work miracles for the miracles' sake; but that His works should be at once wonderful to them that saw them, and true to them that understand them. Thus, one who looks at a manuscript beautifully written, but knows not how to read, will praise the old transcriber's hand, and admire the beauty of the characters; but what those letters signify or mean he knows not, and praises by the sight of his eyes, without understanding by the mind. Whereas the man that cannot only gaze on what is common to all, but also read it, will praise the fine writing, and likewise understand its sense, which the unlearned cannot. Even so, there were some who saw Christ's miracles, and understood not what they meant, nor what they in a manner conveyed to those who understood them; they therefore only wondered at the miracles themselves. But there were others who saw the miracles, wondered at, understood them, and profited by them. And as such we ought to be in the school of Christ.

III. Those who pretend that Jesus wrought miracles only for the miracles' sake, may also say He did not know that it was not the time for fruit, when He sought figs upon the fig-tree, and found only leaves. The Evangelist says: *It was not the time for figs* (Mark 11:

13); yet, being hungry, He sought for fruit upon the tree. Will they say that Jesus was ignorant of a fact not unknown to an ordinary peasant? That the gardener tending the tree knew more than the tree's Creator? When Jesus, being hungry, sought for fruit on that fig-tree, and found only leaves, He wished to tell us that He had a more pressing hunger, and was seeking after something else than this. He found the tree full of leaves and bare of fruit, and He cursed it, and the fig-tree withered away. What had the tree done in not bearing fruit? What fault of the tree for being then fruitless? But this was a figure of those lazy and useless Christians who, by their own fault, do not bring forth any good fruit of penance and salvation; who by their own will are fruitless. The Jews were like this tree, when full of leaves and glorying in the letter of the Law, without any deeds, they cared not for the practice of real works of justice, and bore no fruit. I say this to show you that our Lord, whilst working miracles and thereby manifesting His Divine Power, had in view to teach some special truth by these very miracles which astonished the multitudes.

IV. Let us now ask what our Lord would have us learn in the raising of the three dead persons. The first was the dead daughter of one of the rulers of the synagogue. The father besought Him much, saying: *My daughter is at the point of death, come, lay Thy hand upon her, that she may be safe and may live* (Mark 5: 23). And as He went, it was announced that the daughter was dead. Word was brought to the father: *Thy daughter is dead; why dost thou trouble the Master any further?* But He went on, only saying to the father: *Fear not, only believe.* And when He came to the house, and saw the preparations for the funeral, He said: *Weep not; the maid is not dead, but sleepeth.* He spoke the truth; indeed, she slept, but only in respect of Him, Who could awaken her to life. And so, awakening her, He gave her to her parents. He also raised to life the young man mentioned in this Gospel, of which I wish to speak to you, beloved. You know how He restored him to life. He came nigh to the city of Naim, *and behold a dead man was carried out*, already beyond the gate of the city. And, moved with compassion for that mother who, a widow, and bereaved of her only son, was weeping,

He said: *Young man, I say to thee, arise. And he that was dead sat up, and began to speak. And He gave him to his mother.* And Lazarus also was raised even from his tomb. The disciples knew that Lazarus, whom Jesus loved, was sick, and He said to them: *Lazarus, our friend, sleepeth.* And they, thinking only of a healthful sleep, said: *Lord, if he sleep he shall do well. Then Jesus,* speaking more plainly, *said to them: Lazarus is dead* (John 11). Indeed, He spoke the truth; Lazarus was dead to them, but was only asleep to Him.

V. These three dead persons raised by Jesus under different circumstances, are three kinds of sinners every day awakened by Jesus from a spiritual death. The first are represented by the daughter of the ruler of the synagogue. She was still within the house, though dead, and it was in the house that Jesus raised her to life, so to speak, without difficulty, and gave her to her parents. The young man, spoken of in this Gospel, was already out of the house, but not yet in the grave. He who raised the dead maiden, not yet carried out of the house, also raised the other, who had been carried out, but was not yet buried. To give an image of the third kind of sinners, nothing remained to our Lord but to bring to life one dead and already buried, and this was done in the person of Lazarus. This mystery of the three dead persons, raised to life, may be easily understood, when we consider that there are sinners committing sins in their hearts, but not showing them exteriorly. For our Lord said: *Whosoever shall look on a woman to lust after her, hath already committed adultery with her in his heart* (Matt. 5: 28). Such sinners sometimes awake, hearing the word of God, just as if they heard the voice of Christ, saying: *Arise.* At once they condemn themselves for consenting to sin; they begin to inhale the atmosphere of a new life, and to walk on the road of justice and salvation. Of these sinners it may be said that they are like the daughter of Jairus that is, that they are restored to life, so to speak, within their house, since their hearts, once given up to sin secretly in thought and desire, now revive through the grace of God. By the second kind of sinners we understand those who having given themselves up to sins and vices, do not hesitate to show and commit them in public, and are like the young man who died in the house, but was carried out of it. Is there no hope for such sinners, who show by their exterior and sinful acts that they are spiritually dead? But did not our Lord say to the dead young man: *I say to thee, arise?* Let such sinners hope that if, in the state of death to which they were brought by their exterior sins, they will let themselves be moved and aroused by the words of truth, the voice of Christ will yet call them, and they shall not perish for ever.

VI. As to those who are so hardened in their sins that the evil habit renders them insensible, they become even defenders of their evil deeds, and are angry when they are found fault with. They are, so to speak, buried in their sins, and covered with darkness by the inveterate habit of sin and vice. Such sinners are already in the grave, and we may say of them that, like Lazarus, they begin to be a prey to rottenness and worms. *By this time he stinketh; for he is now of four days.* The heavy stone on the sepulchre is that sinful chain thrown around their neck by habitual sin, from which, as it seems, they are not able to be delivered. Such a sinner seems to be in a hopeless condition, and it may be said of him, as of Lazarus, that he *is now of four days* in the tomb. However, the same Redeemer has the power to open that sinner's eyes, covered for a long time by the terrors and deep darkness of night, and by His grace to raise him to life.

VI. And what is the conclusion to be drawn from all this? That those who enjoy the interior and supernatural life of sanctifying grace should endeavour to preserve it; whereas those deprived of it by sin should make their greatest efforts to recover it. He that carries sin in his heart, though not manifested by exterior acts, let him be penetrated by deep sorrow, and detest the very thoughts that filled his heart. He will thus be delivered from the chains of death by which he was kept in the prison of a sinful conscience. And the sinner who by exterior acts showed to the world the sins and vices that were in his heart, shall he despair? No; he is dead, indeed, not only interiorly, but even exteriorly in the eyes of the world. Nevertheless, he may be raised to life, though he evidently seems to be carried out of the house. Let him be really and interiorly sorry for his sinful and scandalous actions, and let him be careful not to be thrown into the grave, where his unfortunate habit would become the stone closing his sepulchre.

VIII. However, I am perhaps speaking to one groaning under the burden of his sins, who has become a slave of the sins habitually committed; to one, perhaps, who is already feeling the terrors of the tomb, being buried in his grievous sins. Doubtless, such a poor sinner feels wretched and miserable. Yet the arm of the Redeemer is strong enough to take him out of the deepest abyss into which death has precipitated him. God the Almighty knows how to make His voice resound into the most hardened heart, to break the most indissoluble bonds, and to overcome all obstacles opposed to the salvation of sinners. The Lord of all mercy not only knows how to restore to life the most wicked and reprobate sinner, but He also gives to His ministers the power to forgive all sins: *Whatsoever you shall loose upon earth, shall be loosed also in heaven* (Matt. 18: 18). Let such sinners do penance, and they will feel as well and pure as Lazarus, who, after his resurrection, had not a spot of corruption on his body, and came full of life out of the tomb where death had kept him for a time. Behold the useful lesson contained in this mystery. You who are in the happy state of sanctifying grace, persevere therein; but you, unhappy sinners, endeavour to shake off the heavy burden of sins by which you are now oppressed. Amen.

56. SIXTEENTH SUNDAY AFTER PENTECOST

GOSPEL: Luke 14: 1-11. *At that time*: When Jesus went into the house of one of the chief of the Pharisees on the Sabbath day to eat bread, they watched Him. And behold there was a certain man before Him that had the dropsy. And Jesus answering, spoke to the lawyers and Pharisees, saying: Is it lawful to heal on the Sabbath day? But they held their peace. But He, taking him, healed him, and sent him away. And answering them, He said: Which of you shall have an ass or an ox fall into a pit, and will not immediately draw him out on the Sabbath day? And they could not answer Him to these things. And He spoke a parable also to them that were invited, marking how they chose the first seats at the table, saying to them: When thou art invited to a wedding, sit not down in the first place, lest perhaps one more honourable than thou be invited by him; and he that invited thee and him come and say to thee: Give this man place; and then thou begin with shame to take the lowest place. But when thou art invited, go, sit down in the lowest place, that when he who invited thee cometh, he may say to thee: Friend, go up higher. Then shalt thou have glory before them that sit at table with thee; because every one that exalteth himself, shall be humbled; and he that humbleth himself, shall be exalted.

HOMILY BY ST. AMBROSE
On St. Luke 14, Bk. VII

I. THIS MAN, SICK OF THE DROPSY, WHOSE DISease—that is, the swelling of the body—was cured by our Lord, is a figure of a soul so heavy as not to be able to rise above the senses, nor to feel the impression and fire of the Holy Ghost. And our Lord continued giving an important lesson of humility, saying: *When thou art invited to a wedding, sit not down in the first place.* However, He spoke so gently that His rebuke, far from irritating the guests, convinced them of the truth of His teaching. Indeed, there was so much wisdom in the words of Jesus that the reason was convinced, whilst self-love was overcome by His arguments. There we see how the host, by whom our Lord had been invited, was taught by Him to be kind to the poor. It was not without a special motive that the poor and weak were mentioned by our Lord, since they are to be preferred in our acts of hospitality. For is it not a movement of *self-interest* to show courtesy to those—the rich—from whom we expect to receive some thing?

II. The Son of God also fixes the reward of one that has fought generously, and this reward is the kingdom of heaven promised by God to those who make good use of the things of this world. But those, purchasing to themselves earthly possessions, cannot expect to possess that kingdom. We hear our Lord say: *Go sell what thou hast and give to the poor, and follow Me* (Matt. xix. 21). It is evident that those, invited to the supper of the rich man, and making excuse, as he who had bought some yoke of oxen and wanted to try them, were shut out of the eternal kingdom. Eliseus did not act in that manner; *he killed the yoke of oxen, boiled the flesh with the plough, and gave to the people, and they ate* (3 Kings 19: 21). Neither can he win that kingdom, who married a wife, and therefore could not come, for *he that is without a wife, is solicitous for the things that belong to the Lord, how he may please God. But he that is with a wife, is solicitous for the things of the world, how he may please his wife* (1 Cor. 7: 32, 33). This is not to be taken as blaming marriage, but only to say that virginity is the more honourable way, since *the unmarried woman and the virgin* — and the widow — *thinketh of the things of the Lord; that she may be holy both in body and in spirit* (ver. 34).

III. But in all fairness, having thus spoken about widows and unmarried women, let us again return to the married, and with them entertain the opinion held by so many, that there are only three classes of men excluded from the great supper mentioned in the Gospel, and that these three classes are Heathens, Jews, and Heretics. This is the reason why we are warned by the Apostle, saying: *Walk not as also the Gentiles walk,* in malice and uncleanness and covetousness, and so have no entry into the kingdom of Christ; for *no unclean, or covetous person (which is a serving of idols), hath inheritance in the kingdom of Christ and of God* (Eph. 4: 17; 5).

IV. The Jews imposed upon themselves a heavy and useless yoke through the manifold ceremonies by which they are still oppressed. Yet the Prophet said: *Let us break their bonds asunder; and let us cast away their yoke from us* (Ps. 2: 3). As for us, we have accepted Jesus Christ, and bowed our heads under the light and gentle yoke prepared by His goodness. We may also say that the Jews were figured by the man who, having bought five yoke of oxen, excused himself; for the Books of Moses containing the Old Testament are five in number. Our Lord alluded, perhaps, to these five Books, when He said to the Samaritan woman: *Thou hast had five husbands* (John 4: 18).

V. As for heresy, by which the gates of heaven are shut to all its adherents, it tries, like a second Eve, to allure and deceive us by its attractions. For by it our faith is weakened, since faith cannot accommodate itself to our concupiscence. Thus we are dragged into the abyss; for the road to it seems easy and agreeable. The false glitter of error is often preferred to the real and unchangeable beauty of the truth. All those who were invited to the supper by the master of the house, but refused the invitation and made excuse, were justly shut out of the banquet, and this by their own fault. All men are invited by our Lord to the eternal happiness; but by their carelessness or their errors many are made unworthy of it.

57. SEVENTEENTH SUNDAY AFTER PENTECOST

GOSPEL: Matt. 22: 34-46. *At that time*: The Pharisees came to Jesus, and one of them, a doctor of the law, asked Him, tempting Him: Master, which is the great commandment of the law? Jesus said to him: Thou shalt love the Lord thy God with thy whole heart, and with thy whole soul, and with thy whole mind. This is the greatest and the first commandment. And the second is like to this: Thou shalt love thy neighbour as thyself. On these two commandments dependeth the whole law and the prophets. And the Pharisees being gathered together, Jesus asked them, saying: What think you of Christ? whose Son is He? They say to Him: David's. He saith to them: How, then, doth David in spirit call Him Lord, saying: The Lord said to my Lord, Sit on my right hand, until I make thy enemies thy footstool? If David, then, call Him Lord, how is He his Son? And no man was able to answer Him a word: neither durst any man from that day forth ask Him any more questions.

HOMILY BY ST. JOHN CHRYSOSTOM
Seventy-Second Homily on St. Matthew

I. WHEN THE PHARISEES HEARD THAT HE HAD silenced the Sadducees, they came together for a fresh attack, just when it behoved them to keep their peace. But they wished to urge further their former endeavours, and one of them professing to be skilled in law, was put forward. He did not wish to learn, but to lay a snare. He therefore proposed the question: *Which is the great commandment of the law?* Since the first commandment is this: *Thou shalt love the Lord thy God*, they expected that He would make some change or addition in His own behalf, since He made Himself God (John 10: 33). In this expectation they proposed this question; but what did Christ answer? To show that they had adopted this course from having no charity, from pining with envy and jealousy, He answered: *Thou shalt love the Lord thy God with thy whole heart, and with thy whole soul, and with thy whole mind. This is the greatest and the first commandment. And the second is like to this: Thou shalt love thy neighbour as thyself.* But why is the second commandment like to the first? Because the first is the source and support of the second. *For everyone that doth evil hateth the light, and cometh not to the light* (John 3: 20). And again: *The fool hath said in his heart: There is no God* (Ps. 13: 1). And what is the consequence of this? *They are corrupt, and are become abominable in their ways (ibid.* 2). And again: *The desire of money is the root of all evils; which some coveting have erred from the faith* (1 Tim. 6: 10). And one more: *If you love Me keep My commandments* (John 14: 15). The sum of these commandments are these words: *Thou shalt love the Lord thy God, and thy neighbour as thyself.*

II. If, therefore, to love God is to love one's neighbour, as it appears in this: *Simon, son of John, lovest thou Me? And he said: Lord, Thou knowest that I love Thee. He said to him: Feed My sheep* (John 21: 10), and if *love is the fulfilling of the law* (Rom. 13: 17), then with reason does the Lord say that *on these two commandments dependeth the law and the prophets.* And what He did before, He also does here. For, when asked about the manner of the resurrection, He taught a resurrection, instructing them at the same time beyond what they asked. So now, being interrogated concerning the first commandment, He answers them of his own accord touching the second also, which is not much inferior to the first, for the second is like to this; intimating to them that their question had arisen from hatred; *for charity envieth not,* says the Apostle (1 Cor. 13: 4). By this He showed that He was subject both to the law and the prophets.

III. Having answered the Pharisees, our Lord also in His turn asked them: *What think you of Christ? Whose Son is He? They say to Him: David's.* Now consider how Jesus was proceeding in this instance. After many miracles and many signs proving His Divinity; after many positive answers given to prove His dignity; after

57. SEVENTEENTH SUNDAY AFTER PENTECOST

a great display in words and deeds of His unanimity with the Father; and after praising the man who said that there is one God, He asked them what they thought of Christ—that is, of Him. He knew that the miracles wrought before the eyes of the Jews could not be denied by them. Yet He also knew that they would say that, though working miracles, He was an adversary to the Law and an enemy to God. After so many things He asked these questions, secretly leading them on to confess Him also to be God. He had first tried His disciples, asking them what others said of Him, and what they themselves thought of Him. He did not address Himself first to the Pharisees, for He knew they were ready to call Him a deceiver and a wicked man, speaking all things without fear. For this reason He inquired for the opinion of these men. Being about to begin His Passion, He announces David's prophecy, plainly proclaiming Him to be the Lord, and He makes use of the prophet's testimony from a reasonable cause. He introduces this in a suitable manner, so as to overthrow the mistaken opinion of the Jews pretending that He was a mere man, and shows how David proclaimed His Godhead. Indeed, the Jews had said that He was a Son of David; but in this they meant only His humanity. Now, to correct this erroneous opinion, He brings in the words of the prophet bearing witness to His being Lord, true Son of God, and equal to the Father. He does not even stop at this, but that they may be moved by fear, He adds the words: *Until I make Thy enemies Thy footstool;* that He might win them over at least in this way.

IV. And that the Pharisees may not say it was in flattery that David called Him Lord, or that it was a human exaggeration, see what He says: *How, then, doth David in spirit call Him Lord, saying: The Lord said to my Lord, Sit on My right hand?* Admire here the humility and modesty of Jesus, since it concerned His own honour. He had first said: *What think you? Whose Son is He?* in order to get their answer. And when they said *David's,* He did not reply: Yet David said these things of Him—but put another question: *How, then, doth David in spirit call Him Lord?* so that the sayings might not give offence to them. Again, He did not say to them: What think you of Me? but *of Christ*. In the same humble way did the Apostles speak, when, showing that David was not speaking of himself, but of Jesus Christ, they added: *Let us freely speak to you of the patriarch David, that he died and was buried, and his sepulchre is with us to this present day* (Acts 2: 29). Thus, through these questions and answers our Lord s intention was to give testimony to His own Divinity, making use of the words of David. But let us not think that Jesus wished to convey the idea that He was not a Son of David. He had not rebuked Peter for saying so; but He wished to correct the secret and erroneous thoughts of the Pharisees.

V. However, even when they had heard these things, they answered nothing; for they did not wish to learn of these so needful things, but only to lay a snare. He added that He was the Lord, and, saying this, the Prophet was His testimony; for He knew that they distrusted Him, and spread false and evil reports against Him. We ought to have special regard to this fact, and not to be offended if anything said by Him seems humble and lowly; for, as with many other things, He was con descending to their slow understanding. Mark also that, not only by His words and wonders, but also by the words of the Prophet, His Divinity was thoroughly proved to His enemies. For, quoting the words of David addressed to Him: *Sit on my right hand, until I make Thy enemies Thy footstool,* He clearly announced that God, His Father, will revenge Him on His enemies; that the manner in which His Father honoured Him, was a proof of His being equal to the Father; and He put upon this reasoning an end to their contention. From thenceforth they were silent, not willingly, but from their having nothing to say and they received so deadly, a blow as no longer to attempt the same thing any more. *For no man durst from that day forth ask Him any move questions.*

58. EIGHTEENTH SUNDAY AFTER PENTECOST

GOSPEL: Matt. 9: 1-8. *At that time*: Jesus entering into a boat, He passed over the water and came into His own city. And behold they brought to Him one sick of the palsy, lying on a bed. And Jesus, seeing their faith, said to the man sick of the palsy: Be of good heart, son, thy sins are forgiven thee. And behold some of the Scribes said within themselves: He blasphemeth. And Jesus, seeing their thoughts, said: Why do you think evil in your hearts? Whether is it easier to say: Thy sins are forgiven thee; or to say: Arise, and walk? But that you may know that the Son of man hath power on earth to forgive sins (then said He to the man sick of the palsy), Arise, take up thy bed, and go into thy house. And he arose and went into his house. And the multitude, seeing it, feared and glorified God that gave such power to men.

HOMILY BY ST. PETER CHRYSOLOGUS
Sermon 50

I. THAT JESUS WORKED DIVINE MYSTERIES IN those things which He did as Man, and also invisible things under the appearance of things which were seen, is shown in this day's lesson. The Gospel says: *Jesus entering into a boat, He passed over the water and came into His own city.* Was not this He Who once parted the waters, and made the dry ground appear in the depth of the sea, so that the people of Israel passed dry-shod between the masses of water standing still, as through a deep valley in a mountain? Was not this He Who made the waves of the sea solid under the feet of Peter, so that the watery path offered a firm way for human footsteps? Why, then, did He on this occasion deny to Himself a like service from the sea, but crossed over that narrow lake in a boat? *He entered into a boat, and passed over.* Why do we wonder, my brethren? Jesus Christ came to take our weakness upon Him, that He might give us His strength; to seek the things human, that He might give to men the things of God; to receive insults, that He might bestow honours; to bear our weariness, that He might give us health. For the physician, who has no infirmities, knows not how to cure the infirmities of others, nor he that is not weak with the weak, how to give strength to the weak. Had our Lord remained in His strength, what would He then have had in common with man? And if His Flesh had not also taken the infirmities of our flesh, it would have been idle for Him to take Flesh. *He entered into a boat, and passed over into His own city.* The Lord, the Creator of the world and of all things therein, having for our sake imprisoned Himself in our flesh, began to have a human fatherland, to be a citizen of a Jewish city, and to have parents, though He Himself is the Father of all parents. And all this that His love might invite, His charity draw, His tenderness bind, His gentleness persuade all those whom His Majesty, as King, had scared, His awfulness scattered, and His power terrified out of His possessions. It is certain that Jesus had no need of that boat, but the boat was in need of Him; for the Church, figured by it, is like a ship exposed in the midst of the sea to a thousand cliffs, that she will never be able to avoid without the skill of the Divine Pilot.

II. And the Gospel says: *Behold they brought to Him one sick of the palsy, lying on a bed. And Jesus, seeing their faith, said to the man sick of the palsy: Be of good heart, son, thy sins are forgiven to thee.* Now this man, cured of his palsy, remains silent, when, understanding from the words of the Redeemer, that his sins were forgiven to him, he gives no sign of gratitude for the blessing bestowed upon him by Jesus. Is this not a proof that he was more anxious to be delivered from the sickness of his body, than to receive the spiritual health of his soul? that he was more concerned about the temporal pains of his sick body, than about the eternal torments to which his soul would be condemned in the other world? Again, this man, cured of his sickness, only thinks of the present time, without giving any thought to the eternal future.

III. It was not without a special motive that Jesus, seeing the man sick of the palsy at His feet, rewarded the faith of those who had brought him. His intention was to cure the spiritual disease of the man, before giving him the health of the body. *And Jesus, seeing their faith, said to the man sick of the palsy: Be of good heart.* By these words you understand, beloved brethren, that God does not consult the will of the wicked, nor consider the faith of the ignorant; neither does He look on the foolish desires of one only sighing for corporal health; that He is ready to help a generous and living faith, and refuses nothing to a will conformable to His own Will. You know that a physician does not care much about the will of his patients, that he does not even inquire about their wishes and desires, knowing that too often they wish for things that would be injurious to them. In all seriousness he attacks the disease, sometimes prescribes the most bitter medicines, being convinced that his patients, once restored to health, will be most grateful to him for not having yielded to their foolish desires during their illness. Now, since a man has the courage to expose himself to the anger and insults of the patients he wishes to save from death, shall we be surprised at this consoling fact, that Jesus, the true Physician of souls, in His infinite love for them, is ready to deliver them, against their own will, from the abominable disease of sin, and to give them that spiritual health, the value of which they cannot recognise as long as they remain in the folly of their sinful passions? Would to God that we could probe the wounds of our soul! Then we should see it bare and without any virtue amidst the surrounding vices. Then our Redeemer would let His light shine into our darkness, and we should be convinced that He is continually trying by His grace to awaken us, and to persuade us to let ourselves be cured, taking the medicines offered by His helping hand in spite of our dislike and refusal.

IV. By saying to the man sick of the palsy that his sins were forgiven, our Lord wished to show that under the veil of His humanity He was true God. His miracles made Him to be recognised as a Prophet, for by them He was like to the prophets, who had wrought such wonderful things through His Divine assistance.

But by forgiving sins He visibly manifested His Divinity, since no one but God has the power to forgive sins. The envy and hatred of the Pharisees are the strongest proof of this; for when hearing the Son of God say to the man that his sins were forgiven, they were angry, and *said within themselves: He blasphemeth. Who can forgive sins but God alone?* (Luke 5: 21). O ye foolish Pharisees! By your words you show that wisdom and ignorance are united in your minds; you confess the truth, yet you deny it; you accuse the Redeemer, and at the same time you justify Him. If it be true, and it is true, as you confess, that God alone can forgive sins, why do you refuse to recognise Jesus as your God, He Who mercifully takes away the sins of men? *Behold the Lamb of God*, said John the Baptist, *behold Him Who taketh away the sin of the world* (John 1: 29). Do you still look for the proofs of this mystery so incomprehensible to you? then search for it in your own hearts. For, if you seriously consider the fact that this Divine Man discovers all that is in the inmost of your hearts; that He knows your most hidden thoughts; that He reveals before the eyes of men your soul's intentions begotten in darkness; then you will easily understand that the fulness of the Godhead dwells in Jesus. Thus, our Saviour deeply scrutinized the consciences of the Pharisees, revealed their intentions, and proved His Divinity. Yet, to give once more a proof of His Divine power, He granted health and strength of body to the man sick of the palsy. *Arise, take up thy bed and go into thy house.* And, saying this, He wished to teach him the duty of beginning now a different — that is, a better — life. He was to take up the bed on which he had been carried, as a sign of the miraculous manner in which he was cured. This bed, also, the witness of his sufferings, was to give testimony to Him Who wrought the miracle, and by its heaviness prove the health and strength of the man now cured. Lastly, by telling this man to *go into his house,* our Lord desired to give him to understand that, after receiving the gift of the Christian faith, he was not to return to the ways of the unbelieving Jews.

59. NINETEENTH SUNDAY AFTER PENTECOST

GOSPEL: Matt. 22: 1-14. *At that time*: Jesus spoke to the chief priests and Pharisees in parables, saying: The kingdom of heaven is likened to a king, who made a marriage for his son. And he sent his servants to call them that were invited to the marriage; and they would not come. Again he sent other servants, saying: Tell them that were invited: Behold I have prepared my dinner; my beeves and fatlings are killed, and all things are ready: come ye to the marriage. But they neglected, and went their ways, one to his farm and another to his merchandise. And the rest laid hands on his servants, and, having treated them contumeliously, put them to death. But when the king had heard of it, he was angry, and, sending his armies, he destroyed those murderers, and burnt their city. Then he said to his servants: The marriage, indeed, is ready; but they that were invited were not worthy. Go ye, therefore, into the highways, and as many as you shall find, call to the marriage. And his servants, going forth into the ways, gathered together all they found, both bad and good; and the marriage was filled with guests. And the king went in to see the guests, and he saw there a man who had not on a wedding garment. And he saith to him: Friend, how camest thou in hither, not having on a wedding garment? But he was silent. Then the king said to the waiters: Bind his hands and his feet, and cast him into the exterior darkness; there shall be weeping and gnashing of teeth. For many are called, but few are chosen.

HOMILY BY POPE ST. GREGORY, PREACHED IN THE CHURCH OF THE HOLY MARTYR CLEMENT
Thirty-Eighth Homily on the Gospels

I. I REMEMBER HAVING OFTEN SAID THAT IN THE holy Gospel the Church of God, as she is now, is called the kingdom of heaven, for the kingdom of heaven is indeed the assembly of the just. The Lord said by the mouth of His prophet: *Heaven is My throne* (Isa. 66: 1). Solomon says: *The soul of the just is the throne of wisdom* (Wisd. 7: 27); and Paul says: *Christ is the power of God and the wisdom of God* (1 Cor. 1: 24). From these passages we may clearly infer that, if wisdom be God, and wisdom's throne the soul of the just, and God's throne the heaven, then the soul of the just is heaven. Hence the Psalmist, speaking of holy preachers, says: *The heavens show forth the glory of God* (Ps. 18: 1). The kingdom of heaven, therefore, is the Church of the just—that is, of those whose hearts seek not for anything upon earth, but who so sigh for the things that are above, that God does already reign in them, as He reigns in heaven. Let it, then, be said: *The kingdom of heaven is likened to a king, who made a marriage for his son.* You understand, beloved brethren, Who is this Royal Father of a Royal Son. It is indeed He to Whom the Psalmist says: *Give to the King Thy judgment, O God, and to the King's son Thy justice* (Ps. 71: 2) — *Who made a marriage for His Son.* God the Father made a marriage for God the Son, when He wedded Him to the human nature in the womb of the Virgin, when He willed that He, Who is God before all ages, should become Man in the end of the ages.

II. The union of two persons forms the marriage union; but God forbid that we should imagine that the one Person of our Redeemer Jesus Christ, Who is both God and Man, is formed by the union of a human person with a Divine Person. We profess that He is of and in two natures; but we shrink from the blasphemy of saying that in Him there are two persons. It will be clearer and safer to say that the marriage made by the Father for His Royal Son, was the joining Him, through the mystery of the Incarnation, to His mystic Bride, the Holy Church, and that the womb of the Virgin Mother was the bridal chamber in which this union took place. Hence it is that the Psalmist says: *He hath set His tabernacle in the sun, and He as a bridegroom coming out of His bride-chamber* (Ps. 18: 6). Indeed, the Divine Redeemer came out of the purest womb of the Virgin, to unite Himself with the Church chosen by Him as His Bride. He sent out His servants to call His friends that were invited to the marriage. He sent them out twice, to give us to understand that the preachers of the great mystery of the Incarnation of the Son of God were first the prophets and after them the Apostles. The former announced this great mystery in prophecies only, whilst the latter preached to the nations announcing the same, yet being now fulfilled. The proof that the first invited refused to come to the marriage feast is contained in the words addressed to the second: *Behold, I have prepared my dinner; my beeves and fatlings are killed, and all things are ready. Come ye to the marriage.* No mention of this fact was made in the first invitation; but afterwards it was said that the beeves and fatlings were killed, that everything was ready. For when we refuse to hear the words of God, He shows us by examples that, what we think impossible, becomes easy, as soon as we understand that others were able to do the things to which He invites us.

III. The invited guests neglected the invitation, according to the words of the Gospel, *and went their ways, one to his farm, and another to his merchandise.* The one going to his farm is a type of those persons entirely bent on this world's business, whilst the other one represents those who give themselves up to temporal gains and profits. Now, since these two kinds of persons are intent on the cares and goods of this world only, they give no thought to the mystery of God made Man for the salvation of man; neither do they think of conforming their lives to the life of Jesus. It is, therefore, on account of these worldly goods and worldly interests that they refuse to come to the marriage. But what is still worse, they not only refuse to come, but despise the grace of God inviting them; for it is said: They *laid hands on His servants, and, having treated them contumeliously, put them to death.*

IV. *But when the King had heard of it, He was angry, and, sending His armies, He destroyed those murderers, and burnt their city.* He strikes the persecutors, and destroys the murderers. He burns their city — that is, the bodies, in which dwell these sinful souls, will be cast with them into the everlasting fire. The armies, sent to destroy the murderers, are the Angels of God sent with His thunderbolts to take revenge. For what are the hosts of Angels but the armies of our eternal King? Hence God is called the Lord of Sabaoth, and *Sabaoth* means hosts — the Lord of hosts (Isa. 1: 9). The armies of God are composed of the countless multitudes of Angels ordered by God to execute the sentences pronounced against His enemies, and to destroy them. Our fathers heard the Son of God threatening the world with these terrible punishments, and we, their children, have witnessed their fulfilment. Where are now the cruel persecutors of so many holy Martyrs? Where are the proud princes who lifted up their arrogant heads against God, and boasted of their worldly glory? By the death of the holy Martyrs the Christian faith has been spread abroad throughout the whole world; whereas the remembrance even of their persecutors has disappeared with their sudden death. Behold the terrible effects of God's wrath, which is spoken of in the parables of our Lord!

V. And the King, Who invites guests to the marriage of His Son, will easily fill the places of those who refuse to come. For should the word of God remain fruitless in many, it will yet find docile and ready hearts making good use of it. We read: *Then he said to his servants: The marriage indeed is ready, but they that were invited were not worthy. Go ye, therefore, into the highways; and as many as you shall find, call to the marriage.* And our Lord continues in the parable: *And his servants, going forth into the ways, gathered together all they found, both bad and good, and the marriage was filled with guests.* In these different kinds of persons brought to the marriage is seen an image of the Church, including both good and bad Christians. Are you among the good? then during all your life bear generously the presence of the bad. Be not frightened at the enormous number of the wicked, nor saddened by the small number of the just; for *wide is the gate and broad the way that leadeth to destruction, and many there are who go in thereat. How narrow is the gate, and strait is the way that leadeth to life; and few there are that find it!* (Matt. 7: 13, 14).

VI. *The King,* says the Gospel, *went in to see the guests, and he saw there a man who had not on a wedding garment.* What is the meaning of this wedding garment? It is charity. He that came to the marriage without a wedding garment had indeed the true faith, but he had not charity. It was with the garment of love that the Son of God came to celebrate the marriage union with His Bride, the Church, and in this bond of love He continues to be united with His elect. Thus St. John says: *God so loved the world, as to give His only begotten Son* (John 3: 16). Our Saviour, having come to us in love, indicates clearly enough that the wedding garment, in which we are to appear at His marriage-feast, is true charity. Those among you, who believe and belong to the communion of the Church, but have not charity, are in the marriage-hall indeed, but are not covered with the wedding garment. When you are invited to a wedding, beloved brethren, do you not take off your everyday garments and put on your best? By this you intend to show the great interest you take in the happiness and joy of the bride and bridegroom. You dare not appear in garments by which you would be despised by the other guests. Yet, it is God Who invites you to His marriage feast, and you appear without the garment of love. Heaven resounds with songs of praise of the angelic choirs, when the elect are received into their company; but you, assisting by faith at their festivities you are not ashamed to appear without the wedding garment of love, by which alone you find favour with God and His Angels.

60. TWENTIETH SUNDAY AFTER PENTECOST

GOSPEL: John 4: 46-53. *At that time*: There was a certain ruler, whose son was sick at Capharnaum. He, having heard that Jesus was come from Judea into Galilee, went to Him, and prayed Him to come down and heal his son, for he was at the point of death. Jesus therefore said unto him: Unless you see signs and wonders, you believe not. The ruler saith to Him: Lord, come down before that my son die. Jesus saith to him: Go thy way; thy son liveth. The man believed the word which Jesus said to him, and went his way. And as he was going down, his servants met him, and they brought word, saying that his son lived. He asked, therefore, of them the hour wherein he grew better. And they said to him: Yesterday at the seventh hour the fever left him. The father, therefore, knew that it was at the same hour that Jesus said to him: Thy son liveth; and himself believed and his whole house.

HOMILY BY POPE ST. GREGORY, PREACHED IN THE CHURCH OF SS. NEREUS AND ACHILLES ON THEIR FESTIVAL
Twenty-Eighth Homily on the Gospels

I. THE GOSPEL LESSON WHICH YOU HAVE JUST heard, my brethren, stands in need of no explanation. However, lest I should seem to pass it by in idle silence, I will say a few words thereon, but that rather by way of exhortation than of explanation. Indeed, there seems to me to be but one point calling for explanation, namely, this: When the ruler came to Jesus and besought Him to come down and heal his son, how is it that he heard Jesus say: *Unless you see signs and wonders, you believe not*. The very fact that the ruler came and asked Jesus to heal his son is a proof that he believed. Had he not believed Him to be a Saviour, he would not have asked Him to save his son. Yet Jesus said: *Unless you see signs and wonders, you believe not.* He had not seen any signs, yet he believed. Now, think of his prayer, and you will clearly understand wherein his faith was weak. *He prayed Him that He would come down and Heal his son.* He asked for the corporal presence of Him Who is spiritually present everywhere. He did not believe enough in Jesus, since he thought His bodily presence was required for the healing of his son. Had his faith been perfect, he would doubtless have known that God is everywhere. His faith was, therefore, imperfect for attributing the virtue of healing, not to Christ's Majesty, but to His bodily presence. Thus, even while he was asking for his son's health, his faith was not yet sound. He believed concerning Him, Whom he had come to ask, that He was mighty enough to save, yet he thought that at that very moment Jesus was absent from his son. But the Lord, being asked to go, showed that He is there, wherever He is called on; and He gave health by a single command, He Who by a single act of His will had created all things.

II. What we are to consider in this case is the answer given by Jesus, on another occasion, to the centurion asking Him to heal his servant grievously tormented by the palsy. According to the Evangelist, our Lord said: *I will come and heal him* (Matt. 8: 7). How is it that our Lord, being asked by the ruler to come to his house and heal his son, refused to go, whereas He promised the centurion to go down and heal his servant, though He had not been asked to come down and see that servant? The reason is that the Lord wished to put down our pride, that sees and esteems in others their dignities and riches, more than their nature, the image of God. Indeed, when we consider man in the things without, like riches and honours, we do not see what he is in himself, neither do we know his real merit, when considering only his body, that seems contemptible on account of its infirmities. Our Saviour judges differently. To give us to understand that whatsoever seems great in the eyes of the world, is often low and contemptible, and whatsoever is despicable in the estimation of the worldly-minded,

60. TWENTIETH SUNDAY AFTER PENTECOST

is not so before God, He goes to the servant of the centurion, whilst refusing to visit the son of the ruler.

III. Indeed, should we be asked by a servant to go down to him, our pride would tell us not to do such a thing. To yield to his prayer would be to lower ourselves, to esteem our honour very little; certainly such a place as the dwelling of an humble menial does not deserve this condescension. Yet there we see God Himself coming down from heaven, and not despising to go to a poor servant, whilst we, being nothing but living dust, feel great difficulty in humbling ourselves. We are the more to be despised, since, wishing to guard our honour before the world, we fear not the eyes of that Divine Majesty searching the thoughts and hearts of men. Hence the Son of God said to the Pharisees: *You are they who justify yourselves before men; but God knoweth your hearts; for that which is high before men, is an abomination before God* (Luke 16: 15). Carefully consider those words, beloved brethren. If it is true that the things which seem great to men, are abominable before God, then our conclusion will be that our thoughts are despised by God, as much as they are esteemed by men. Humility produces a different effect, since it makes us the greater before God, the less we are considered by men. Now let us look at our doings; let not even our most praiseworthy undertakings flatter our pride; neither let our vanity be tickled by honours and riches. For if we are puffed up by our possessions, whatsoever they may be, we shall be despised by God. Speaking of the humble, the Psalmist says: *The Lord is the keeper of little ones* (Ps. 114: 6). The little ones are the humble. And, speaking of his own experience, he adds: *I was humbled, and He delivered me* (ibid.).

IV. Now, consider these truths well, beloved brethren, and carefully ponder on them. When honouring your brethren, look not so much at their perishable riches, as at the fact that men are the image and likeness of God, their Creator. Honour them for the sake of God. Yet this will not be possible, as long as your proud thoughts are not banished from your hearts. He that esteems himself on account of passing things cannot honour another for his durable goods. Consider as nothing what you *have*, but think of what you *are*, for the world you love will one day perish. The Saints, before whose tomb we are now standing, despised the flowers brought forth by the world, and trampled upon them. A long life, good health, a prosperous state, a numerous posterity, tranquillity in continual peace, were flowers at which their hearts did not rejoice; they blossomed in the world, but in their own hearts they were withered. Like a tree drying up before our eyes, the world is getting weaker and darker, yet it is still blossoming in our hearts and minds. Everywhere there is death, everywhere mourning, everywhere desolation! We are struck from all sides; we are filled with bitterness; nevertheless, with lamentable blindness, we desire and love the bitter fruits of carnal concupiscence. The world flies away, and we run after it; it is shaken under our feet, and we cling to it; and since we cannot prevent its fall, we still take hold of it, and are thrown into the same abyss. At the beginning we were attracted by the deceitful world; now, seeing it is so full of scourges and misery, we ought to be brought back to God by this very world. Reflect upon all this, and know that the things disappearing in time are to be considered as nothing. By the fall of all the things once existing in the world, we understand that they were but a shadow now vanished, for they are destroyed. The ruins of those splendid monuments, which once were thought of as defying all future times, clearly tell us that nothing is durable in this world. These are subjects worthy of your meditations; such thoughts will encourage you to have only contempt for worldly greatness, and to desire what is eternal. They will also help you to obtain that eternal glory revealed to you by faith through the grace of Jesus Christ our Lord, Who, with the Father and the Holy Ghost, liveth and reigneth one God, world without end. Amen.

61. TWENTY-FIRST SUNDAY AFTER PENTECOST

GOSPEL: Matt, 18: 23-35. *At that time*: Jesus spoke to His disciples this parable: The kingdom of heaven is likened to a king, who would take an account of his servants. And when he had begun to take the account, one was brought to him that owed him ten thousand talents. And as he had not wherewith to pay it, his lord commanded that he should be sold, and his wife and children and all that he had, and payment to be made. But that servant, falling down, besought him, saying: Have patience with me, and I will pay thee all. And the lord of that servant, being moved with pity, let him go, and forgave him the debt. But when that servant was gone out, he found one of his fellow-servants that owed him a hundred pence; and, laying hold of him, he throttled him, saying: Pay what thou owest. And his fellow-servant, falling down, besought him, saying: Have patience with me, and I will pay thee all. And he would not; but went and cast him into prison, till he paid the debt. Now, his fellow-servants, seeing what was done, were very much grieved, and they came and told their lord all that was done. Then his lord called him, and said to him: Thou wicked servant, I forgave thee all the debt, because thou besoughtest me; shouldst not thou, then, have had compassion also on thy fellow-servant, even as I had compassion on thee? And his lord, being angry, delivered him to the torturers until he paid all the debt. So also shall My heavenly Father do to you, if you forgive not every one his brother from your heart.

HOMILY BY ST. JEROME
Commentary on St. Matthew 28, Bk. III

I. IT IS A USUAL WAY WITH THE SYRIANS, AND especially with the inhabitants of Palestine, to illustrate their discourses with parables, so that what the hearers may not be able to understand so easily when spoken plainly, they may catch by the means of comparisons and example. Thus our Lord made use of a parable to teach St. Peter. By an allegory about a king, a master, and a servant who owed him ten thousand talents, and who, entreating, obtained forgiveness of his debt, He taught His Apostle how it was his duty to forgive his fellow-servants their comparatively small offences, Indeed, if that royal master so readily forgave his servant the debt of ten thousand talents, should not his servants much more readily forgive smaller debts to their fellow-servants?

II. In order to put this more clearly, let us take an example: If one of us were to commit adultery, or murder, or sacrilege, such sins, great as a debt of ten thousand talents, would be forgiven to us in answer to prayer, if we also from our heart forgive our brethren their offences against us. But if we refuse to forgive a slight, and keep up a continual enmity on account of an unkind word, does it not appear just, indeed, that we should be cast into prison, and, by the example of our own actions, be shown that our debt is not forgiven to us?

III. And our Lord adds: *So also shall My heavenly Father do to you, if you forgive not every one his brother from your heart.* What an awful sentence! Yet God's purpose may be turned and changed. But if we will not forgive our brethren small things, God will not forgive us great things. And if we forgive them, it must be from our heart. Someone may say: I have nothing against such a one; he knows what he has done, and God will judge him for it; I do not care what he is doing; I have forgiven him. But the Lord's sentence is clear, and He destroys such simulation of feigned peace, when He says: *So also shall My heavenly Father do to you, if you forgive not every one his brother from your heart.*

62. TWENTY-SECOND SUNDAY AFTER PENTECOST

GOSPEL: Matt. 22: 15-21. *At that time*: The Pharisees, going, consulted among themselves how to ensnare Jesus in His speech. And they sent to Him their disciples, with the Herodians, saying: Master, we know that Thou art a true speaker, and teachest the way of God in truth, neither carest Thou for any man; for Thou dost not regard the person of man. Tell us, therefore, what dost Thou think, is it lawful to give tribute to Caesar, or not? But Jesus, knowing their wickedness, said: Why do you tempt Me, ye hypocrites? Show Me the coin of the tribute. And they offered Him a penny. And Jesus saith to them: Whose image and inscription is this? They say to Him: Caesar's. Then He saith to them: Render, therefore, to Caesar the things that are Caesar's, and to God the things that are God's.

HOMILY BY ST. HILARY
Commentary on St. Matthew, Can. 23

I. OFTENTIMES THE PHARISEES HAD BEEN PUT TO confusion, and could not find any cause to accuse Him of anything that He had hitherto said or done. Though His words and actions were faultless, these men, still from spite, set themselves to seek in every direction for some cause to accuse Him. They knew that He was calling all to turn away from the corruption of the world and the superstitious practices of devotion invented by men, and to fix their thoughts and hopes upon His kingdom of heaven. Therefore the Pharisees arranged a question calculated to entrap Him into an offence against the civil government, namely: *Is it lawful to give tribute to Caesar or not?* But since there is nothing in the heart of man that God does not see, Jesus, knowing their wickedness, said: *Why do you tempt Me, ye hypocrites? Show Me the coin of the tribute. And they offered Him a penny. And Jesus said to them: Whose image and inscription is this? They said to Him: Caesar's. Then He saith to them: Render, therefore, to Caesar the things that are Caesar's, and to God the things that are God's.*

11. How wonderful this answer, and how perfect the fulfilment of the prescribed Divine Law! So beautifully does He here indicate the middle way between not caring for the things of the world, on the one hand, and the offence of injuring Caesar, on the other, that He proves the perfect freedom of minds, however devoted to God, to discharge all human duties by commanding them to render to Caesar the things that are Caesar's. If we possess nothing that is Caesar's, we are not bound to render anything to him; but since we are concerned with the things which are his, since we make justly use of his power, and are subject to him as paid servants to take care of property not our own, we cannot question our duty to render to Caesar the things that are Caesar's. But all of us are always bound to render to God the things that are God's — that is, our body, our soul, and our will. These things we hold from Him, for He is our Creator. It is, therefore, just and meet that those who acknowledge that they owe to Him their being, life, and preservation, should render to Him all that they are and have.

63. TWENTY-THIRD SUNDAY AFTER PENTECOST

GOSPEL: Matt. 9: 18-26. *At that time*: As Jesus was speaking to the multitude, behold a certain ruler came up and adored Him, saying: Lord, my daughter is even now dead; but come, lay Thy hand upon her, and she will live. And Jesus, rising up, followed him with His disciples. And behold a woman who was troubled with an issue of blood twelve years, came behind Him, and touched the hem of His garment. For she said within herself: If I shall touch only His garment, I shall be healed. But Jesus, turning and seeing her, said: Be of good heart, daughter; thy faith hath made thee whole. And the woman was made whole from that hour. And when Jesus was come into the house of the ruler, and saw the minstrels and the multitude making a rout, He said: Give place, for the girl is not dead, but sleepeth. And they laughed Him to scorn. And when the multitude was put forth, He went in, and took her by the hand. And the maid arose. And the fame hereof went abroad into all the country.

HOMILY BY ST. JEROME
Commentary on St. Matthew 9, Bk. I, Chapter 9

I. THIS IS THE EIGHTH MIRACLE WROUGHT BY Jesus, when a certain ruler, desiring not to be kept out of the true circumcision, besought Him to recall his daughter to life. The ceremony of circumcision, which usually took place on the eighth day after the birth, seems to be indicated by this miracle. Jairus, the ruler of the synagogue, certainly deserved the preference; but a woman, diseased with an issue of blood, thrust herself in, and her own cure occupies the eighth place, so that the resurrection of the ruler's daughter is postponed, and made the ninth in the enumeration. Indeed, it seems that by this case our Saviour wished to call our attention to the vocation of the Gentiles; for we read in the Psalms: *Ambassadors shall come out of Egypt; Ethiopia shall soon stretch out her hands to God* (Ps. 67: 32). A great mystery, spoken of by the Apostle, saying: *Blindness in part has happened to Israel, until the fulness of the Gentiles should come in. And so all Israel should be saved, as it is written: There shall come out of Sion He that shall deliver, and shall turn away ungodliness from Jacob* (Rom. 11: 25, 26).

II. *And behold a woman who was troubled with an issue of blood twelve years, came behind Him, and touched the hem of His garment.* Now, compare these two miracles in this Gospel: the first, a woman troubled with her disease for twelve years; the second, the resurrection of the daughter of Jairus who, according to St. Luke (8: 42), was twelve years old; and you will come to the conclusion that the woman, a type of the Gentiles, had been diseased for the same time that the Jewish nation, typified by the ruler's daughter, had been living in faith. It is only by comparing good with evil—that is, idolatry—that we see the hideousness of the latter. Note also that this woman with the issue of blood came to our Lord, not in a house nor in a city, for such as she were by the law banished out of cities (Lev. 15: 25), but in the way, as He walked. Thus our Lord healed one even whilst He was on the road to heal another. Whence the Apostles said: *To you it behoved us first to speak the word of God; but because you reject it, and judge yourselves unworthy of eternal life, behold we turn to the Gentiles. For so the Lord has commanded us: I have set thee to be the light of the Gentiles, that thou mayest be for salvation unto the utmost parts of the earth* (Acts 13: 46, 47).

III. According to the Law, whosoever touched a woman with an issue of blood was declared unclean. Here, however, we see a woman touch Jesus to be cured of that issue by which she seemed to be unclean. *Be of good heart, daughter,* said Jesus; *thy faith hath made thee whole.* Our Saviour calls her *daughter,* and justly, on account of her faith, by which she was cured. Note, again, our Lord did not say to the woman that her faith would make her whole—that is, clean—but *thy faith hath made thee whole.* It was to give her to understand that, as soon as she believed, she was cured. *And when Jesus was come into the house of the ruler, and saw the minstrels and the multitude making a rout, He said.* The deceased daughter of Jairus was the type of the Jewish nation, even now, after so many years, in a state of death. The Rabbis, entrusted with the instruction of that nation, may be compared to the minstrels playing a mournful and useless tune. The Jews, as we know, are only a noisy society of infidels, not of believers; and when Jesus said, *Give place, for the girl is not dead, but sleepeth,* He wished to teach us that every being, under the dominion of the living God, is alive. *And when the multitude was put forth, He went in.* Indeed, these people, *laughing to scorn the One* Who had power to give life, were not worthy to assist at the miraculous resurrection of this maiden.

IV. Finally, consider the last point of likeness between the Jewish nation and the ruler's daughter who, being dead, received life. *He took her by the hand. And the maid arose. And the fame thereof went abroad into all the country.* The synagogue, typified by this daughter, is dead; for her sinful hands are covered with the blood shed by the Jews. To rise from that death her stained hands must be washed in the same innocent Blood of Jesus Christ, the Author of all life.

64. TWENTY-FOURTH SUNDAY AFTER PENTECOST

GOSPEL: Matt. 24: 15-35. *At that time*: Jesus said to His disciples: When you shall see the abomination of desolation, which was spoken of by Daniel the Prophet, standing in the holy place: he that readeth let him understand. Then they that are in Judea, let them flee to the mountains; and he that is on the house-top, let him not come down to take anything out of the house; and he that is in the field, let him not go back to take his coat. And woe to them that are with child, and that give suck in those days. But pray that your flight be not in the winter, nor on the Sabbath. For there shall be then great tribulation, such as hath not been from the beginning of the world until now, neither shall be. And unless those days had been shortened, no flesh should be saved: but for the sake of the elect, those days shall be shortened. Then if any man shall say unto you: Lo! here is Christ, or there, do not believe him. For there shall arise false Christs, and false prophets, and shall show great signs and wonders, insomuch as to deceive (if possible) even the elect. Behold I have told it to you, beforehand. If therefore they shall say to you: Behold he is in the desert, go ye not out: Behold he is in the closets, believe it not. For as lightning cometh out of the east, and appeareth even unto the west: so shall also the coming of the Son of Man be. Wheresoever the body shall be, there shall the eagles also be gathered together. And immediately after the tribulation of those days, the sun shall be darkened, and the moon shall not give her light, and the stars shall fall from heaven, and the powers of the heavens shall be moved; and there shall appear the sign of the Son of Man in heaven; and then shall all tribes of the earth mourn; and they shall see the Son of Man coming in the clouds of heaven with much power and majesty. And He shall send His Angels with a trumpet and a great voice; and they shall gather together His elect from the four winds, from the farthest parts of the heavens to the utmost bounds of them. And from the fig-tree learn a parable: when the branch thereof is now tender, and the leaves come forth, you know that summer is nigh. So you also, when you shall see all these things, know ye that it is nigh, even at the doors. Amen, I say to you, that this generation shall not pass, till these things be done. Heaven and earth shall pass away, but My words shall not pass away.

HOMILY BY ST. JEROME
Commentary on St. Matthew 24, Bk. IV

I. WHEN THE MEANING OF THE WORDS OF HOLY Scripture is not quite clear, it is a sign that there is something mysterious in them. In Daniel, the prophet, we read as follows: *And in the half of the week the victim and the sacrifice shall fail: and there shall be in the temple the abomination of desolation: and the desolation shall continue even to the con summation, and to the end* (Dan. 9: 27). It is of the same thing that the Apostle speaks, saying: *The man of sin is revealed, the son of perdition, who opposeth, and is lifted up above all that is called God, or that is worshipped, so that he sitteth in the temple of God, showing himself as if he were God, whose coming is according to the working of Satan, in all power, and signs, and lying wonders, and in all seduction of iniquity* (2 Thess. 2: 3-9). This prophecy may be understood simply of the Antichrist, or of the statue of Caesar, set up by Pilate in the temple, or also of the statue of the Emperor Hadrian on horseback, which has been standing, even until our own time, upon the site of the Holy of Holies. In the Old Testament the word abomination is very often used for an idol, and the other title, desolation, is added to indicate an idol erected upon the site of the desolate and ruined temple.

II. *Then they that are in Judea, let them flee to the mountains; and he that is on the house-top, let him not come down to take anything out of the house; and he that is in the field, let him not go back to take his coat.* We may also understand by the abomination of desolation any perverse doctrine, and when we see such a thing as standing in the holy place — that is, in the Church of God — and showing itself that it is God that is, pretending that it is His revealed truth then will be the time when we must flee from Judea into the mountains that is, to leave the letter that passes away and all appearance of Jewish superstition, and to hasten to the *everlasting hills*, from whence God does wondrously cause His light to shine forth (Ps. 75: 5). Then it will be our duty to find ourselves under a roof and in a house, wherethrough the darts of the devil can never pierce to strike us, and not to come down to take anything out of the house of our old conversation, or to have regard to those things which are behind us. But rather to sow in the field of the spiritual Scriptures, that we may reap therefrom a plentiful harvest; neither to have two coats, a thing forbidden to the Apostles (Matt. 10: 10). *And woe to them that are with child, and give suck in these days.* Woe to those souls that have not brought forth the fruits of virtue which make the perfect Christian; or woe to those weak souls, still standing in the beginning of faith, wanting the spiritual food, and who, through that want, are in this abomination of desolation. The words may also be explained in this way, that, when the conquered city of Rome will be the prey of tyrants, or when the persecution of the Antichrist arises, then the comfortless mothers will not know how to save themselves, because of their being with child or giving suck. *But pray that your flight be not in the winter, nor on the Sabbath.* These words refer either to the taking of the city of Jerusalem, under the Emperors Titus and Vespasian, or to the general destruction of the whole world. Were we to understand them as meaning the destruction of Jerusalem, then we should say that it will be a great misfortune to the Jews to flee from the city either in the winter or on the Sabbath. For, in the first case the excessive cold, prevailing in the deserts and mountains, would prevent the fugitives from finding shelter therein; whereas in the second case the Jews were forbidden by the Law to travel on the Sabbath, therefore certain destruction awaited those who remained in the city. Should we understand these words as meaning the end of the world, then we infer that by the winter our Lord meant the coldness of both our faith in, and our love for, Him; and that by the word 'Sabbath' He wished to urge us on not to remain idle in God's service, but continually to make progress in virtue and perfection.

III. *And unless those days had been shortened, no flesh should be saved; but for the sake of the elect, those days shall be shortened.* Let us not believe, as some pretended, probably when in a state of insanity, that the different parts of time shall then be changed. Those sharing such opinion, forget the words of Holy Scripture: *By Thy ordinance the day goes on* (Ps. 118: 91). There is no question here about the measure of the time, which remains unalterable, but about the number of the days that is to be shortened. For, as in giving His blessing, God says: *I will fill him with length of days* (Ps. 90: 16), so also will these days be shortened, lest by their great number the faith of the elect would be shaken. And Jesus added: *Then if any man shall say unto you: Lo! here is Christ, or there, do not believe him.* These words may perhaps mean what we know about the events that happened at the time of the Jewish captivity, when many princes of that people called themselves Christ; for when Jerusalem was besieged by the Romans, there were three parties in the city, each claiming to be the rightful heir to the old kingdom. However, it will be safer to say that by these words is meant the end of the world. *For there shall arise false Christs, and false prophets, and shall show great signs, and wonders, insomuch as to deceive (if possible) even the elect. Behold I have told it to you, beforehand.* As I said before, this may refer to three different events, namely, to the siege of Jerusalem by the Romans, or to the end of the world, or also to the stormy assaults, of heretics against the true Church, for these are the Antichrists waging war against Christ, under the exterior appearance of seducing and deceiving science. *If therefore they shall say to you: Behold he is in the desert, go ye not out; Behold he is in the closets, believe it not.* By the word *desert* we understand the sects of philosophers and the false religion of the pagans, who vainly boast of announcing the truth through their mythical doctrines. The *closets*, or secret chambers, mean the assemblies of the heretics trying to make us believe that they alone are capable of thoroughly searching and explaining the Divine mysteries. Do not believe them, neither go out to them. It is specially in times of persecutions and distress that false prophets make their appearance, and try to deceive us. We hear, therefore, our Lord warning us not to listen to them. *For as lightning cometh out of the east, and appeareth even unto the west: so shall also the coming of the Son of Man be.* He means to say, do not believe that the Son of Man is in the desert of the pagans, or in the secret chambers of the heretics; for the faith of the Catholic Church is shining from the east to the west, and she alone can show to the world Jesus Christ, the Son of God. Again, consider that the second coming of Christ will not be like His first, in humility, but in glory and majesty. It would, therefore, be a thoughtless act to search for Him in the darkness and the corners of the earth, since by His splendour and glory He will be then the astonishment of the whole world.

IV. *Wheresoever the body shall be, there shall the eagles also be gathered together.* This is a natural fact, seen every day; yet, however common it may seem, in it appears the image of Jesus Christ. Birds of prey — that is, eagles and vultures — are said to be sensible of the smell of corpses even across the seas, and to fly in crowds together in order to devour them. If irrational birds, by their natural instinct, discover a far-off corpse, shall not reasonable beings and Christians, having the true faith, so much the more run to Him, *Whose lightning cometh out of the east, and appeareth even unto the west?* The word *corpse*, or *dead body*, reminds us also of the Passion of Jesus Christ. Indeed, we may say that, when we read the Scriptures, in which the Passion of our Lord is clearly spoken of, we are, so to speak, gathered around the Body of Christ, and that, meditating on that Body crucified for us, we are attracted by the Word of God. The truths of the Passion and Death of the Son of God are described in all their details in the Holy Scriptures, for they say of our Saviour: *They have dug My hands and feet* (Ps. 21: 17). Isaias also says: *He shall be led as a sheep to the slaughter* (Isa. 53: 7). Other passages of Holy Scripture are as clear as those. The eagles represent the just who, like the eagles, renew their years; and who, according to Isaias, are covered with feathers, and take wings to fly to Christ and meditate on His Passion.

V. *And immediately after the tribulation of those days, the sun shall be darkened, and the moon shall not give her light, and the stars shall fall from heaven, and the powers of the heavens shall be moved.* When hearing these words, let us not think that the sun shall then lose its rays, for it is said: *The light of the moon shall be as the light of the sun, and the light of the sun shall be sevenfold* (Isa. 30: 26). But we learn thereby that the light of the sun and the stars will then seem like darkness in comparison with the brilliant light of the Son of God. It follows that, when even the sun now shining in the firmament, when the moon, taking the second place among the luminaries, when the stars, now like lighted lamps in the night, when the powers of the heavens — the multitude of Angels — will seem like shadows or darkness at the coming of Christ, it follows that man, now thinking himself pure enough not to be afraid of the terrible Judge, is grossly deceiving himself. *And there shall appear the sign of the Son of Man in heaven.* This sign is the Cross, at the sight of which the Jews shall be filled with astonishment, according to Zachery 22 and John 19. We may also understand by this *sign* the victories won by Jesus over His enemies. *And then shall all tribes of the earth mourn; and they shall see the Son of Man coming in the clouds of heaven with much power and majesty.* These words do not refer to the elect, the inhabitants of heaven, but to the wicked, called the children of the earth, since they chose it for their inheritance. They shall not be in the company of the elect, whom *the Angels with a trumpet shall gather together from the four winds.* Meanwhile, *heaven and earth shall pass away,* says Jesus, *but My words shall not pass away.* Namely, the form of heaven and earth shall be changed, but not destroyed; for how could we understand the words about the sun being darkened, the moon not giving her light, and the stars falling down, were heaven and earth no longer in existence at the time of these astounding events?

65. FEAST OF SS. PETER AND PAUL, APOSTLES

GOSPEL: Matt. 16: 13-19. *At that time*: Jesus came into the quarters of Cesarea Philippi, and He asked His disciples, saying: Whom do men say that the Son of Man is? But they said: Some, John the Baptist, and other some, Elias, and others, Jeremias, or one of the prophets. Jesus saith to them: But whom do you say that I am? Simon Peter answered and said: Thou art Christ, the Son of the living God. And Jesus, answering, said to him: Blessed art thou, Simon Bar-Jona: because flesh and blood hath not revealed it to thee, but My Father, Who is in heaven. And I say to thee: That thou art Peter, and upon this rock I will build My Church, and the gates of hell shall not prevail against it. And I will give to thee the keys of the kingdom of heaven. And whatsoever thou shalt bind upon earth, it shall be bound also in heaven: and whatsoever thou shalt loose on earth, it shall be loosed also in heaven.

HOMILY BY ST. JEROME
Commentary on St. Matthew 16, Bk. III

I. HOW WONDERFUL THE QUESTION ADDRESSED by our Lord to His disciples: *Whom do men say that the Son of Man is?* For those who speak of Him as the Son of Man are men; while those who know Him as God are called not men, but gods. *But they said: Some, John the Baptist, and other some, Elias, and others, Jeremias, or one of the prophets.* I wonder why some interpreters of the Holy Writ have thought it worth their while to search into the origin of each of these errors, and to engage in a lengthy discussion as to why some thought that our Lord Jesus Christ was John the

Baptist, *other some, Elias, and others, Jeremias, or one of the prophets.* Their mistakes about Elias and Jeremias were like that of Herod concerning John the Baptist. It is *John the Baptist, whom I beheaded; he is risen again from the dead, and therefore mighty works show forth themselves in him* (Mark 6: 14, 16).

II. *Jesus saith to them: But whom do you say that I am?* Intelligent reader, notice from the context, that there is a distinction drawn between the Apostles and mere men; they are called gods. *Whom do men say that the Son of Man is?* asked the Lord; but, on the other hand: *Whom do you say that I am?* They, being but men, only think of human things; but you, whom I call gods, whom are you convinced that I am? Then Peter, in the name of all the Apostles, pronounced these words: *Thou art Christ, the Son of the living God.* He called Him *living God,* to mark the difference between Him and all those gods adored by the pagans: Saturnus, Jupiter, Minerva, Bacchus, Hercules, and all other pagan gods, who are indeed dead.

III. *And Jesus, answering, said to him: Blessed art thou, Simon Bar-Jona: because flesh and blood hath not revealed it to thee, but My Father Who is in heaven.* The Apostle, having given testimony to the Lord, the Lord in turn gave testimony to the Apostle. Peter said: *Thou art Christ, the Son of the living God,* and he received as a reward for his testimony to the truth these words: *Blessed art thou, Simon Bar-Jona.* Why *blessed? Because flesh and blood hath not revealed it to thee, but My Father.* What flesh and blood could not reveal, was revealed by the grace of the Holy Ghost. This name was given him on account of his confession, as the name of one who has revelation from the Holy Ghost, whose son he is called. *Bar-Jona* in our tongue means the *son of the dove,* the symbol of the Holy Ghost. We may also compare these words: *Flesh and blood hath not revealed it to thee* with those of the Apostle, saying: *When He called me by His grace to reveal His Son in me, that I might preach Him among the Gentiles, immediately I condescended not to flesh and blood* (Gal. 1: 15, 16). By the words *flesh and blood* the Jews are here meant by the Apostle, thus indicating, though under other circumstances, that not by the doctrine of the Pharisees, but by the grace of God, it was revealed to men that Jesus Christ is indeed the Son of God.

IV. *And I say to thee: That thou art Peter, and upon this rock I will build My Church.* And by these words our Lord seems to say: Thou hast confessed Me to be the Son of God, and I confess, not in words only without any meaning, but in deed, that thou art Peter — a rock — and that upon this rock I will build My Church. The Divine light was given by Jesus to the Apostles, called *the light of the world* (Matt. 5: 14), and to each of them was given a special name. But Simon was called *Peter*, because he firmly believed in Jesus Christ, the true Rock. This rock is alluded to when Jesus said to the Prince of the Apostles: *Upon this rock I will build My Church, and the gates of hell shall not prevail against it.* I believe that by these words, *the gates of hell*, not only the sins and vices of men are to be understood, but especially the doctrines of heretics and apostates, by which men are deceived and cast into hell. Let no one imagine that by the words *gates of hell* our Lord meant a temporal death, from which the Apostles were to be preserved; for we know that all of them suffered a glorious martyrdom.

V. *And I will give to thee the keys of the kingdom of heaven; and whatsoever thou shalt bind upon earth, it shall be bound also in heaven; and whatsoever thou shalt loose on earth, it shall be loosed also in heaven.* Bishops and priests, not understanding the meaning of these words, could perhaps in pharisaical pride imagine that power was given to them arbitrarily to condemn the innocent, and to absolve the guilty; just as if God did not regard the disposition of the sinner, before pardoning or condemning him, more than the sentence of the priest. We read in the Book Leviticus (chap. 14) that the lepers were to show themselves to the priest, who declared them to be unclean if infected with leprosy. However, they were not made unclean by the priest, whose office it was to judge of leprosy, and declare some clean and others unclean. What was done in the Old Testament about lepers happens now, when the Bishop or the priest, after examining the stains of sins, is able by his office and power to declare who are those to be bound and those to be loosed.

66. THE ASSUMPTION OF THE BLESSED VIRGIN MARY

GOSPEL: Luke 10: 38-42. *At that time*: Jesus entered into a certain town, and a certain woman, named Martha, received Him into her house. And she had a sister called Mary, who, sitting also at the Lord's feet, heard His word. But Martha was busy about much serving, who stood and said: Lord, hast Thou no care that my sister hath left me alone to serve? speak to her, therefore, that she help me. And the Lord, answering, said to her: Martha, Martha, thou art careful, and art troubled about many things. But one thing is necessary. Mary hath chosen the best part, which shall not be taken away from her.

HOMILY BY ST. AUGUSTINE
Twenty-Seventh Homily on the Words of the Lord

I. WHEN THE HOLY GOSPEL WAS READ OUT, WE heard that our Lord was received by a pious woman into her house, and the woman's name was Martha. And while she *was busy about much serving*, her sister Mary was sitting at the Lord's feet, hearing His words. The one worked, the other was idle; the one was ministering, the other was being filled. However, Martha, though working hard in that occupation and bustle of serving, appealed to the Lord, and made complaint of her sister, because she did not help her in her work. But the Lord answered Martha for Mary, and He Who had been appealed to, to be her Judge, became her Advocate: *And the Lord, answering, said to her: Martha, Martha, thou art careful, and art troubled about many things. But one thing is necessary. Mary hath chosen the best part, which shall not be taken away from her.* We have heard both the appeal of the complainant and the sentence of the Judge—sentence which replied to the appellant and defended the cause of the other whom the Lord had received. Mary was wrapped up in the sweetness of the Lord's word. Martha was intent how she might feed the Lord, and Mary was intent how to be fed by the Lord. By Martha a banquet was being prepared for the Lord, at Whose banquet Mary was already delighting herself. And as Mary was listening in peace and delight to His most sweet words, when Martha came and complained of her to the Lord, how do we imagine that she feared, lest the Lord should say to her: Arise, and help thy sister. For she was held by a wondrous sweetness, the relish of which is felt more by the mind than the belly. She was excused, and she sat all the safer. But on what ground was she excused? Let us consider, examine and investigate it thoroughly, as far as we can, that we also may be fed.

II. What then? For what do we imagine that Martha's serving was blamed, she who was busy with the cares of hospitality, and who had received the Lord into her house? How could she be blamed, whose heart was gladdened by so great a Guest? If this be true, then let men give up their service to the poor; let them choose for themselves *the best part, which shall not be taken away from* them; let them give themselves entirely to the word, and long after the sweetness of doctrine; let them be occupied about the salvation-giving knowledge; let there be no care in them to find out what stranger is in the street, or whether there be one who wants bread, or clothing, or to be visited, to be redeemed, or to be buried; let works of mercy cease, and attention given only to knowledge. If this be the *best part*, why do not all men do so, since we have the Lord Himself as our Advocate in this case? We do not fear in this matter to offend His justice, since we have the support of His sentence.

III. And yet it is not so; but as the Lord said, so it is. It is not as you understand, but it is as you ought to understand it. Mark, then: *Thou art troubled about many things; but one thing is necessary. Mary hath chosen the best part.* Thou hast not chosen a bad part, but she a better one. And how better? Because thou art *about many things*, she about *one thing*. One is preferred to many; for one does not come from many, but many from one. Many are the things that were made; He Who made them is One. Heaven and earth, the sea, and all things in them, how many are they? Who can number them? Who can conceive their multitude? Who made them? God made them all, and *they are very good* (Gen. 1: 31). And how much better is He Who made them? Let us consider our occupations *about many things*. Much work is required for refreshing our bodies. How is this? Because we hunger and thirst. Mercy is necessary for the wretched. You break bread to the hungry, for you have found a hungry man. Take hunger away, to whom do you break bread? Take homeless travellers away, to whom do you offer hospitality? Take nakedness away, whom will you cover with clothes? Let there be no sickness, whom do you visit? No captivity, whom will you redeem? No quarrelling, whom do you reconcile? No death, whom do you bury? In the future world these evils will not exist, therefore these works of mercy will not be required. Martha did well to serve the Lord's mortal body in those things which concerned, shall I say, His bodily want or His bodily will. But Who was within that mortal flesh? *In the beginning was the Word, and the Word was with God, and the Word was God* (John 1: 1). See what Mary was listening to! *And the Word was made flesh, and dwelt among us.* See Whom Martha was serving! Therefore *Mary hath chosen the best part, which shall not be taken away from her.* For she has chosen what shall abide for ever and ever, and it shall not be taken away from her. Mary was careful about *one thing* only, and she held to the belief of the psalmist, saying: *It is good for me to adhere to my God* (Ps. 72: 28). She sat at the feet of our Head. The more lowly she sat, the more fully she received. Water, that runs down from the summits of the hills, flows to the lowest depths of the valleys. The Lord did not blame Martha's work, but distinguished between the service of the two sisters. *Thou art troubled about many things; but one thing is necessary.* Mary has already chosen that one thing for herself. The labour of manifold things passes away, and the love of one thing abides; therefore what she has chosen *shall not be taken away from her.* But what thou hast chosen, O Martha (it follows, of course, and must be understood) — what thou hast chosen shall be taken away from thee. But it shall be taken away from thee for thy good, so that what is best may be given to thee.

Labour shall be taken away from thee, that rest may be given to thee. Thou art still on the sea; Mary is already in port.

IV. You see, then, beloved brethren, and, as I suppose, you understand already, that in these two women, who were both well pleasing to the Lord, both lovely, both disciples, you see, I say, and whosoever you be who understand, you understand something great, which you also, who do not understand, ought to hear and know, that in those two women two lives are figured, the present life and the life to come, the life of labour and the life of rest, the life of sorrow and the life of blessedness, the temporal life and the eternal life. There are two lives; think more fully about them. Whatsoever this life contains, I speak not of a life of evil, of wickedness, of crime, of uncleanness, or of ungodliness; but of labour and full of troubles, chastened by fears, and tried by temptations, even such guileless life I mean, as was suitable for Martha; such a life examine as well as you can, and, as I said, think more about it than I speak. There was no wicked life in that house, neither with Martha nor with Mary. If it ever had been, it fled when the Lord made His entrance. In that house, therefore, which received the Lord, there remained in the two women two lives, both guileless, both praiseworthy, the one of labour, the other of ease; neither vicious, neither slothful, both harmless — both, I say, praiseworthy, but one of labour, and one of rest. Neither vicious, of which the life of labour must beware; neither slothful, which the life of rest has also to beware of. There were in that house those two lives, and He Himself the Fountain of life. In Martha was the image of the present things; in Mary of future things. What Martha was doing is what we do now; what Mary was doing is what we hope for. Let us do the first well, that the second may be granted to us fully. What of this have we now, and how far is it ours? As long as we are in this world, how much of that life have we? In some measure we are employed in it now; for when removed from business, and laying aside domestic cares, you meet together, you stand and listen; and, in so far as you do this, you are like Mary at the feet of Jesus. And you do what Mary did with greater facility than I who have to distribute to you. Yet if I speak anything to you, it is Christ's; therefore you are fed by my words, for they are Christ's. The Bread, of which I live as well as you, is common to us all. *Now we live, if we stand in the Lord* (1 Thess. 3: 8) — not in us, but stand in the Lord. For *neither he that planteth is anything, nor he that watereth; but God that giveth the increase* (1 Cor. 3: 7).

67. THE FEAST OF ALL SAINTS

GOSPEL: Matt. 5: 1-12. *At that time:* Jesus, seeing the multitudes, went up into a mountain, and when He was sat down, His disciples came unto Him. And opening His mouth, He taught them, saying: Blessed are the poor in spirit: for theirs is the kingdom of heaven. Blessed are the meek: for they shall possess the land. Blessed are they that mourn: for they shall be comforted. Blessed are they that hunger and thirst after justice: for they shall have their fill. Blessed are the merciful: for they shall obtain mercy. Blessed are the clean of heart: for they shall see God. Blessed are the peacemakers: for they shall be called the children of God. Blessed are they that suffer persecution for justice sake: for theirs is the kingdom of heaven. Blessed are ye when they shall revile you, and persecute you, and speak all that is evil against you, untruly, for My sake; be glad and rejoice, for your reward is very great in heaven.

HOMILY BY ST. AUGUSTINE
On the Lord's Sermon, Bk. I

I. IF THE QUESTION BE ASKED, WHAT THE MOUNtain signifies, it may well be understood as meaning the higher and greater commandments of justice, since there were lesser ones given to the Jews. The one God, according to an excellently arranged distribution of times, gave by His prophets and servants the lesser commandments to a people who as yet required to be bound by fear; but by His Son He gave the greater ones to a people whom it now behoved Him to set free by love. But whether it be the lesser to the lesser, or the greater to the greater, all are alike the gift of Him Who alone knows what is at each time the best medicine to be presented to the human race. Nor is it surprising that the greater commandments are given for the kingdom of heaven, and the lesser for an earthly kingdom, since both are the gifts of one and the same God Who made heaven and earth. This higher and greater justice, then, is that spoken of by the Prophet: *Thy justice is as the mountains of God* (Ps. 35: 7). This may well mean that the one Teacher, alone fit to teach matters of such importance, teaches on a mountain. *And when He was sat down.* He teaches sitting, as it pertains to the dignity of the Instructor's office. *His disciples came unto Him*, that they may be nearer in body, to hear those precepts, by the fulfilment of which they should also be nearer in spirit. *And opening His mouth, He taught them.* The circumstance before us, which runs, *And opening His mouth*, perhaps gracefully intimates that the sermon will be somewhat longer than usual. Unless the meaning be the declaration that He now opened His own mouth, whereas under the Old Law He used to open the mouths of the prophets.

II. And now what does He say? *Blessed are the poor in spirit: for theirs is the kingdom of heaven.* We read in Holy Scripture concerning the lusting after temporal things: *All is vanity and presumption of spirit* (Eccles. 6: 9). Presumption of spirit means rashness and pride. Usually the proud are said to be men of high spirit, and rightly so, since *spirit* is only one of the Latin names for wind. Hence it is written: *Fire, hail, snow, ice, stormy winds* (Ps. 148: 8). Who has not heard that the proud are spoken of as *puffed up*, as if blown out with wind? Hence also the Apostle says: *Knowledge puffeth up; but charity edifieth* (1 Cor. 8: 1). By the *poor in spirit*, here called blessed, are justly to be understood the humble and God-fearing — that is, those not having a spirit puffed up with windy vanity. Blessedness ought not to begin at any other point, if, indeed, it is to reach the highest wisdom. For *the fear of the Lord is the beginning of wisdom* (Ps. 110: 10). Whereas, on the other hand, it is written: *Pride is the beginning of all sin* (Ecclus. 10: 15). The proud covet and love earthly kingdoms.

III. *Blessed are the meek: for they shall possess the land.* The land they shall possess, I suppose to be that of which it is said in the Psalm: *Thou art my hope, my portion in the land of the living* (Ps. 141:

6). The inheritance of the meek in this land is everlastingly sure and safe, where the soul, being of a good disposition, rests, as it were, in its own home, just as carnal owners rest at home in sure earthly possessions. And they live on the income from that land, as earthly owners from the income of their possessions; this is the home and abiding-place of the Saints. The meek, therefore, are those who yield to acts of wickedness, and do not resist evil, *but overcome evil by good* (Rom. 12: 21) Let those, then, who are not meek, quarrel and fight for earthly and temporal things; but *blessed are the meek: for they shall possess the land*, from which they cannot be driven away.

IV. *Blessed are they that mourn: for they shall be comforted.* This mourning is sorrow for the loss of things loved and now lost. Now, those converted to God lose in this world things which they once loved; for they do not rejoice in the things in which they formerly rejoiced. Until the love of eternal things be in their hearts, they are wounded by some measure of grief; but they will be comforted by the Holy Ghost, Who on this account chiefly has the title of the Paraclete — that is, the Comforter. They lose the temporal joy, but they gain the enjoyment of eternal things.

V. *Blessed are they that hunger and thirst after justice: for they shall have their fill.* Those who are here spoken of by Jesus, are the lovers of a true and indestructible good. And they shall have their hunger satisfied with that meat of which the Lord Himself says: *My meat is to do the will of Him that sent Me, that I may perfect His work* (John 4: 34). And their thirst shall be slaked with that water which the Lord Himself gives them, whereof whosoever *drinketh*, as the Lord says, *shall not thirst for ever. It shall become in him a fountain of water springing up into life everlasting* (John 4: 13, 14).

VI. *Blessed are the merciful: for they shall obtain mercy.* He calls blessed those who relieve the miserable and needy; for with the measure wherewith they have meted, it shall be measured to them, and they shall not be left unhelped in their own misery. *Blessed are the clean of heart: for they shall see God.* What fools, therefore, are those who seek God with their outward eyes, since He is seen with the heart, as it is written: *Seek Him in simplicity of heart* (Wisd.

1: 1). A simple heart is a pure heart. And just as this earthly light cannot be seen unless the eyes be clean, so cannot God be seen, unless that is pure by which alone He can be seen.

VII. *Blessed are the peacemakers: for they shall be called the children of God.* The perfection of peace is the absence of opposition and contrariety, and the peace makers are called the children of God, because they offer no opposition against the will of God. As becomes children, they have their Father's likeness. Now they are peacemakers in themselves, because they order all the movements of their own mind in obedience to reason — that is, to mind and soul — and by so doing and so taming the lust of the flesh, they become a kingdom of God. In such a kingdom all things are so arranged that the chiefest and noblest part of man rules without resistance over those lower things which we have in common with beasts. And in the same way that nobler part of man — that is to say, his mind and reason — must be brought under subjection to something better and higher still, namely, TRUTH, the only begotten Son of God. He only can rule well, who has learned to obey. And this is the peace given on earth to men of good will; this is the life of one completely and perfectly wise. The prince of this world, who rules over perversity and disorder, is cast out of such a most peaceful and orderly kingdom. When once this peace has been inwardly established, whatsoever persecutions he that has been cast out shall stir up from without, he only increases the glory that redounds to God. He will be unable to bring to the ground anything in that stronghold, and by the failure of his machinations he will make known how strongly it was built inwardly. Hence there follows: *Blessed are they that suffer persecution for justice sake: for theirs is the kingdom of heaven.*

VIII. In this eighth sentence, which goes back to the starting point — *for theirs is the kingdom of heaven* — and makes manifest the perfect man, is perhaps contained a connection with the fact that, according to the Old Law, circumcision was to be performed on the eighth day, and that the resurrection of our Lord took place on the day after the Sabbath — that is, the eighth day and at the same time the first day of the week. There is, perhaps, also

67. THE FEAST OF ALL SAINTS

a connection with the celebration of the eight festival days celebrated in the case of the regeneration of the new man, and by the very number of Pentecost—being interpreted, the Feast of the Fiftieth Day. For this number of fifty days is reckoned by counting seven weeks multiplied by seven days, which is forty-nine, to which *one* is added—that is, an eighth—thus making up fifty. Hence we return to the starting point, the day whereon the Holy Ghost was sent, by Whom we are led into the kingdom of heaven, receive the inheritance, and are comforted. We are fed, and obtain mercy; we are purified, and are made peacemakers. And being thus made perfect within, we bear all troubles brought upon us from without for the sake of truth and justice.

IX. *Blessed are ye*, says Jesus, *when they shall revile you, and persecute you, and speak all that is evil against you, untruly, for My sake; be glad and rejoice, for your reward is very great in heaven.* Let anyone who is seeking after the pleasures of this world and the possession of temporal goods, under the name of a Christian, consider that our blessedness is within, as it is said of the soul of the Church by the mouth of the Prophet: *All the glory of the king's daughter is within* (Ps. 44: 14). For outwardly reviling, and persecutions, and evil reports are promised her. Yet for these very things her reward is great in heaven, and it is felt in the hearts of sufferers, at least of those who can now say: *We glory also in tribulations, knowing that tribulation worketh patience, and patience trial, and trial hope. And hope confoundeth not, because the charity of God is poured forth in our hearts by the Holy Ghost Who is given to us* (Rom. 5: 3-5). To suffer such things is not in itself advantageous, but the bearing of them for the name of Christ not only calmly but gladly. For many heretics, deceiving souls under the name of Christians, suffer many such things, yet they are excluded from the reward; for it is not merely written: *Blessed are they that suffer persecution; but it is added, for justice sake.* Where there is not sound faith, there cannot be justice; for, *my just man liveth by faith* (Heb. 10: 38). Neither let schismatics promise themselves anything of that reward; for as justice cannot exist where there is no faith, so neither can it exist where there is not love. And schismatics have no love; for *love of our neighbour worketh no evil* (Rom. 13: 10). If they had love, they would not tear asunder the Body of Christ, *which is the Church* (Col. 1: 24).

Also available from
AROUCA PRESS

Meditations for Each Day
Antonio Cardinal Bacci (pbk & hb)

Fraternal Charity
Fr. Benoît Valuy, S. J.

The Epistle of Christ:
Short Sermons for the Sundays of the Year
on Texts from the Epistles
Fr. Michael Andrew Chapman

Our Lady, A Presentation for Beginners
Dom Hubert van Zeller, O.S. B.

A Centenary Meditation on
A Quest for "Purification" Gone Mad
Dr. John C. Rao

Integrity, Volume 1:
The First Year (October–December 1946)
Ed. Carol Jackson, Ed Willock

Christ Wants More:
Ignatian Principles and Ideals on Prayer and Action
Fr. Frank Holland, S. J.

Breaking the Chains of Mediocrity:
Carol Robinson's Collected Works (The Marianist Articles)
Carol Jackson Robinson

The Eightfold Kingdom Within:
Essays on the Beatitudes and the Gifts of the Holy Ghost
Carol Jackson Robinson

Louis Cardinal Billot, S.J.
Liberalism: A Critique of Its Basic
Principles and Various Forms
(Newly translated by Thomas Storck)

AROUCAPRESS
REPRINTS
Dogmatic Theology (Msgr. Van. Noort)
Volume 1: The True Religion
Volume 2: Christ's Church
Volume 3: The Sources of Revelation, Divine Faith

www.ingramcontent.com/pod-product-compliance
Lightning Source LLC
Chambersburg PA
CBHW060349080526
44583CB00012B/231